Contemporary Catholic Education

Contemporary Catholic Education

edited by

Michael A. Hayes
and
Liam Gearon

GRACEWING

First published in 2002

Gracewing
2 Southern Avenue, Leominster
Herefordshire HR6 0QF

UK ISBN 0 85244 528 8

Typesetting by
Action Publishing Technology Ltd, Gloucester, GL1 5SR

Printed in England by
MPG Books Ltd,
Bodmin PL31 1EG

Contents

Introduction

Michael A. Hayes and Liam Gearon

'Learn the heart of God through the Word of God' so wrote St Gregory. The word of God as outlined in the Vatican II document *Dei Verbum* includes scripture and tradition, 'tradition and scripture make up a single sacred deposit of the word of God, which is entrusted to the church' (DV 10). Places of learning include both an intellectual discourse and moral engagement in community. This focus on community is highlighted by *Gravissimum Educationis*. This key Vatican II document on education states that a decisive change in the history of Catholic schools is marked by 'the move from school as institution to school as community' (GE 27).

The worldview of the Catholic Christian is inspired by the revelation of scripture and Church tradition. The universe is a meaningful if often mysterious place. Though our worlds are often fraught by suffering, our place in the world, though sometimes unclear, is fundamentally purposeful. It is this which gives Catholic education a hopefulness which is more than short term but rather eternal. Such words seem sometimes to jar in a society that lives for the moment and which gives little outward credence to the sacred and divine, going so far so often even to deny them legitimacy. Catholic education is undertaken with a purposefulness, taking teaching and learning beyond a mere earthly context.

The guiding theological principles of Catholic education remain a constant across national and international borders. And no emphasis other than the theological – 'a caring atmosphere', 'a community spirit', 'the concern for social justice', nor even a concern for spirituality – makes Catholic education distinctive: for all of these and other concerns are shared by secular schools. The Catholic Christian worldview – the universal understanding of human beings as beings created by God for a divine purpose, contextualised in community – is the only thing which makes Catholic education distinctive from a secular education.

What this book attempts to do is to look at some of the particular issues facing Catholic education in the United Kingdom at the beginning of the twenty-first century. In other words, the book is an examination of the theologically universal in a particular social, political, economic situation – at a given time in the history of England, Northern Ireland, Scotland and Wales. The book is divided into three parts and part one looks explicitly at these particular regional issues.

The second part of the book looks at some key educational issues in more detail as they affect the contemporary Catholic school. Topics raised by contributors here include the Christian ministry of the teacher and the distinctive roles and responsibilities that this will involve. Other chapters in this section deal with the management of the whole school and subject leadership, together with an analysis of the role of the governing body. The distinctive theological dimension of Catholic education – historically central and remaining so today – is brought out by chapters on the Catholic school as a worshipping community and an assessment of chaplaincy as a ministry rooted in Christ which is consistent, realistic, and audacious.

The final, third part of the book critically explores selective major challenges for Catholic education. This is not to say that some of the challenges are new – though the chapter on 'Discovering the Alternatives' does address this – but issues raised here do highlight areas of critical importance for the future of all Catholic education including inter-faith perspectives, continuing professional development and the role of the Catholic Church within the university sector of education.

The editors would like to thank most gratefully all contributors – many who have written from the perspective of a practitioner. The book does not aim to provide comprehensive coverage for all aspects of Catholic education in the United Kingdom but it is hoped that the book will make a contribution to debate amongst educators and will provide a useful tool for reflection in the training of Catholic teachers.

It is hoped that this volume will be a useful companion to our previously published *Contemporary Catholic Theology: A Reader* and in particular for students who follow the 'professional studies' modules of the Catholic Certificate in Religious Studies. Furthermore it is our hope that anyone with an interest in Catholic education – teachers, governors, parents, students – will find it helpful.

Abbreviations

AQW	Answers to Written Questions
CCAC	Council of Church and Associate Colleges
CCC	Catechism of the Catholic Church
CCMS	Council for Catholic Maintained Schools
CCRS	Catholic Certificate in Religious Studies
CES	Catholic Education Service
CRHR	Centre for Research in Human Resources
CTS	Catholic Truth Society
DENI	Department of Education in Northern Ireland
GCSE	General Certificate of Secondary Education
GDC	General Directory for Catechesis
GE	*Gravissimum Educationis*
HMSO	Her Majesty's Stationery Office
ILEA	Inner London Education Authority
JSEA	Jesuit Secondary Education Service
LEA	Local Education Authority
NA	*Nostra Aetate*
NICIE	Northern Ireland Council for Integrated Education
OFSTED	The Office for Standards in Education
PGCE	Post-graduate Certificate in Education
PRU	Pupil Referral Unit
RCIA	The Rite of Christian Initiation of Adults
RE	Religious Education
ROSLA	Raising of the School Leaving Age
SACHR	Standing Advisory Committee on Human Rights
SC	*Sacrosanctum Concilium*
UNESCO	United Nations Educational, Scientific and Cultural Organization

Part One

Catholic Education
in the
United Kingdom

Chapter 1

Catholic Education in England and Wales[*]

Gerald Grace

Introduction

The future of the Catholic school (in this case, of Catholic voluntary-aided and grant-maintained schools in England)[1] is, from one perspective, an occasion for hope and optimism. Catholic schools, both primary and secondary, have been well placed in the public league tables of academic and test results which are, in contemporary England, an important source for the making or breaking of a school's reputation and public image. In addition to support from local Catholic communities, the schools are much sought after by parents of other Christian faith communities and by members of other faiths. In many areas, therefore, Catholic schools are filled to capacity and are, in fact, oversubscribed by parents who are attracted by the Catholic school's reputation for academic success and for taking spiritual and moral formation seriously. As Cardinal Hume (1997, pp. 25–26) has put it:

> The Church's aim has always been to provide a place at a Catholic school for every Catholic child. Great strides have been taken towards achieving that goal. Today, Catholic schools are increasingly popular, not only because of the good academic results they often achieve, but also because many parents sense that a Catholic

---

[*] This chapter also appears in Feheney, M. (ed.), as 'The Future of the Catholic Church: An English Perspective' in *From Ideal to Action: The Inner Nature of a Catholic School Today* (Dublin, Veritas, 1998). First published by Veritas Publications and used with permission.

[1] McLaughlin, T., O'Keefe, J. and O'Keeffe, B. (eds), *The Contemporary Catholic School: Context, Identity and Diversity* (London, Falmer, 1996).

school might help their children to develop the self-discipline, moral resilience and spiritual maturity so necessary in surviving exposure as young adults to the winds of secularism and materialism in our society.

The decision by the British Prime Minister (an Anglican) and his wife (a Catholic) to send their [children] to a Catholic grant-maintained school in London appeared to confer public and political legitimacy upon a schooling system that has, even as late as the 1970s, been subject to political calls, especially from the Left, for its abolition on the grounds of social divisiveness, covert selection and the general undermining of the effectiveness of the state system of schooling.[2]

If we distinguish in educational analysis between *surface level analysis* and *deep structure analysis*[3] it is possible to conclude that, at a surface level, the future for Catholic schools in England looks bright. The schools have most of the surface and visible indicators of success and effectiveness, i.e. good academic and test scores, a reputation for spiritual and moral excellence and for the 'good discipline' which exemplifies this, a strong position in the competitive internal market for schooling which developed in the 1980s, the support of parents ('customers'/'consumers') extending well beyond the Catholic community, and official and political legitimacy and approval at a high level in the British state. There is much here to give confidence for the future.

However, analysis at the deep structure level prevents the development of triumphalism about Catholic schooling and encourages, instead, thoughtful reflection about its visible success and more systematic research into the changing culture of Catholic schooling. This paper is written as a contribution to deep structure analysis by looking carefully at some of the contemporary challenges for the future of Catholic schooling in England and with reference to the available research.

[2] James Arthur (1995) notes that the Inner London Education Authority (ILEA), in evidence to the Taylor Committee in 1976, argued that 'Catholic schools did not take their fair share of really difficult children' (105) and the Association of Metropolitan Education Authorities, as late as 1989, passed a resolution which asserted that voluntary-aided schools were 'damaging' to the interests of state education in some localities (119).

[3] Deep structure analysis refers to a mode of social and educational inquiry which goes beyond surface indicators of performance or 'success' to attempt in-depth assessment of culture, process and values. A fundamental concern of this approach is to evaluate the extent to which an educational institution realises in its practice what it claims in its mission statement.

Challenges for the future of Catholic schooling

1. Common good v individual self-interest

The Sacred Congregation for Catholic Education, in publications such as *The Catholic School* (1988), asked all Catholics to consider 'the Catholic school's fundamental reasons for existing' (p. 2). The Sacred Congregation provided a basic framework to guide such thinking, as follows:

> To provide a service which is truly civic and apostolic. (p. 9)

> This is the basis of a Catholic school's educational work. Education is not given for the purpose of gaining power but as an aid towards a fuller understanding of, and communion with, man (*sic*), events and things. Knowledge is not to be considered as a means of material prosperity and success but as a call to serve and to be responsible for others. (p. 43)

> First and foremost the Church offers its educational service to 'the poor or those who are deprived of family help and affection or those who are far from the faith' (pp. 44–45)

> For the Catholic school mutual respect means service to the Person of Christ. Co-operation is between brothers and sisters in Christ. A policy of working for the common good is undertaken seriously as working for the building up of the kingdom of God. (p. 46)

This fundamental call to be of service to the poor (in economic, family and spiritual terms) has been a powerful constituent of the culture of Catholic schooling since the Second Vatican Council in many countries, including the USA, England, Ireland and Australia. Bryk *et al.* (1993), in a major research study, *Catholic Schools and the Common Good,* have argued that many Catholic schools in the USA serving inner-city communities have been informed by 'an inspirational ideology' (p. 301) which has made them qualitatively different from public (state) schools. This inspirational ideology has celebrated the primacy of the spiritual and moral life, the dignity of the person, the importance of community and the moral commitments to caring, social justice and the common good as the visible fruits of the faith. Catholic school principalship in these contexts has been strongly influenced by the spiritual, economic and moral capital of the various religious orders, which have provided most of the leadership

positions until recently. Working with such a culture of 'the preferential option for the poor', Bryk *et al.* have demonstrated that
Catholic schools have made considerable contributions to the
common good of American society by their effective academic,
spiritual, moral and social service to the most deprived and disadvantaged communities.

The detailed research reported in *Catholic Schools and the Common
Good*, while celebrating these achievements in the past, concludes
in sombre terms. Contemporary conditions in the USA are beginning to demonstrate that market forces and market values in
education and the inexorable circumstances shaping institutional
survival and financial solvency are threatening the historical
mission and values of Catholic schooling. As the strategic subsidy[4]
which the religious orders provided in personnel and in cultural
and economic capital for the educational mission to the poor
weakens over time, Catholic schools in areas of the greatest need
are closing while those in the affluent suburbs are prospering.
These trends are confirmed by the research of O'Keefe (1996) in
a paper evocatively entitled, 'No Margin, No Mission'. Surveying
the pattern of Catholic school closures in poor inner-city areas of
the USA, O'Keefe calls for renewed efforts in the Catholic
community as a whole to sustain the educational mission to 'some
of the most underprivileged children in the United States'
(p. 193). What is being described here is the growing triumph of
profit margin (market culture in education) over educational and
spiritual mission (the option for the poor). As market forces in
education grow stronger, and as the ability of the Catholic Church
and of the religious orders to countervail these economic forces
becomes weaker, the future of Catholic schooling may look bright
in the suburbs but grim in the inner city, where its priority mission
should be.

For English Catholic schools in the maintained sector of education there are similar challenges for the future, but realised within
different socio-political and cultural contexts, the most significant
of which is the existence of substantial state funding for denominational education. However, developments in the 1980s and
1990s arising from the educational reforms of governments influenced by the ideologies of the New Right have led to major
changes in the culture of education and in the general working

---

[4] The 'strategic subsidy' of the religious orders has been particularly crucial in
urban poverty areas in the past. The question for the future is: Will the state, or
the wider Catholic community, be prepared to take over this subsidy? In both
cases, the answer seems likely to be 'no'.

environment of schools. The introduction of local management of schools (with individual devolved budgetary responsibility), empowered school governors (to strengthen the parental voice in education), grant-maintained status (to encourage autonomous independence from local education authorities), open pupil enrolments (to encourage 'customer'/'consumer' choice among schools) and a political and ideological climate celebrating a competitive market in education, the survival of the fittest as demonstrated by public academic league tables and the need for the closure of 'failing' schools; all of these radical changes have attempted to transform the culture of English schooling so that all schools are subject to the discipline of the individual competitive success, measured, visible and cost-effective.

Catholic schools in England face challenges in the future from a new culture of education which, at its worst, involves the commodification of education,[5] the marketisation of school cultures and processes and the celebration of an ethic of individual and autonomous school 'success', regardless of the fate of other schools. These developments do not articulate easily with Catholic values in education, where spiritual and moral culture is given precedence over material success, where education is seen as a service and not a product, and where notions of the common good and of the well-being of community institutions take precedence over individual self-interest. In other words, the space, identity and voice of contemporary Catholic schooling in England is now more directly challenged by individualistic and market values than ever before in history. In these circumstances, the critical question for Catholic school leaders (the hierarchy, the head teachers and the school governors) is: Can a legitimate balance be found between Catholic values and market values or will market forces in education begin to compromise the integrity of the special mission of Catholic schooling? Can Gospel values survive in the face of a more direct relationship with the market-place and education?

Richard Pring (1996) has argued that the philosophy of the market-place is incompatible with the distinctive idea of the nature and purpose of schools. In particular, in placing the market and individual self-interest at the centre of educational arrangements, the reforms of the 1980s, he argues, undermine Catholic educational values, which emphasize the importance of community and

[5] For a discussion of the commodification of education, see Grace, G., 'Education is a Public Good', in D. Bridges and T. McLaughlin (eds), *Education and the Market-Place* (London, Falmer, 1994).

concern for the common good. My own research (Grace, 1995, 1996) demonstrates that the struggles between concern for the common good and the advancement of school self-interest constitute major ethical and professional dilemmas for Catholic head teachers in England. Stated in its starkest form, it is beginning to be realized by head teachers that there is little market yield or measurable return for schools which continue to operate a preferential option for the poor or even a fully open-door policy for all the children and youth of the local community. In a market economy for schooling, the imperatives of visible and measurable success, financial balance and high league table positions, all combine against commitment to 'customers' who are lacking in both cultural and economic capital and the 'right attitudes' to schooling. The temptation is, therefore, to 'play the market' or to 'go upmarket' by adopting a more calculating policy on who is admitted to the school, who is excluded from the school, who is entered for external examinations at secondary level, etc. At present, Catholic head teachers are struggling with these market temptations and dilemmas:

> Catholic schools really must keep the explicit link between Christ and person-centred education.... How do we square our vocational vision of pupils as persons with the market vision of economic units? How does this affect our treatment of special educational needs? How does this affect our admissions policy? (Female secondary head teacher, quoted in Grace, 1995, p. 176.)

The moral and professional dilemma that is currently facing Catholic head teachers (primary and secondary) in England is the recognition that a competitive market culture in schooling is making it much more difficult to be in the service of the poor, the troublesome, the alienated and the powerless. Success can be achieved with such children and young people (as the Catholic Bishops' report, A Struggle for excellence, 1997, demonstrates), but at a greater cost in terms of time, resources, staff commitment and educational support, and it can only be fairly judged in relative rather than in absolute terms. As questions of cost and cost-effectiveness become more dominant in English schooling culture, and as public and visible 'success' continues to be judged in absolute terms, the integrity of Catholic schooling in the future is, at a deep structure level, under threat. Catholic schools may continue to score successes in the new culture of schooling in England but this may be at the price of fidelity to 'the poor or those who are deprived of family help and affection or those who are far from the faith'.

It is clearly in recognition of this threat to the spiritual, moral and educational integrity of Catholic schooling in the future that the Bishops' Conference of England and Wales has issued an authoritative commentary on *The Common Good in Education* (1997). In calling for more solidarity, partnership and co-operation among Catholic schools, the bishops say:

> it remains the Christian duty of individual schools themselves to promote the common good and support 'the poor, vulnerable, powerless and defenceless' by:
>
> • reviewing and, where necessary, amending their selection procedures
> • sharing specialist resources wherever possible with those that have few or none
> • helping unpopular schools to improve their public image
> • working at local, diocesan and national levels to ensure an equitable distribution of the resources available to education. (*The Common Good in Education*, p. 17)

Future research will have to investigate the extent to which Catholic schools remain faithful to their own mission statements, the exhortations of the Sacred Congregation for Catholic Education, and the call from the bishops for solidarity and commitment to the common good. In the struggle between moral purpose and material success, an important values audit will have to be undertaken of the integrity and distinctiveness, at a deep structural level, of Catholic schooling culture in England.

2. The nature of future Catholicity

In considering 'the Catholic school's fundamental reasons for existing' (p. 8), the Sacred Congregation for Catholic Education laid emphasis upon the contribution of the Catholic school to the salvific mission of the Church. Thus it asserted 'the Catholic school forms part of the saving mission of the Church, especially for education in the faith' (1988, p. 13). What 'education in the faith' entails, what the evidence of its relative success or failure can be said to be, and what forms of Catholicity are actually realized in the living cultures of different types of Catholic school are currently topics for debate and for research in England.

Thomas Groome (1996) has claimed that what makes a school

Catholic is, among other things, the presence of five theological characteristics:

- a positive anthropology of the person i.e. a realistic but optimistic understanding of people as capable of sin but essentially good;[6]
- a sacramental life and a sacramental consciousness i.e. an awareness of the presence of God as mediated by the liturgical sacraments;
- a communal emphasis i.e. that we find our identity, our true selves and our salvation in a relationship with others;
- a sense of tradition i.e. the importance of tradition and history in the development of the Christian story;
- an appreciation of rationality and learning i.e. the illumination of faith by reason wherever possible.

To what extent in the past Catholic schools in England actually realized a culture of Catholicity of this type is difficult to assess, given the paucity of systematic research with such a focus. However, there are influential writers who believe that the Catholicity of the schools was much stronger in the past than it is in the present or will be in the future. James Arthur (1995), in *The Ebbing Tide: Policy and Principles of Catholic Education*, argues that Catholic schools in England, which were originally founded on a 'holistic' model ('concerned with the transmission ... of Catholic faith – its beliefs, values, character and norms of conduct' (p. 233)), are being transformed over time into educational cultures based upon 'dualistic' and 'pluralistic' models. For Arthur, the 'dualistic' Catholic school separates the secular and religious elements of education, regarding the Catholic ethos of the school as something additional to its secular academic programme, and 'it does not assume that a majority of children come from believing families' (p. 227). The 'pluralistic' school is based on the assumption that all single-faith schools offer an educational setting which is narrow and divisive ... and this school model would involve accepting other faiths into Catholic schools' (p. 229). The analysis contained in *The Ebbing Tide* suggests that English Catholic schooling of the holistic type is giving ground, especially at secondary-school level, to dualistic and pluralistic

---

[6] There is, of course, no shortage of accounts of pre-Conciliar Catholic schooling which assert that the anthropology of the person was based upon a different principle, i.e. capable of good but essentially evil.

models of schooling, and that this constitutes part of the ebbing tide of Catholicity. In support of this thesis, Dr Arthur constructs an illuminative (although fictional) case study of St Michael's secondary school in which the Blessed Sacrament is reserved in the school chapel at the opening of the school in 1960 and removed from a very different St Michael's in 1996. The symbolism is power-ful and intentional: a central feature of Catholicity in the schools, the sacramental life and the consciousness that goes with it, is disappearing, and Catholic schools in England in the future will 'become institutions practically indistinguishable from those under LEA control' (p. 253).

This analysis has provoked much controversy within the Catholic educational community in England. For some, it has given expres-sion to their deepest fears that Catholic schools are undergoing a process of incorporation into a multi-faith pluralism which will extinguish the rich distinctiveness of the Catholic faith. Worse than this, the dualistic school appears to relegate religion to being a footnote to the serious academic text of achieving measurable successes. However, for others, Arthur's analysis is based upon a golden-age construct of Catholicity in the past and a too pessimistic reading of the different forms that Catholicity can take in contemporary schooling. Peter Hastings (1996), for instance, believes that much of the Catholicity of English schooling in the past was oppressive in its culture and immature in its outcomes. For Hastings, the future for a mature Catholicity must be found in schools that value openness and intellectual challenge.

From a research standpoint, there is much to be done in this contested area. This is why I have worked to establish a Centre for Research and Development in Catholic Education at London University, Institute of Education.[7] James Arthur's thesis of ebbing Catholicity is not actually based on extensive fieldwork research in Catholic schools.[8] While intuitively appealing, it remains at the level of a hypothesis to be tested. Similarly, the notion that a vital and authentic Catholicity is tied to a particular form of the sacra-mental life must be investigated in detail. As part of a pilot study for a more extensive inquiry into the contemporary role of Catholic secondary schools in inner-city areas of England, I have

[7] It seems remarkable that no designated agency for research into Catholic education in England and Wales has been established in this century. The CRDCE was inaugurated in September 1996 with an initial grant from The Society of Jesus.

[8] Fieldwork research for *The Ebbing Tide* was based upon a study of Catholic schools in Oxfordshire only.

been involved in research consultations with a sample of head teachers. This has revealed that, while the celebration of the Mass may be relatively infrequent in such schools, many of the head teachers assert that Catholicity is being 'realized in other ways'. Future research will need to probe the validity of such claims and to explore what head teachers, teachers and pupils understand by other forms of Catholicity. The question of what constitutes the Catholic ethos of a school is another contested area which needs investigation. For some the issue is necessarily tied to the proportion of Catholic pupils (practising or nominal) who are present on the school roll. For others, this is a narrow and mechanistic view which fails to take into account the contemporary faith pluralism of inner-city communities and the need for Catholic schools to be of service to 'those who are far from faith'[9] (Sacred Congregation, p. 45).

Just as Catholic school leaders have to consider what legitimate balance can be made in the future between the imperative demands of market survival and those of spiritual and moral mission, so too they have to consider what is the proper balance that should be made between the generation of a distinctive Catholic ethos on the one hand and a pluralistic and ecumenical openness to all faiths or even to non-faith on the other.

Those who support the analysis given in *The Ebbing Tide* argue that a great strength of Catholic religious and educational culture is the richness of its symbolic life and its ritual practices. This richness, in their view, should not be lost to Catholic school culture in the future in the mistaken pursuit of modernity, pluralism or ecumenism. Thus, McClelland (1992, pp. 6–7) argues:

> The crucifix should not be discarded from classrooms as a gesture to religious pluralism. Neither should representation of saints be relegated ... in the interests of a false ecumenism. Nor should pious religious practices be abandoned on the altar of individual freedom. All these things are daily reminders of that communion of saints which lies at the heart of the theology of the Catholic school. Such schools will not overcome the materialism of the age ... (in this way).

---

[9] It is not only Catholic inner-city schools which are dealing with significant numbers of 'those who are far from the faith'; it is also, at the other end of the financial spectrum, Catholic independent schools. As Bishop David Konstant noted in his address to the Conference of Catholic Independent Schools, 'roughly half of all pupils in your schools are Catholics; there is no indication as to the religious background of the other 50 per cent' (1997, p. 64).

Peter McLaren (1993) has suggested that ritual and symbolism have a powerful effect on the formation of young people and on the process of 'making Catholics'. The power of ritual and symbolism is to be found precisely in their appeal to the imagination, the emotions and the sense of dramatic, which are particularly salient during adolescence. In his ethnographic study of a conservative Catholic school, 'St Ryan's', McLaren concluded that:

> Overall, a broad range of Catholic symbols were translated by class-room rituals into graphic and readily comprehensible messages which constituted a compelling way of viewing reality and the student's location within that reality. (p. 184)

While such observations seem to support the case for renewing a strong form of Catholic ethos in the future, there are also counter-arguments which suggest that a 'strong' form of Catholic ethos may, in practice, be oppressive and alienating in religious formation and inhibiting to open and critical intellectual inquiry. As well as this, it may seem to signal Catholic exclusiveness and closure to other faith communities rather than inclusiveness and openness to the challenges of contemporary pluralism.

For Bernadette O'Keeffe (1992), the future for Catholic schools in England must be in the direction of greater openness. Such openness is already a *de facto* feature of many Catholic schools in inner-city areas where substantial 'other faith' school populations exist. For O'Keeffe, it should now become a principled development for the future, where faith rather than denomination 'would seek to achieve the integration of differences into a collaborative and fruitful whole' (p. 45).

There is a wariness in the English Catholic community about greater openness and the possibility of inter-faith schools. The historical legacy of the citadel school (as a bulwark against enemies of the Faith) and of triumphalist truth claims (against the truth claims of other faiths) is far from exhausted. At this present juncture, there appears to be a sincere commitment to dialogue with other faiths (which is an advance over no dialogue) but little evidence of such dialogue being realized in many concrete educational projects which advance the inter-faith educational mission.[10] It is significant, in this connection, that Bishop Vincent Nichols, addressing Catholic educators on 'The Church's mission

---

[10] For an account of the progress and the difficulties associated with inter-denominational schools, see Chadwick, P., *Schools of Reconciliation: Issues in Joint Roman Catholic-Anglican Education* (London, Cassell, 1994).

in education in a multi-faith society', observed:

> Catholicism is not a breakaway movement or a protest. It is not a
> denomination. Rather it is a response to the revealed truth – a truth
> which possesses it, and not a truth which a Catholic can ever
> pretend to possess. (1997, p. 58)

Much more debate and much more research will be required in
the future to assist the Catholic educational community in England
and its deliberations about what sort of Catholicity should be
looked for in the schools.

Conclusion

There is not space here to do justice to the full range of issues that
will impinge upon the future of Catholic schooling in England.
Among these are questions to do with the tensions between
Catholic grant-maintained schools and Catholic voluntary-aided
schools; tensions between hierarchical counsel and guidance on
the future of schools and the voice of a more confident and
assertive group of parents; issues to do with the future of Catholic
independent schools and the matters relating to the future role of
religious orders and their changing mission in education. While all
of these are important, it is the argument of this paper that the two
most profound questions are the nature of the educational mission
being realized in the schools in an age of market culture, and the
nature of Catholicity being realized in the schools in a more
secular and pluralistic age.

Catholic schools in England are currently enjoying great surface
structure success, popularity and acclaim from official sources.
What their status is at the deep structure level of educational, spiritual, moral and ethical integrity, is a more complex issue, in need
of much more debate, dialogue and research inquiry.[11] Catholic
schools, by reason of their special mission, have to pay particular
attention to the verse in St Matthew's Gospel which asks: 'What
shall it profit a man to gain the whole world and to lose his own
soul?' It is not being suggested here that Catholic schooling in
England has lost its soul, but it is being suggested that, for the

---

[11] For a discussion of the importance of Catholic school mission statements in
guiding such research, see Grace, G., 'Realising the Mission: Catholic
Approaches to School Effectiveness', in R. Slee *et al.* (eds), *Effective for Whom?
School Effectiveness and the School Improvement Movement* (London, Falmer, 1997).

future, more investigation should be undertaken on the state of its educational soul.[12]

Acknowledgements
I would like to thank Professor Richard Pring and Professor James Arthur for comments received on the first draft of this paper.

Bibliography
Arthur, J., *The Ebbing Tide: Policy and Principles in Catholic Education*, (Leominster, Gracewing, 1995).

Bryk, A. *et al.*, *Catholic Schools and the Common Good* (Cambridge, Mass., Harvard University Press, 1993).

Catholic Bishops' Conference of England and Wales, *The Common Good in Education* (London, Catholic Education Service, 1997).

Chadwick, P., *Schools of Reconciliation: Issues in Joint Roman Catholic-Anglican Education* (London, Cassell, 1994).

Department for Catholic Education and Formation, *A Struggle for Excellence* (London, Catholic Education Service, 1997).

Grace, G., 'Education is a Public Good', in D. Bridges and T. McLaughlin (eds), *Education and the Market-Place* (London, Falmer, 1994).

Grace, G., *School Leadership: Beyond Educational Management* (London, Falmer, 1995).

Grace, G., 'Realising the Mission: Catholic Approaches to School Effectiveness', in R. Slee *et al.* (eds), *Effective for Whom? School Effectiveness and the School Improvement Movement* (London, Falmer, 1997).

Groome, T., 'What Makes a School Catholic?', in T. McLaughlin *et al.* (eds), op. cit.

Hastings, P., 'Openness and Intellectual Challenge in Catholic Schools', in T. McLaughlin *et al.* (eds), op. cit.

Hume, B., 'The Church's Mission in Education', an address given in April 1995 and reprinted in *Partners in Mission* (London, Catholic Education Service, 1997).

Konstant, D., 'The Church and Catholic Independent Schools', an address given in April 1995 and reprinted in *Partners in Mission* (London, Catholic Education Service, 1997).

McClelland, V., 'The Concept of Catholic Education', in V. McClelland (ed.), *The Catholic School and the European Context* (Hull, University of Hull, 1992).

McLaren, P., *Schooling as a Ritual Performance* (London, Routledge, 1993).

McLaughlin, T., O'Keefe, J. and O'Keeffe, B. (eds), *The Contemporary Catholic School: Context, Identiy and Diversity* (London, Falmer, 1996).

---

[12] At a more general theoretical level, Philip Wexler, *Holy Sparks: Social Theory, Education and Religion* (London, Macmillan, 1997) has called for the 'resacralising' of social and educational theory and of research inquiry in education.

Nichols, V., 'The Church's Mission in Education in a Multi-Faith Society', an address given in April 1995 and reprinted in *Partners in Mission*, op. cit.

O'Keeffe, B., 'Catholic schools in an Open Society: The English Challenge', in V.A. McClelland (ed.), *The Catholic School and the European Context* (Hull, University of Hull, 1992).

O'Keefe, J., 'No Margin: No Mission', in T. McLaughlin *et al.* (eds), op. cit.

Pring, R., 'Markets, Education and Catholic Schools', in T. McLaughlin *et al.* (eds). op. cit.

Sacred Congregation for Catholic Education (ed.), *The Catholic School* (Homebush, NSW, St. Paul's, 1998).

Wexler, P., *Holy Sparks: Social Theory, Education and Religion* (London, Macmillan, 1997).

Chapter 2

Catholic Education in Scotland

James C. Conroy

Christian, what
went wrong with your art?...

I'm sorry that the daring
dream you had has faded,
that your truth isn't everlasting,
that today your souls are merely
empty, lightless houses
the wind of your fear sweeps through,
of your unwillingness to admit
that your words have lost all meaning!...

And so all you could do
was to reject even art
and set your God on a throne of ugliness

Christopher Whyte (1989–90)
(Whyte, 2000, pp. 224–227)[1]

---

[1] A Chriosdaidhean, carson a chaill
bhur n-ealain-se a brigh...

Is truagh leamsa gun do chrion
am bruadar dana sin a bh'agaibh.
bhur firinneachd a bhith gun chrisoch,
's nach eil nur n-anmannan an duigh
achtaighean falamh dubharach
gaoth fhuar bhur n-eagal a'sguabadh trompa,
bhur neo-thoil a bhith 'g aideachadh
gun do chaill bhur cainnt gach brigh!...

Mar sin b'fheudar dhaibh
an ealain fhein a mhasladh
's bhur dia a chur air cathair duaichneachd

Introduction

Undoubtedly the most critical issue for Catholic education in the twenty-first century is the loss of meaning to which the Scottish poet Christopher Whyte gives such eloquent testimony. The loss of meaning can come as a result of the withdrawal of legitimacy by those outside the institution or by the loss of belief of those within. This is as true in Scotland as it is elsewhere. Either way the challenge to Catholic education comes from those who see no meaning in its words and symbols and who would replace its rhetoric of the created person with that of the economic cipher. Here I am primarily concerned to explore the erosion of legitimacy in the wider Scottish polity. This does not absolve Catholic educationalists and the Catholic Church in Scotland from a continuing responsibility to persuade both those inside and outside Catholic education that Catholic Christianity has much to offer them as a system of meaning and import. To return then to the central theme of this essay, it is the case that those who would bring an end to Catholic education come from many walks of life, united only in their core belief that religiously denominated education is at best anachronistic and at worst positively dangerous. This essay is an attempt to understand this process from one particular angle. It does not offer a taxonomy of critical issues in Scottish Catholic education but suggests a line of argument which brings together a number of issues under one broad heading. So what might this be?

As I sat down to reflect on the particular way in which this challenge manifests itself in Scotland I began a search for some kind of understanding of the distinctions to be made between the Scottish variety of Catholic education and its counterparts in England and Wales and Northern Ireland. After all they are all supposedly located in parts of the same political entity and, as such, it might be expected that they are roughly equivalent in terms of status, structure and legal frameworks. But this is not the case; there are quite marked distinctions to be made between the provision in Scotland and that made elsewhere in the United Kingdom. Indeed the current legal frameworks offer quite a different understanding of the relationship between the State and the Catholic school, or more generally Catholic education. These differences are a consequence of three important and interrelated features of Scottish history. Firstly, the religious history of Scotland has had a profound impact on the evolution of educational provision and the consequent place of Catholic education. Secondly, and not unrelated, were the particular patterns of migration which affected Scotland, in particular from the end of the eighteenth century through to the early part of the twentieth century. Finally, the distinctive legal and legislative history of Scotland has been important in producing subtle but important differences in major education acts of the late nineteenth and early twentieth centuries. In order to understand something of the challenges facing Scottish Catholic education it is necessary to reflect on these features of its historical context and evolution. After this brief historical survey I will outline some of the implications which it has had and continues to have for the maintenance and mission of Catholic education. In this way I will demonstrate that the most critical issue facing Scottish Catholic education is rooted in but not limited to its historic context. In doing so I hope to illustrate the point that the withdrawal of legitimacy by those who no longer ascribe meaning to the language of religion in general and to Catholicism in particular but who continue to hold political sway represents the greatest threat to the continuation of Catholic education in Scotland. Despite this I would also wish to suggest that there continues to be a way forward for Catholic education. However, if Catholic education is to thrive in a post-devolution Scotland it must address the loss.

The Historic Context for Scottish Catholic education

This section, then, deals with the historic development of Catholic education in Scotland.

1. Catholic burgh schools represented the backbone of Scottish education prior to the Reformation and ensured that it was among the most successful offerings anywhere in Europe. After Oxbridge it has the third, fourth and fifth oldest Universities in the United Kingdom in St Andrew's, Glasgow and Aberdeen. These three pre-Reformation universities were established to counter heresy but were also a testament to the central importance of education to Scottish public life. Peculiarly in Scotland, after the thirteenth century the secular clergy grew in stature, eventually becoming more important than the religious orders. This in turn led to the establishment of burgh schools. In the later Middle Ages local schools developed which were managed by the burghers; an arrangement which sometimes led to conflict with the local cathedral or monastery.
    It was this established network of burgh schools which were

to be so vital to the transformation of Scotland into a Presbyterian country and were wholeheartedly embraced by the Reformers who recognised their evangelising importance. Given that, from the outset, the Scottish Reformation was much more ideologically driven than its English counterpart and that the individual was seen to be at the centre of his or her own salvation, and further, given that the Bible (*scriptura sola*) was the guide to this individual salvation, schools which taught reading and writing were profoundly important to the Protestantizing of Scotland. It would be hard to overestimate the importance of the Reformation on Scottish education *per se* or indeed the importance attached to education by the Reformers with the maintenance of Grammar schools falling to local burghs and the Kirk showing an intense interest in education from its inception. Knox and others quickly produced a book of discipline as an appendix to his *History of the Reformation in Scotland* with two chapters on education. As an integral part of the plan for a changed religious landscape the Reformers decided to maintain the parish as the administrative unit and wished for each parish to have a school attached. It should also be remembered in this connection that the curriculum in Scottish schools was more comprehensive than elsewhere in Europe and was to include reading, catechism, grammar, Latin, arts, philosophy and languages (Scotland, 1969). The Reformation project in Scotland was indeed very successful with its framers regarding education as the right of all children and such education to be founded upon a systematic presentation of the faith. Indeed so successful was it that by the time of the passing of the 1872 Education (Scotland) Act the provision of education here compared favourably with that in other European countries including England (at least it was better for the middle classes). As Knox indicates, in respect of the whole population this meant that 1 in 140 (in private schools) had a secondary education in Scotland (1 in 205 if only public schools counted). The comparable figures for Prussia was 1 in 249; for France 1 in 570; for England 1 in 1300. This was probably little comfort to the few remaining Catholics post-Reformation who were restricted to isolated areas of the highlands and a few islands in the Outer Hebrides and this right of education did not extend to them.

2.   The position of Catholics remained pretty much the same until the second decade of the nineteenth century (Handley, 1947)

when Scotland experienced substantial Irish Catholic immigra-
tion. Most of these Irish Catholics were economic migrants and
much too poor to consider education to have any significance.
In Scotland, at least, this Catholic migration was accompanied
by Protestant migration, largely from the province of Ulster, to
feed the industrial growth of Glasgow. The industrial growth of
Glasgow in particular required large numbers of manual
labourers and the Irish immigrants were competing not only
with each other for employment but also with the large
number of Highland Scots moving south in the wake of the
Clearances. In Glasgow and elsewhere these groups were effectively fighting each other for the scarce resources which
attended manual labour in the nineteenth century. However
Irish Protestants had a significant advantage. Not only were
many of them co-religionists with their Scottish hosts but the
political and ecclesial establishments of the Reformed Church
in Scotland and Ireland had very close ties. Indeed it might be
argued that the Presbyterian communities of Scotland and
Ireland were significantly overlapping with Glasgow University
being the education centre for both and Ministers of the
Presbyterian congregations moving back and forth between the
two parts of the United Kingdom (Stewart, 1993, pp. 81–89).
While it is undoubtedly the case that Presbyterian émigrés
faced privations on their arrival in the Scottish industrial
centres – especially Glasgow, Edinburgh and Dundee – these
were not as stark as those faced by Catholics. Catholics were at
a further disadvantage in the early part of the nineteenth
century in having virtually no middle class to represent their
interests. Drawing on a number of sources, O'Hagan (1996,
p. 8) points out that, 'the Chairman of the Catholic Schools
Society [founded 1817] for its first thirty years [was] the
merchant and member of parliament, Kirkman Finlay ... not
himself a Catholic, and [that] the original syllabus was drawn
up by a board of thirty, only half of whom belonged to the
Roman Catholic Faith' having very few co-religionists of social
standing to plead their cause.

Nevertheless as the century progressed the Catholic Church
began to establish schools beginning in Glasgow where a
number of schools were created from 1817 onwards. Fitzpatrick
(1985) points out that some 20,000 pupils were receiving some
kind of education but he also indicates that this provision was
indeed basic. This rudimentary provision was maintained
throughout the century but the quality of the education on

offer generally lagged behind that available elsewhere in the country. Gradually the Catholic community through its Bishops and their representatives became more organized, first with the establishment of the Catholic Schools Society (ibid.), the Catholic institute, and most importantly, the Catholic Poor Schools Committee established by the Bishops of England and Wales and subsequently joined by the Scottish hierarchy (O'Hagan, op. cit., pp. 9f). The Catholic Poor Schools Committee gradually encouraged the development of elementary education by way of providing for trained teachers and encouraging improved religious instruction (ibid., p. 10f). However the quality of education on offer remained woefully inadequate despite the gradual improvement wrought by virtue of the establishment of the first three Catholic Teacher Training establishments (St Mary's, Hammersmith, 1850; Notre Dame, Liverpool, 1856; and Sacred Heart Hammersmith, 1870) all of which served Scotland as well as England and Wales. There was no indigenous Scottish college prior to the establishment of Notre Dame College in 1895.

Following the 1870 Forster Education Act, the 1872 Education (Scotland) Act was passed which retained much that was in the parent Act and had similar general aims: the provision of an efficient education for the children of all the people of Scotland. As much as it was significant educationally, it was more important politically as it offered the possibility for Catholics to maintain schools of a reasonable standard and to gradually create a small but significant middle class. The Act provided for any ecclesiastical body to transfer its schools to local school boards which would then assume financial responsibility for their maintenance. This offer must have appeared tempting given the relative material poverty of Catholic schools and the generally poor quality of their teaching. Nonetheless, like the Episcopalians, the Bishops of Scotland decided to continue, where possible, to provide their own schools. As Treble has pointed out, 'this conscious repudiation of the State system ... owed much to the emphasis which was placed by bishops and clergy upon the value of religious education. But in arriving at that verdict they were also consciously influenced by their own perception of the limited potential of the board school' (Treble, 1978, p. 111). Their great fear was that Board schools could only lead down two pathways – the first was into the hands of the Church of Scotland and the second into the hands of creeping secularization.

While Catholic schools were not transferred to the local school boards they were nevertheless able to receive grant funding and after 1872 the number of Catholic schools in receipt of grant aid rose sharply from 65 to 224 by 1918 (ibid., p. 113). Thus, despite their material and social disadvantage Catholics were extremely active in the creation, development and promotion of their schools. However these establishments remained hampered by teacher shortages, poor wages, high teacher-pupil ratios and cramped accommodation, and the high preponderance of unskilled, low wage workers in the Catholic community. This last point had a significant effect on Catholic schooling as many parents felt compelled to withdraw their children from school as soon as they were capable of earning a wage. Attendance was more irregular here than in the board counterparts which in turn led to substantially poorer achievement. This under-development of elementary education meant that the post-elementary provision was in an equally poor condition with only 3% of pupils in Glasgow undertaking post primary study (Skinnider, 1967) and so it remained until the passing of the 1918 Education (Scotland) Act.

3. The 1918 Education Scotland Act has entered into the mythology of Scottish Catholic education as the moment of deliverance for a system creaking at the seams. Many of the aspirations of Catholics for schools to be established on equal terms with their board counterparts were realized. The Bishops and the Catholic community agreed to the transfer of control of their schools to the State; in effect they became state schools. In return the Church was given 'statutory power to approve teachers and appoint supervisors of religious education. Catholic teachers had to be qualified under the national regulations and also be approved by a bishop 'as to their religious belief and character'. They would be the principal witnesses to the religious nature of the education provided' (Fitzpatrick, 1999, p. 257). However the 1918 Act carried dangers as well as hope. Certainly it is true that the quality of provision in Catholic schools was substantially enhanced by its passing but the relationship between the State and the Church has and continues to remain uneasy. The price of the 1918 Act was the effective loss of control over not only the curriculum but the manner in which Catholic schools were to be, and are to this day, managed. The next section sets out some of the critical issues which have arisen out of the difficult history of Scottish

education. In doing so it suggests that the withdrawal of legitimacy alluded to above is to be seen as rooted in the
relationship which modern Scots have to their own legislative
and social history.

Critical Issues

In this section I wish to outline a number of interrelated critical
issues for Scottish Catholic education. It would be possible to
rehearse a large number of issues for Catholic education generally
and no doubt Scottish Catholic education partakes in these by
virtue of its position in the world but they are too many and diffuse
to be dealt with in this essay. Rather the issues dealt with here are
local, determined by the topography of local politics but they are
undoubtedly affected by these more generic challenges to Catholic
education with which I have dealt elsewhere (Conroy, 2000). Such
issues include the continuing impact of the Irish Legacy of
Catholic education in the anglophone world; the nature of Power
and Control; the language of managerialism; the loss of tradition;
the loss of imagination; the absence of a substantial relationship
between Catholic education and contemporary notions of political
economy; the impulses of postmodernity; changes to Information
and medical technologies and the cultural shift from dogma to
discourse.

Local Issues

Focusing on the local critical issues as the centre piece of this essay
is not to ignore their connectedness to these wider concerns.
Indeed it will be apparent in the ensuing discussion that the local
represents a particular refraction of some of the issues listed above,
most especially the relationship between Catholic schooling and
the wider polity. Of course local identification of the religious
purposes of schools can produce distorting effects but such distor-
tions are an integral part of the landscape and consequently
impact on the practices and perspectives of those working in such
institutions. Take as an example an Irish-based student who was
asked to write an essay justifying the continued existence of
Catholic schools in a plural society: one of the central planks of her
response was that such schools continued to be necessary because
without them 'there would be nowhere to learn to play camogie or

learn the Irish language'.[2] Of course such particular and cultural identifications of religion with place may be deplored by those who perceive the Church to be universal and not to be too closely identified with the collective aspirations of this or that group but to do so would be to deny a fundamental feature of all religion; that it is shaped as much by political exigencies as by ecclesial pronouncements on the faith. And so it is that in Scotland to understand some of the critical issues facing Catholic education is to understand something of its history and contemporary politics.

At the end of the first section I indicated that the 1918 Act was seminal in Catholic education. The Church was struggling to pay for its schools, its teachers were more poorly paid than their state counterparts and the Catholic community was still regarded as alien and suffered from significant and substantial discrimination. The Act was also important in Scottish public life as a marker of a changing relationship between the Irish-Catholic community and the wider civic society. In the wake of the Second World War it was recognised, albeit temporarily, that many Catholics had fought for Britain and could be seen in some sense to be loyal. To the extent that it drew the then existing 226 Catholic schools into a National system it might be regarded as an act of public reconciliation. Catholic schools (and, indeed, their Episcopalian counterparts which had also remained outside the Board school system set up in 1872) were to become State schools.

This sense of national cohesiveness was to be short-lived and, as Finn points out, 'A truly national education system, one that recognized and accepted diversity, now began to operate in Scotland. Unfortunately, the spirit of reconciliation that was apparent at the conclusion of the Great War was not to last much longer' (1999, p. 874). For many, the idea that Catholic schools could be paid for on the rates (never mind that Catholics too paid rates) was, and continues to be, anathema. Since the passing of the Act there has been opposition to the maintenance of Catholic schools. For much of the twentieth century this opposition was framed in quite openly bigoted, indeed racist, terms with the Presbyterian Church in the forefront of calls for the repatriation of Irish Catholics and the repeal of the 1918 Act (ibid., p. 876).

While the more virulent attacks on Catholic schools have gradually lost much of their potency, the calls for the closure of Catholic

---

[2] Camogie is a game for women played almost exclusively among Catholic women and girls in Ireland using sticks and a ball. This example comes from the author's personal experience.

schools continue unabated to the present day albeit in a different, more nuanced form. Of course the terms in which this debate are couched are no longer held to be openly prejudiced though the virulent reaction to a speech given by the Scottish Catholic composer, James MacMillan, at the Edinburgh Book Festival in 1999 now published in a collection of essays entitled *Scotland's Shame* (MacMillan, 2000) may give the lie to this. MacMillan argued that Scotland continues to harbour deep rooted anti-Catholic prejudices and systemic, institutionalised bigotry. The response in some sections of the Scottish press was as swift as it was vitriolic and MacMillan was roundly condemned for opening up such a hornets' nest and accused of an over active imagination. The political, social and cultural elites of Scotland were appalled that they might be labelled prejudiced, especially in view of the creation of their fledgling model democratic institutions. However, it is only necessary to look at the manner in which Macmillan's speech was reported to recognize the structural flaws in Scottish public life. In his speech, MacMillan had been critical of the role the Catholic Church had played in Scottish public life and had then gone on to examine the anti-Catholic sentiment which lurks below the surface in Scottish institutions. His observations about the limitations of the leadership of the Catholic Church were not taken up in the press. Was this because the Press were afraid to be seen to be critical of the Church? It would be difficult to uphold such a claim in the light of the constant stream of criticism levelled at the Church in the Scottish press. Rather, it would appear that much of the press did not wish to muddy the waters by exposing the balanced and thoughtful manner in which MacMillan couched his arguments. In a classical *ad hominem* move it was seen to be more 'productive' to brand MacMillan as extreme. In this way broadsheets such as the *Glasgow Herald* could more easily dismiss the arguments. What impact do these wider considerations have on the continuance of Catholic schools?

Despite the claims that anti-Catholic prejudice is a thing of the past, the advent of the Scottish parliament has seen an interesting rise in renewed clarion calls for the closure of Catholic schools. These calls are not confined to fringe members of Presbyterian sects or to bigots on football terraces as is sometimes imagined. Calls for the closure of Catholic schools come from, among others, senior academics, Steve Bruce, Professor of Sociology at the University of Aberdeen (Bruce, 1998, p. 5), Senior politicians, Lord MacKay and John Maxton (Conroy, 1999a), senior Trades Union officials, Fred Forrester, recently retired Deputy General

Secretary of the Educational Institute of Scotland (EIS) (Forrester, 2000) and leading broadsheet newspapers (*Glasgow Herald*, 1998, p. 15). The justification for these calls is not couched in terms of the poverty of what is on offer in Catholic schools, nor in terms of the unpatriotic nature of Irish-Catholics but is rooted in the claim that Catholic schools are, by virtue of their very existence, either unjust or sectarian. This challenge to Catholic education manifests itself in a number of related ways. Firstly there is the position artic- ulated by Bruce, who claims that, 'irrespective of any virtues that Catholic education may have, and irrespective of the rights of any group of parents to raise their children as they wish, a segregated school system is divisive [because] the dual system separates young people' (Bruce, op. cit., p. 5). Secondly, as with the EIS position, the provision of the 1918 Act which gives the Church the right of approval of teachers is regarded as an impediment to justice. At the time of writing the Educational Institute for Scotland is mount- ing a legal challenge on the grounds that teachers in the Catholic school from other traditions are being discriminated against in their attempts to seek employment and promotion in the Catholic school. Thirdly, there is the critique mounted in the pages of the *Glasgow Herald*; that Catholic schools are past their 'sell-by' date since most of the children in attendance are no longer practising Catholics and that Catholic schools no longer pass on the Catholic faith. Since the passing on of the Catholic faith was the reason for their establishment and since that reason no longer has any purchase in the actual life of the school they should close or be closed. The *Glasgow Herald* claims (without any substantive evidence) that, 'members of Catholic school boards have boasted that Catholic schools today take the same "neutral" approach to religious belief and practice as non-denominational schools and religiously indifferent parents fighting school closures declare that they do so not on religious grounds, but either because the school has a good academic record or on grounds of proximity. Proof that the constant references to the "distinctive Catholic ethos" in defence of the separate school system has become a meaningless soundbite comes from a Catholic teacher recently quoted in the Scottish press as saying that "Catholic schools have the same educa- tion aims in RE as do the non-denominational schools"' (*Glasgow Herald*, 1998, p. 15).

Are these claims against the continuance of Catholic schools justified? Let me take them one at a time.

Undoubtedly Bruce is correct, children are separated by virtue of the existence of Catholic schools but such an observation is neither novel nor useful since children are separated one from the other by all kinds of discrete social and cultural groupings. And, in any event, they are only separated for part of their daily existence (15% of a child's waking life is spent in school). It is a strange argument which suggests that the existence of something which has no inherent malign intent is bad simply because it exists. People need to separate themselves from each other, they need to live in different kinds of communities within a wider society and, providing the aims and objectives of that particular grouping are not inimical to the wellbeing of society as a whole then the kind of stance adopted by Bruce has very limited intellectual or practical appeal. If it were to be established that x or y school promoted bigotry and intolerance then there would be a case for saying such a school should be closed. Equally, if Catholic schools as a species were promoting sectarianism or withdrawal from public, political and social life then there would be a case for closing them forthwith. Neither of these appear to be the case so Bruce's argument must de facto fall. Further it can hardly be argued that a school which bases its mission on a Gospel of forgiveness and reconciliation, and in doing so establishes practices which give concrete expression to such a mission, is promoting bigotry. In any event there is no evidence that the 'melting pot' approach in and of itself does anything to break down barriers. All that may happen is that the conflicts which Bruce implies exist on the streets will be imported into the school. There are important lessons to be learned from the Balkan experience where religiously and culturally discrete groups were forced to integrate without having first resolved a host of outstanding grievances and antinomies. Bruce spends much of his time challenging the continued existence of Catholic schools on the grounds that they provide an excuse and opportunity for bigots to exercise their prejudices. As Finn has pointed out (op. cit., pp. 872ff), such a realist account of bigotry rests on extremely shaky foundations. To attack the object of prejudice on the grounds that their existence excites antagonism is to avoid the real issue. One might as well say that the existence of so many Jewish shopkeepers in Berlin provided a reason for the rise of the most appalling anti-semitism. Notice in this that Bruce doesn't claim that such anti-Catholic prejudice is justified; he simply implies that it is understandable. Finally, as a sociologist he will undoubtedly be aware that similar anxieties do not exist in other parts of the United Kingdom which rather begs the question as to why Catholic schools are under so much attack in Scotland only – is it something peculiar to Scotland? I suggest that it might be profitable to explore the extent to which such antagonism is part of the continuing legacy of the bitter anti-Catholic sentiment evident in Scotland, before, during and after the passing of the 1918 Act.

The second issue involves the belief that Catholic schools embody discriminatory employment practices. It certainly is the case that they do but the main question is whether or not such discrimination is legitimate. The existence of such separate provision is not in itself unjust. There may be perfectly good reasons why we discriminate between one person and another. In the case of Catholic schools the grounds are that the particular religious culture and the practices which emanate from it are better nurtured by those who believe in the basic assumptions which underpin that culture. It would indeed be strange if someone who claimed not to believe in God were to become the Principal of an institution which founded itself upon precisely such a belief. To do away with appropriate and justifiable discriminatory employment practices would indeed represent the death knell for Catholic schools as their distinctiveness would inevitably be obliterated.

A further dimension to this particular critical issue hangs on the need for the Catholic education system to retain their right of approval exercised through the office of the local Bishop. Can anyone who calls him or herself a Catholic have a right to approval? I think that the answer must be no. For example, in so far as someone displays behaviours which flout the Gospel in their treatment of others they provide scandal. In Scotland, however, the main barrier to approval in practice tends to be the state of one's personal/sexual relationship. Individuals do not fail to receive approval because they are mean-spirited, sanctimonious or corrupt in their dealings with others. The almost universal reason provided for their failure to receive such approval is that they are divorced and remarried or that they are living with a partner without being married. Given that 'approval' in the sense used here has a legal status, proof is necessary and it would be somewhat difficult to stand in a court of law and 'prove' that someone was 'mean-spirited'. Therefore, given that the structural visibility of an individual's sexual relationship is self-evident, it is understandable that the nature of that relationship assumes such importance in the 'approval' process – it is not difficult to establish that the individual is in a position which is not in accordance with the official teaching of the Church. It is much more difficult to prove that they are 'mean-spirited'! The issue is further complicated in that Scotland has a small Catholic population (around 800,000) and 'local knowledge' assumes rather too much importance. This in turn can lead to a culture of 'whispering' which itself undermines those Gospel values to be embedded in the Catholic school. One of the challenges facing the Scottish Catholic church in its educational dealings is to persuade those within and without that it harbours no institutionalized neurosis about human sexuality while maintaining the dignity of the person in relationship.

'Approval' represents one part of a larger jigsaw of concerns about the particular requirements placed upon Catholic teachers. Other concerns surround their beliefs and attitudes which will play a critical role in the continuance of effective Catholic education. Central to this is the preparation and education of such teachers, and Scotland lost its only remaining independent College of Education in 1999. The historic mission of St Andrew's College was taken over by the University of Glasgow. While this may represent an opportunity for Catholic teacher education to be rooted in a wider cultural and educational context it has not been universally welcomed and is regarded by many as the beginning of the end for Catholic education (Conroy and McCreath, 1999). The argument of opponents of the merger is that the distinctive preparation for all teachers for Catholic schools in religious education and in the theology of Catholic education will not survive long in the new institution. The particular emphasis on the development of a Christian ethos was decried by the *Glasgow Herald* article (despite the large number of reports from her Majesty's Inspectorate which are quite specific about the contribution of the distinctively Catholic ethos to the quality of the provision offered in Catholic schools) (Conroy and McCreath, 1995, Information paper 1).

The third issue, which is raised by the the *Glasgow Herald* feature, is that the historic mission of Catholic schools, embodied in the 1918 Act, was to protect the freedom of religious belief and worship. The schools distinctive denominational purpose was to 'pass on the faith'. But, so the argument goes, schools no longer claim this as a purpose. They are indistinguishable from their State counterpart; they have no special ethos rooted in the Gospel and their religious education is rooted in a phenomenological approach recognizable in any school. Further, now that the Scottish polity no longer harbours deep anti-Irish-Catholic resentments, Catholics need no institutionalized protection for the faith. These arguments deserve to be taken seriously since they echo an extant and more sophisticated discussion within Catholic education itself. Arthur claims that the adoption of a number of programmes of Religious Education in Catholic schools (throughout Britain) has seen the replacement of catechetical intent with phenomenological intent (1995, pp. 65–67 and p. 227f) and that, allied to the lack of definition and direction in theology and practice of Catholic education, has rendered as suspect many of the claims Catholics make for the continuation of a separate State funded system.

It is certainly true that the debate within Catholic education has been and continues to be robust. There are divided opinions as to the nature of the religious education within Catholic schools but on what evidence does the *Glasgow Herald* make its assertion – perhaps a little hearsay from 'pub chats'? Better, I suggest to compare the rationale available in the State version of the 5–14 Curriculum Guidelines with those in the parallel Roman Catholic document (Conroy, 1999b, p. 391f). Whatever the claims of individuals as to what they do or do not do the official position is fairly unequivocal – religious education broadly conceived is undoubtedly part of the educational project of the Catholic school but it is not the object of a Catholic school. Rather it sits alongside a catechetical claim which is clearly derived from the document, 'The Religious Dimension of Education in the Catholic School', where it states that 'a Catholic school cannot relinquish its own freedom to proclaim the Gospel and to offer a formation based on the values to be found in a Christian education; this is its right and its duty. To proclaim or to offer is not to impose, however; the latter suggest a moral violence which is strictly forbidden, both by the Gospel and by Church law' (Congregation for Catholic education, 1988, p. 5). In view of this it may be claimed that Scottish Catholic schools continue to exercise their catechetical obligations. But there is a difference between official Church teaching and what happens in practice and the practice rates among Scottish children appear to be little different from those elsewhere in the United Kingdom, and so, it might be suggested even where the broad intent is in line with the historic mission success is far from assured. Catholic primary schools do continue to offer broadly catechetical programmes and prepare children for the Sacraments of Initiation. But it would be naïve to suggest that the same approach can or will work in secondary schools. Should the Church abandon its secondary schools as some would like? Given the plethora of secondary school closures in recent years, especially in the West of Scotland, there does appear to be some retreat from the historic position. Some Catholic schools appear to be developing the status of magnet schools – special interest institutions which increasingly serve middle class interests for religion as a form of civic support. If such a pattern persists it will become ever more difficult for Catholic education to maintain its historic mission. And, given the origins of Catholic schooling in the provision of a service to the poor it might well be important to continue to offer such service to the poor – even where the demography and religious allegiance of the poor has shifted. Thinking about such a shift refocuses our attention on the extent to which it should change to meet changed circumstances and the consequent question of how far such change should be allowed within the spirit of the 1918 Act. In other words can Catholic schools be retained where their primary purpose is not to catechize? From the Catholic perspective the answer can and should be yes. Catholic schools do contain the possibility of offering alternative ways of constructing and making sense of the world (Davis, 1999). Newman's dictum that, 'Christian history and theology change in order to remain the same' may be equally applied to education. Indeed it would be bizarre to imagine that the purposes of Catholic education would not undergo significant modification with the passage of time. It is worth speculating on whether or not Catholic schools would be accused by the *Glasgow Herald* of being anachronistic had they not embraced some changes with respect to the delivery of their historic mission. The mission of making the world a more humane, generous and whole pace – a mission shared by many if not most educationalists – is entirely consistent with the Gospel. Catholic schools base their approach to education on a reading of the Gospel which supports the claims of justice and service to the poor. Where the support and provision of education is seen to do this it may be regarded as in accordance with Gospel imperatives. This is especially the case where the imperatives of the market have themselves replaced those of human value (Conroy, 1999c, pp. 490–494). In such circumstances supporting education as part of that process seems not unreasonable.

However, given that the State is quite clear about the imperatives for education and that some of these are not truly in harmony with those of the Catholic Church should the State then be required to continue to provide funding for Catholic schools? This is indeed a complicated question and one which it is impossible to do justice to here. However, it is worth making a few observations. Firstly, it is important to distinguish the State from the polity; the State may be seen to embody our modes of governance whereas the polity is the embodiment of the people. While the Government may have, as far as possible, to speak with one voice that is not the case for the polity. The polity brings together such a range of different voices, some of them contesting and challenging. The Catholic Church through its influence in education continues to represent one such voice. Democracy needs contesting voices if its systems of Government are truly to remain democratic. Scotland does not enjoy the variety of educational provision available elsewhere in Britain. There are very few private schools, and State schools, be they Catholic or non-denominational, enact uniform policies across the country. Catholic schools provide for the possibility of some difference. Secondly, parents choose Catholic schools because they wish to introduce their children to a world mediated through some kind of moral/theological lens. Of course they may not be able to articulate this particularly well and may have only a dim recognition of what it is they want but it cannot be deducted from this that they don't wish for such schools. Many of Scotland's Catholic schools continue to be oversubscribed. As long as such parents express a preference for Catholic schools and that such preferences are not inimical to the State it is possible to stand the argument of the *Glasgow Herald* on its head and suggest that the State should support the continued existence of Catholic schools as a sign of its inclusiveness.

Conclusion

In this essay I have concentrated on a number of arguments publicly espoused against the continuation of separate provision for Catholic education in Scotland. These arguments represent the most critical challenge to the continuation of this provision. However it would be too easy to suggest that the key issue for the Church is dealing with and combating the continuing antagonism to Catholic education. Nevertheless to thrive it has to come to terms with these criticisms. In doing so it needs to develop a greater clarity of purpose and be able to articulate the Church's evolving purposes and interests in education with greater coherence and force. Some of these will be expressed in terms of the provision of high quality education within a faith framework. Others will emphasize the contribution to the maintenance of our democratic institutions, others again will stress the importance of holding together inclusiveness and difference. Certainly if Catholic education is to make a contribution to the polity then the conversation about the nature of such schooling must go beyond catechises and faith development. Nevertheless these issues cannot be ignored or glossed over. The quality of teachers in Catholic schools and their commitment to a coherent set of aims and practices is imperative to the continuation of effective Catholic education within a State system. To have Catholic educators who see the future as well as remember the past is vital for Catholic education.

It is equally important that Catholic educators involve themselves in a robust defence of what is good and positive in Catholic schooling while avoiding the defence of the indefensible. In responding to these outside pressures it is too easy to become introspective and self-absorbed worrying away at questions of internal consistency and governance. While the arguments of Bruce and others may not be persuasive inside the cabal of Catholic education they do hold sway in the wider polity and may not be ignored. Further, there is a point to many of their criticisms and those promoting Catholic education must be prepared to argue their position. Thus while the current arrangements for 'approval' are not indefensible, justice and integrity demand that the Church constantly keep them under review and reflect on their implementation.

At the beginning of this paper I offered a lengthy quotation from a poem reflecting the theological, spiritual and cultural emptiness that marks Scottish public religious life. Properly conceived of from within and without Catholic education offers some colour into that void but only if it is prepared to meet criticism head on and reflect on its own limitations.

Bibliography

Arthur, J., *The Ebbing Tide* (Leominster, Gracewing, 1995).

Bradley J.M., *Ethnic and Religious Identity in Modern Scotland: Culture, Politics and Football* (Avebury Press, 1995).

Bruce, S., 'Mission: Impossible', *Glasgow Herald*, 28 January 1998.

Conroy, J. and McCreath D., *Leadership in Catholic Schools* (Glasgow, Strathclyde Regional Council, 1995).

Conroy, J. and McCreath D., 'The Challenge to Catholic Teacher Education in Scotland', *Catholic Education: A Journal of Inquiry and Practice*, 2:3, 1999, 312–327.

Conroy, J., 'The Long Johns and Catholic education', in J. Conroy (ed.), *Catholic Education: Inside/Out – Outside/In* (Leamington, Lindisfarne, 1999a).

Conroy, J., 'Religious and Moral Education', in T.G.K. Bryce and W.M. Humes (eds), *Scottish Education* (Edinburgh, Edinburgh University Press, 1999b).

Conroy, J., 'Poetry and Human Growth', *Journal of Moral Education*, 28:4:491–510, 1999c.

Conroy, J. 'The Challenges to Catholic Education', in M. Potterton (ed.)

The Catholic School and the Common Good (Conference Proceedings, Johannesburg, 2000).

Davis, R.A., 'Can there be a Catholic Curriculum?', in J. Conroy (ed.), *Catholic Education: Inside/Out – Outside/In,* (Leamington, Lindisfarne, 1999).

Finn, G.T.P., 'Sectarianism and Scottish Education', in T.G.K. Bryce and W.M. Humes (eds), *Scottish Education* (Edinburgh, Edinburgh University Press).

Fitzpatrick, T., 'Catholic Education in Glasgow, Lanarkshire and South West Scotland Before 1972', *The Innes Review*, XXXVI:2, Spring 1985.

Fitzpatrick, T., 'Catholic Education in Scotland', in T.G.K. Bryce and W.M. Humes (eds), *Scottish Education* (Edinburgh, Edinburgh University Press, 1999).

Forrester, F., 'Schools Beyond Saving', *The Scotsman*, 31 May 2000.

Glasgow Herald Feature, 'Challenge to the separate schools system in Upfront on Saturday', *Glasgow Herald*, 30 May 1998.

Handley, J., *The Irish in Modern Scotland* (Oxford, B.H. Blackwell, 1947).

MacMillan, J., in T. Devine (ed.), *Scotland's Shame: Bigotry and Sectarianism in Modern Scotland* (Edinburgh, Mainstream, 2000).

Newman, J.H., *The Development of Christian Doctrine*, Notre Dame, Indiana, University of Notre Dame Press, 6th edition, 1989.

O'Hagan, F., *Change, Challenge and Achievement: a Study of the Development of Catholic Education in Glasgow in the Nineteenth and Twentieth Centuries* (Glasgow, St Andrew's College, 1996).

Sacred Congregation for Catholic Education, *The Religious Dimension of Education in the Catholic School* (London, Catholic Truth Society, 1998).

Scotland J., *The History of Scottish Education* Vol. 1 (London, University of London Press, 1969).

Stewart, A.T.Q., *A Deeper Silence: The Hidden Origins of the United Irishmen* (London, Faber and Faber, 1993)

Skinnider, M., in T. Bone (ed.), *Studies in the History of Scottish Education: 1872–1939,* SCRE, No. 54 (London, ULP, 1967).

Treble, J.H., 'The Development of Roman Catholic Education in Scotland, 1878–1978' in *The Innes Review*, 29, Autumn 1978.

Whyte, C., 'An Trath Duilich', in J. McGonigal, D. O'Rourke and H. Whyte (eds), *Across the Water: Irishness in modern Scottish writing* (Glendaruel, Argyll Publishing, 2000).

Chapter 3

Catholic Education in Northern Ireland

Aidan Donaldson

'Take up the Irish problem at whatever point you may, you inevitably find yourself in the end back at the education question.' Thus wrote Patrick Pearse, poet, author, educationalist and revolutionary, in *An Claidheamh Soluis* in 1903.[1] And he was right. Any student of Irish politics would be well advised to examine the development of education in Ireland, for the history of formal education over the past centuries – even pre-dating the rise of formal schooling in the 1830s – in many ways reflects the political and national questions which have dominated the history of this island.[2] It is not that the Irish educational experience is unique or so peculiar that it shares no parallels with other countries' experiences. Similar experiences in Europe can be found also in England, Scotland, and the Netherlands as well as, later, in the Catholic sectors of Germany. In short, the impact of the religious question on the educational sphere is nothing new or unique. And yet, Ireland is unique in Europe on this issue. Unlike Scotland, England or the Netherlands all of which sought to impose restrictions on Catholic education in order to eliminate the religious belief of one section of the community and impose another set of religious beliefs, as well as to

[1] Patrick Pearse, *An Claidheamh Soluis* (Dublin, 1903), p. 4.
[2] While no definitive work on the subject of education and the national question in Ireland has yet been published, some valuable insights into this issue can be found in the excellent and timely work by Michael McGrath entitled *The Catholic Church and Catholic Schools in Northern Ireland* (Dublin, Irish Academic Press, 2000). Also see Farren, S., *The Politics of Irish Education* (Belfast, QUB, 1995) and McCann, J., *A Theological Critique of Christian Education, with special reference to Developments in Northern Ireland since 1944,* (a Ph.D. thesis submitted to the Department of Theology, the University of Durham, 1993).

reinforce, particularly in the case of Ireland, a new set of economic relations – the attempt to use education as an ideological weapon against Catholicism failed in Ireland – like the rest of the Penal Laws – precisely because it attempted such in a country which was overwhelmingly of the opposite faith of the rulers.

The aim of this paper is to introduce the reader to the educational debate in Northern Ireland today – a debate which has lessons for the future of Catholic education throughout both the United Kingdom and Ireland and, indeed, beyond. It is the writer's view that the experience of the Catholic educational sector in Northern Ireland over the entire history of that State (and, indeed, even proceeding the establishment of Northern Ireland in 1921), while being somewhat unique, reaches beyond that sector and that, through the struggle to provide a Catholic education for Catholic children, strong and enduring bonds between the Catholic community and Church have been established, bonds which, if recognised and nurtured, may indeed have implications for spiritual and social formation far beyond the educative realm.

The Rise of Formal Education in Ireland

In order to understand education in Northern Ireland today it is necessary to be aware of the factors that gave rise to that system. While it is not possible in this article to give a comprehensive account of the history of formal education in Ireland from its very origins, it is of value to examine the rise and development of formal schooling in Ireland in order to give the reader an insight into the inherited education system which prevails in Northern Ireland today and which still heavily influences and conditions the current debate on education.

The context for Catholics in Ireland in the period preceding the establishment of wide-scale formal education was set by the Penal Laws, the anti-Catholic set of laws and legal restrictions passed during the period 1695–1728 and which remained in force until the end of the eighteenth century.[3] The Penal Code was directed against all aspects of life for Irish Catholics – religious, social, political and economic. The expressed purpose of the laws was to eliminate Catholic opposition to the Protestant ascendancy

---

[3] There are numerous works on the Penal Laws and their effect on Irish society. One of the most accessible and informative is Corish, P.J., *The Catholic Community in the Seventeenth and Eighteenth Centuries* (Dublin, Helicon Ltd, 1981), especially pp. 73–81.

through a process of disempowering and impoverishing the native Irish, with the elimination of the Catholic Church as a significant element in Irish society as the ultimate aim. The same areas were consistently identified for legislative consideration throughout most of the eighteenth century: religion, politics, economics, land and education. And with no little effect. In 1704 in Ireland, a little more than a decade after the end of the Williamite War, Catholics owned less than one-seventh of the land, reducing to 7% by 1750. Catholics could not vote in parliamentary elections, serve on a jury, hold any government office, or become a lawyer or army officer. Failure to attend Anglican service was punishable by fine. Bishops and members of religious orders were banished. No new priests could be ordained. The expectation was that the episcopacy would literally die out within a few decades and, with that, so too would the structural Catholic Church in Ireland. Yet, if restrictions made the practice of Catholicism difficult and adherence entailed many financial hardships, the harrying failed in its primary purpose to eliminate the presence of Catholic priests in Ireland. Unlike in Scotland, however, which from 1560 until the restoration of the hierarchy in 1878 was, in Church terms, *in paribus infideles*, a mission region served mainly by religious orders, the Church in Ireland mounted a more successful defence. Indeed, so successful was the Church in resisting destruction that by 1730 it was able to reorganize not as a mission but as a fully episcopal Church with bishops in almost every diocese – albeit living a somewhat furtive and dangerous existence.

Education did not escape the attention of the framers of the Penal Laws. Some of the fullest rigours of the Penal Laws were reserved not only for clergy but also for those engaged in the practice of Catholic teaching. Indeed, it is of significance that the first penal law included a clause stating that 'no person of the popish religion may publicly teach school or instruct youth'.[4] The earliest efforts at providing education in Ireland were driven, to a considerable extent, by a desire on the part of the various Protestant Churches to proselytise. The education laws enacted in Ireland in 1703 and 1709 which gave rise to the Charity School Society included the intention that 'the children of Popish natives may be so won by affectionate endeavours that the whole nation may become Protestant and English' and encouraged the heavily subsided Charter schools to set an agenda to 'rescue the souls of thousands of poor children from the dangers of Popish superstition

---

[4] Cited Corish, op. cit., p. 79.

and idolatry and their bodies from the miseries of idleness and beggary'.[5] Nor did these attempts finish with the lifting of the Penal Laws. Interestingly, as a result of a clause inserted into the Suppression of (Religious) Orders Act (1791) following the Act of Emancipation in 1829 'to make provision for the gradual suppression and final prohibition of the religious orders' the Christian Brothers, in fact, remained technically illegal in Ireland until 1922 and the founding of the Irish Free State.[6]

The Penal Laws came and went and, while their legacy had an enormous effect on the collective historical consciousness of Irish Catholics, it is with the rise of formal schooling in the nineteenth century that we find, perhaps, the most telling and clearly stated attempts at social engineering via education. While the debate concerning the future development of education was carried out largely in theological terms, the dispute was also of a political nature, i.e. whether or not the Catholic authorities should be able to determine the education of Catholic children. The celebrated aims of national education were laid down by E.G. Stanley, the Chief Secretary for Ireland, in a report to the Duke of Leinster, the Lord Lieutenant of Ireland. According to Stanley, 'one of the main objects must be to unite in one system children of different creeds'.[7] Yet the 1831 Act did present the Catholic Church with a serious dilemma and problem. On the one hand, the leaders of the Church were only too aware of the dangers of accepting unconditioningly and unquestioningly a system, which explicitly was to be based on nondenominational principles. The opportunity for the advancement of secularist education – as was being actively promoted at that time in England – and the fear of a resurgence of Protestant proselytism was clearly contained in the Stanley principles.[8] Ambrose McAuley points out that the Church of Ireland Archbishop of Dublin, Richard Whatley, 'one of the most industrious and influential members' of the National School Board from 1831 to 1853, expressed his favourable opinion of the envisaged system of nondenominational education thus:

[The National School system] was gradually undermining the vast

[5] Cited Crilly, J., 'Education for a Divided Community', in D. Breen and A. Donaldson (eds), *Ethos and Education* (Belfast, 1995), vol. 2, p. 38.
[6] On the history of the Christian Brothers and the legacy of the Penal Laws see Rushe, D., *Edmund Rice, a Man of His Times* (Dublin, Gill and Macmillan, 1981), especially pp. 1–20.
[7] Cited Farren, op. cit., p. 3.
[8] McGrath, op. cit., p. 17.

fabric of the Irish Roman Catholic Church ... and if we give it up, we give up the only hope of weaning the Irish from the abuses of Popery.[9]

On the other hand, however, the Catholic authorities were only too aware of the difficulties facing Catholic education in the era of Catholic emancipation. Simply stated, they could not retain a position of total opposition. In the educative sphere they were unable to offer a viable educational alternative, which would have been to provide the masses of the Catholic population with an adequately funded formal education system. Despite the enormous and, indeed, heroic efforts of the religious orders only a small minority of schools in Ireland were administered by the Catholic authorities.[10] Simple demography was a major ally in ensuring that the vast majority of National Board schools were *de facto* denominational in make-up and character. In addition, Ireland in the nineteenth century was, and still is in many ways, a deeply religious country. Secular education was simply a non-starter. The Catholic authorities showed themselves to be very adept at thwarting the secularizing desires contained in the National Schools legislation. Hislop correctly points out that 'it was obvious that any generally acceptable educational scheme would have to recognize the realities of denominational control.'[11] The decades of debate also occurred at a painful and almost nation-defining time in Irish history. Ireland's own national disaster, indeed, its holocaust – the Great Hunger of 1847 and the subsequent economic and social deprivation – conditioned the climate in which the educational debate took place.[12]

It is scarcely surprising in these circumstances that the educational debate in Ireland was a most acrimonious and bitter one. A microcosm of the struggle, which took place during this period, can be seen in the withdrawal of the Christian Brothers of their schools from National Board control in 1836 over interference by National Board inspectors in the teaching of religion,

[9]   Macauley, A., 'Catholics in the North: Survey of a Century, 1870–1970', in *The Newman Review*, vol. 2, no. 1, Summer 1970, p. 22, cited McCann, op. cit., pp. 111–112.

[10] McGrath informs us that as late as 1824 only 423 of Ireland's schools were under the administration of the Catholic Church. See ibid., p. 117.

[11] Hislop, H., 'The Management of the Kildare Place School System 1811–1831', *Irish Educational Studies* (Dublin, 1992), p. 65.

[12] See Larkin, E., *The Consolidation of the Roman Catholic Church in Ireland, 1860–1870* (Chapel Hill and London, The University of North Carolina Press, 1987), pp. xvi–xvii.

the presence of a crucifix in the classroom and the saying of prayers.[13] The Catholic authorities had entered the National School system in good faith in the hope that they would be able to secure the conditions for the education of their flock's children, which would also accommodate their spiritual welfare. McCann points out that 'at almost every turn, however, they were frustrated both by sectarian prejudice and a pervasive proselytism'.[14] The Powis Commission of 1870 proved a significant victory for the Catholic authorities in their struggle for Catholic schooling, while in 1880 the National Board finally allowed Catholic religious instruction and worship to take place in Catholic National Schools – some forty years after this right had been granted to their Protestant counterparts – as well as accepting the display of religious emblems.[15] By 1883 the Church authorities had the right to place clergy in classrooms, train and appoint teachers and had secured effective control over the boards of management in those schools that were predominantly Catholic in character. Auchmulty informs us that by the end of the nineteenth century almost ninety per cent of all national schools were, in fact, 'clerical schools'.[16]

Formal Education and Northern Ireland: a Battleground Revisited

The National Schools debate, which had raged throughout the middle decades of the nineteenth century, had been largely settled by the end of the century to the satisfaction of the main Christian denominations. Other factors – particularly the question of Home Rule and Irish independence – dominated the final years of the nineteenth century and the opening decades of the twentieth century. The resolution to the conflict was the partition of the country with the largely Catholic and nationalist two-thirds of the country establishing a Free State of dominion status, achieved only after a protracted and bloody struggle against the British authorities and, subsequently, a civil war among the nationalists themselves. The six northeastern counties were permitted to establish their own regional parliament and retain their links with

[13] On opposition of sections of the Catholic Church to the National Board system see McGrath, op. cit., pp. 18–20.
[14] McCann, op. cit., p. 137.
[15] On the Powis Commission and other related events during this period see ibid., pp. 22–25.
[16] Auchmuty, J., *Irish Education, a Historical Survey*, (London, G.G. Harrap & Co., 1937), p. 149.

Westminster. Unlike the Free State whose population was, being overwhelmingly Catholic and nationalist, homogenous, the new Northern Irish state, while containing a Protestant and unionist majority, was deeply split on both religious and political lines, with approximately forty per cent of the population Catholic and nationalist.[17] In the newly emerging Free State education was not a contested area of political life. Indeed, the ruling Irish authorities were able to use the educational system as a means of legitimising and moulding their vision of a new Ireland.[18] In Northern Ireland, however, things were different. Cut off from their fellow Irishmen and women northern Catholics felt a deep sense of isolation and powerlessness. Locked into a State that they felt to be alien, which they felt to resent their collective identity, their very presence – cultural, aspirational and, indeed, physical – northern Catholics looked inward.[19] It is in this context that education once again became a major issue for the first time in some years. After all, it was the only institution that northern Catholics felt they owned. Input into the political or civic culture, indeed, even into many of the elements of the economic life of Northern Ireland was severely restricted by barriers on the grounds of religion being erected against Catholics at many official levels. In such circumstances it is scarcely surprising that northern Catholics would not simply give up the only institution they felt they owned. As Osborne, Cormack and Gallagher point out:

> [I]n a society that is intolerant and inequitable, it should come as no surprise that ethnic and religious minorities will seek to defend their identity and traditions, and that one of the routes they will follow is to demand the right to their own schools.[20]

And in any case, there were sound economic reasons for holding onto the Catholic education sector. Excluded from many sectors of the economy many Catholics saw education as their only means of social advancement.

In the context of insecurity and perceived threats the education

---

[17] J.D. Brewer has produced a most insightful and highly significant work on the nature of the Northern Ireland state and on the entire Plantation period. See Brewer, J.D. (with Higgins, G.I.) *Anti-Catholicism in Northern Ireland, 1600–1998* (London, MacMillan, 1998).

[18] On this see S. Farren, pp. 35–36.

[19] See Brewer, J.D., op. cit., pp. 87–94.

[20] Osborne, R., Cormack, R. and Gallagher, A., 'Education in Northern Ireland', in *After the Reforms: Education and Policy in Northern Ireland* (Aldershot, Avebury, 1993), p. 191.

debate, which appeared to have been settled some decades previously, once again emerged centre stage. In 1921 the new Minister of Education, Lord Londonderry, established a committee of inquiry, the Lynn Committee, which was charged to produce proposals as to the future structures of education in Northern Ireland. The result of this committee's deliberations became the basis of the 1923 Education Act that had far-reaching implications for education in Northern Ireland.[21] Among the more contested and controversial aspects of the Act were those that envisaged a fully integrated (non-denominational) system of education and those that sought to treat religious education as no longer part of the school curriculum.[22] Londonderry is generally seen very much in the mode of E.G. Stanley who sought to remove all religious influence from the educative sphere. Political and religious forces in Northern Ireland, particularly in the Unionist/Protestant side, ensured that the educational debate would once again almost mirror the early decades of the National Schools issue – except that this time, many of the key factors which aided the Catholic Church in the earlier struggle, such as demography and political influence, were decidedly outside of Catholic influence. The Catholic community in Northern Ireland would be required to make massive sacrifices if it was to retain its right to educate its children. And it did.

It is not an exaggeration to state that education provision in Northern Ireland exemplified the role of Catholics in the new state. The 1923 Education Act invited existing schools to transfer control and management to local committees that would then assume responsibility for the running and management of those schools. Schools that refused to transfer according to the format laid down in the Act would not be able to avail themselves of the grants that had been available to them for more than five decades. According to the Act trustees of those schools which wished to transfer would be invited to negotiate on the terms of transfer, thus obstensively guaranteeing the interests of the trustees.[23] As a result of a combined and intensive campaign by the Protestant churches, the Orange Order and many of the leading Unionist politicians against the 1923 Education Act, Protestant schools were able to transfer to state control with their interests safeguarded.[24] The 1930 Education Act ensured that the obstacles placed before Catholic schools were almost insurmountable. Changes in the

---

[21] On Londonderry and the Lynn Committee see Farren, pp. 38–39 and 58–85.
[22] See Education Act (Northern Ireland) (Belfast, H.M.S.O., 1923) section 26.
[23] See Farren, op. cit., pp. 59–61.
[24] See McGrath, op. cit., pp. 15–66.

provision of religious education effectively excluded the possibility of Catholic schools transferring to state control. Section four of the 1930 Education Act decreed that each education authority was required to provide religious instruction based solely on 'the holy scriptures according to some authoritative version or versions [of the Bible], but excluding instruction as to any tenet which is distinctive of any particular religious denomination'.[25] For a church such as the Catholic Church, with its emphasis on the relationship between school and Church, the idea of education as involving the holistic social and spiritual formation of the child, the value-laden nature of knowledge itself and, not least, the role which schools have traditionally played in sacramental preparation, such a limited vision of religious instruction could scarcely be seen as anything other than unacceptable. Nor could it be seen as 'accidental' or an 'oversight'. David Harkness assesses the implications of this legislation thus:

> This was to skate over one of the great dividing lines of the Reformation (the Protestant interpretation of the Scriptures by private judgement being opposed to the Catholic insistence upon a church interpretation) so that for the Catholic community the whole measure rendered the state school network, whether 'transferred' or 'provided', Protestant in character and inappropriate for Catholic children, further justifying its initial determination to retain its own voluntary schools.[26]

Schools which refused to transfer – i.e., the Catholic sector – found their capital funding cut, initially to fifty per cent of the cost of approved, amended in 1947 to sixty-five per cent, in 1968, to eighty per cent and later, in 1975, to eighty-five per cent. Indeed, it was only as recently as 1994 that Catholic schooling received full capital funding and even that was only after a series of studies carried out by the Standing Advisory Committee on Human Rights (SACHR). After these studies, carried out between 1988 and 1993, moves were finally completed to cease structural injustices and funding restrictions.[27] The legacy of meeting the capital shortfall – which fell on that section of the community which was at a severe economic disadvantage to its Protestant counterpart – will last for considerable decades as almost every parish in Northern Ireland has inherited a considerable educational debt from these times. And the shortfall

[25] Cited McCann, op. cit., p. 22.
[26] Harkness, D., *Northern Ireland since 1920*, quoted ibid.
[27] See Standing Advisory Commission on Human Rights, *Reports* (London, HMSO, 1988–1993).

was indeed considerable. Referring only to the period 1947–68 the Northern Catholic Bishops stated the following:

> A conservative estimate would indicate that since the passing of the 1947 Education Act the Catholic community has contributed something in the region of twenty million pounds in present-day money values towards the erection and maintenance of their schools.[28]

The total cost of voluntary contribution made by the Catholic community over the history of the Northern state is estimated to amount to (in 1996 value) almost two hundred million pounds with Catholics paying more than four million pounds each year in 1991.[29] Little wonder that Seamus Dunn states that 'the response of the Catholic community to the challenge is something of which they are rightly proud'.[30] Nor was the cost limited to the financial burden placed upon the Catholic laity. The SACHR reports also noted that Catholic schools had less space for the provision of technology, ICT and craft and design.[31] Furthermore, the SACHR Report of 1991 illustrated that even in non-capital recurrent costs – the actual money spent on each child within the school – Catholic schools fared badly, receiving more than ten per cent less than controlled or Protestant schools.[32] In addition, the Protestant community also had greater access to the grammar sector with thirty-one per cent of Protestant post-primary pupils attending grammar schools as compared to only twenty-six per cent of Catholic students in the 1980s.[33]

It was in this context two parallel school systems developed in Northern Ireland, with the overwhelming majority of both communities using their respective parental right to send their children to their respective schools. Recent enrolment figures indicate that almost half – forty-seven and a half – of children of school age currently attend Catholic schools. The Protestant sector accounts for approximately the same percentage, while the integrated schooling system is attended by approximately four per cent.[34] Catholic

---

[28] Cited Wallace, M., *Northern Ireland: Fifty Years of Self-Government* (Newton Abbott, David and Charles, 1971), p. 111.

[29] On the contribution of the Catholic community to Catholic schooling see McGrath, op. cit., pp. 245–248.

[30] Dunn, S., 'A Short History of Education in Northern Ireland, 1920–1990', (SACHR, 1990), p. 75.

[31] See SACHR (1991) pp. 139–140.

[32] SACHR (1991) p. 145.

[33] See McGrath, op. cit., p. 248.

[34] I am indebted to the Research Department of the Council for Catholic Maintained Schools for these statistics.

pupils make up a clear majority in both primary and secondary (i.e., non-grammar) schools. One other educational sector, Irish-medium schools, deserves mention. From very small beginnings, and in the face of massive obstacles placed before it by both unionist and, later, British authorities this most interesting experiment is growing at a very fast rate and does, perhaps, indicate the way forward for a new partnership in education based on an alliance between parents and other interests in the educative process. Parental involvement and ownership, very much key concepts in modern educational development, is very evident in this sector.[35] Indeed, the demand for an enhanced role for the Irish language appears to have been recognized by mainstream parties within the maintained sector. Whereas traditionally it was left to those such as the Christian Brothers to actively promote the Irish language, culture and Gaelic sports, the increasing importance of this dimension to many within the Catholic community has led to the Catholic authorities placing greater emphasis on all aspects of Gaelic culture in their schools, particularly in those working-class areas where the Gaelic revival is strongest. An example of this new emphasis on Irish was the response from the powerful Council for Catholic Maintained Schools (CCMS) to the initial DENI educational reform proposals made in March 1988. Surprisingly the CCMS response document contained no less than three full pages urging the Department to recognise the importance of Gaelic for many parents and to increase its scope within the curriculum.[36] The White Paper of October 1988 and the subsequent Education (Northern Ireland) Order of 1988 explicitly committed the Department to concrete steps in facilitating Irish-medium schools and in the promotion of Irish in the curriculum.[37] Following the Good Friday Agreement of 1998, a central element of which is a recognition of the principle of parity of esteem for both those who espouse an Irish identity and those who define themselves in terms of being British, these developments in education were further enhanced and advanced by the language provisions of the Education (Northern Ireland) Order of 1998 which, for the first time, places a statutory duty on the DENI to promote the Irish language. The future may well see a steady growth in Irish-medium schools and an enhanced position of Gaelic within the curriculum in line with parental demand.

[35] See McGrath, op. cit., pp. 249–251.
[36] The Council for Catholic Maintained Schools, *Responses to the Consultative Document 'Education in Northern Ireland'* (Belfast, CCMS, 1988) pp. 13, 22 and 29.
[37] See The Department of Education for Northern Ireland, *Education: the Way Forward* (Bangor, Co. Down, DENI, 1988) p. 7.

Issues Facing Catholic Education in Northern Ireland Today

Today, the education system in Northern Ireland is as denominational as might be imagined. The Council for Catholic Maintained
Schools – a non-departmental statutory body established in 1987
to, in consultation with the Department of Education and the
Educational and Library Boards, 'negotiate, establish and implement policy both in general educational matters and in areas of
management of the Catholic maintained sector in accordance with
the *Statement of Aims of Catholic Schools*'[38] – has given the Catholic
educational authorities and other interested parties in the Catholic
sector a degree of control over their schools hitherto only dreamed
about. The issue of capital funding as well as other financial areas
appears to have been satisfactorily addressed. Attempts to eliminate the autonomy of Catholic teacher training, such as the
Chilver's Report, were, largely, successfully fought off. The
Catholic College of Education, St Mary's, is now a fully recognized
university college and a part of Queen's University Belfast. The
Education Reform (Northern Ireland) Order (ERO) (1989) introduced many of the education reforms established in England and
Wales as a result of the Education Reform Act (1988) but with a
number of important features which are specific to the context of
Northern Ireland. These include a common curriculum specific to
Northern Ireland which must be delivered in all grant-aided
schools, local management of schools and a considerable degree of
parental choice as to the school their children might attend. The
common curriculum includes a common core syllabus for religious
education, a core of aims, concepts, and content areas, which was
identified and developed by a joint working party, established by
the four main Christian churches (Catholic, Church of Ireland,
the Presbyterian Church in Ireland and Methodist) and ratified by
the respective church authorities. In this way the question of religious education – so much a contentious issue throughout much
of the history of formal schooling in Ireland – could be seen to
have been resolved to the satisfaction of all of the main churches,
including the Catholic Church. This might lead the reader to
conclude that Catholic education is safe. And yet, this would be
incorrect. Catholic schooling today faces crucial challenges and
choices. In particular two issues – the question of selection and the
right of Catholic parents to have their children educated in their

---

[38] The Council for Catholic Maintained Schools, *Response to Proposal for a Draft
Order-in-Council* (Belfast, CCMS, 1989), p. 8.

own chosen system – now confront those who are in positions of leadership in Catholic education.

Selection: an Unjust System?

The education system in Northern Ireland is not only divided according to religious lines. Northern Ireland, unlike any other region in the UK, has retained a selection procedure by which children are effectively separated at the age of eleven on the basis of a form of testing into two distinct schooling systems – secondary and grammar – through which they pursue the rest of their formal education until, at least, the age of sixteen. The educational reforms of the 1960s and 1970s in England and Wales, which saw the abolition of the eleven-plus and the replacement of the grammar/intermediate divide by the comprehensive system, were not extended to Northern Ireland. Selection at eleven remains the predominant form of transfer from primary to post-primary education in Northern Ireland with approximately ninety per cent of pupils being involved in the transfer procedure. The remaining ten per cent of pupils avail themselves of alternative transfer arrangements, usually of a local nature.[39] The Transfer Procedure ensures that twenty-seven per cent of pupils are awarded a non-fee paying grammar place. The rest of the pupils are awarded places in secondary schools. All post-primary pupils follow the same common curriculum.

Supporters of the current system often point to the academic results which are achieved, particularly in the grammar sector. School performance data published by DENI each year provides comfort for those who wish to retain the current system with almost ninety-five per cent of Year Twelve grammar school students achieving five or more GCSE passes at grades A*–C – a standard school performance indicator – during the academic year 1997/98.[40] These very commendable results are, however, achieved at a cost. The downside of the Northern Ireland two-track educational system is clearly illustrated when one compares the academic achievements of the grammar schools with those of the secondary sector with only approximately thirty-one per cent of Year Twelve secondary school students achieving five or more

[39] See Gallagher, A., *Education in a Divided Society* (Coleraine, University of Ulster, 1995), pp. 1–3.
[40] Calculated from School Performance Tables, (Belfast, DENI, 1998).

GCSE passes at grades A*–C.[41] One further particular problem in Northern Ireland which may illustrate the negative effects of selection on those who are deemed 'failures' at the age of eleven is the relatively high proportion of pupils leaving school with no GCSE passes or equivalent. Gallagher points out that in 1986/7, for example, 21.9% of Northern Ireland school leavers had no qualifications compared with 9.6% of school leavers in England and 16.1% in Wales.[42] The Northern Ireland Economic Council makes the following point:

> Selection can be criticised [for]... the apparent polarisation in attainment between grammar and secondary school leavers. This may occur as a result of the de-motivation of students who are assessed as academically less able and because more able students, whose presence may help raise the attainment of less able groups, are educated separately. Recent research on the Northern Ireland educational system raises real doubts about whether it is possible to raise the standards of secondary students substantially within the present system of selection at the age of eleven.[43]

That selection impacts on achievement irrespective of other socio-economic factors is made by Shuttleworth who, in taking into account the differential impact of socio-economic status (SES) on performance notes that 'for any given parental labour market status a grammar school pupil performed better than an equivalent secondary school pupil'.[44] Shuttleworth's findings give support to the refutation made by Blakely and Heath of the oft-stated claim made by some supporters of the selection system that it is better to be a 'high flyer' in a secondary school than struggle at the lower end of the grammar sector.[45]

Of course social class plays an important role in the attainment of the academic results of the selection tests themselves. The predominance of children from middle-class backgrounds in

---

[41] Calculated from ibid.

[42] See Gallagher, op. cit., pp. 36–37.

[43] The Northern Ireland Economic Council, *Reforming the Educational System in Northern Ireland* (Belfast, NIEC, 1995), p. 73.

[44] Shuttleworth, I., 'The Relationship Between Social Deprivation, as Measured by Individual Free Meal Eligibility, and Educational Attainment at GCSE in Northern Ireland', in *The British Educational Research Journal*, Vol. 21, No. 4 (1995).

[45] See Blakely, L. and Heath, R., 'Differences Between Comprehensive Schools: Some Preliminary Findings', in D. Reynolds and P. Cuttance (eds), *School Effectiveness* (London, Cassell, 1992).

grammar schools is well documented. In a range of research educationalists such as Sutherland, Spelman and Gallagher suggest that
approximately twice as high a percentage of middle-class children
secure grammar school places as children from a working-class
background.[46] Indeed, the SACHR Report of February 1990 notes
that evidence from a range of studies covering the period 1975 to
1989 indicates that 'social class affected grammar school enrolment over and above performance in the selection test'.[47]

Selection and a Catholic Vision of Education

The Catholic Church has long viewed education as a spiritual,
incarnational and formative activity through which each becomes
in reality what each possesses in potentiality. The Catholic school,
if it is worthy of that descriptor, must aim at forming Christian
people of competence and conscience, people who will play a full
role in society, guided by the Christian vision and value system
and seeking to put their talents at the service of others. The ultimate aim of Catholic schooling is not simply the attainment of
academic results but the full growth of the person, a fully alive
person for self and others who is in full communion with Christ
and his/her fellow men and women. And herein also lies the challenge for Catholic education in Northern Ireland. Catholic
education is about a commitment to people's 'personhood', to
their life-affirming, fundamental being, created in the image and
likeness of the Creator. It is about the sacramentality of living
itself, of the Thomist sense of 'seeing God in all things', or what
Karl Rahner called 'the liturgy of life'. The distinctiveness of
Catholic education rests upon Catholicism's commitment to
'catholicity' – a universal concern for and identification with the
other – that involves a deep eucharistic sense of sharing, commu-
nality and, above all, justice.[48] How, therefore, can such a radical
vision of education based on the profound sense of proclamation,
liberation and solidarity sit easy with an education system largely

[46] See Sutherland, A., 'Selection in Northern Ireland: from 1947 Act to 1989
Order', *Research Papers in Education* (Belfast, 1990) 5 (1); B. Spelman,
'Developments in Post-Primary Education in Northern Ireland', in *The Northern
Teacher* (Belfast, 1975) 11 (4); and A. Gallagher, *Transfer of Pupils at* 16 (Belfast,
Northern Ireland Council for Educational Research, 1988).
[47] SACHR (1990) op. cit., p. 101.
[48] See Groome, T., 'What Makes a School Catholic?', in T. McLaughlin, J. O'Keefe
and B. O'Keefe (eds), *The Contemporary Catholic School: Context, Identity and
Diversity* (London, Falmer, 1996) pp. 107–125.

conditioned by a selection procedure which is manifestly unjust and which alienates, fragments and makes victims of many within that system?

Catholic schooling has a long-standing tradition of service world-wide to the disadvantaged and marginalised. Bryk, for example, points out that the 'inspirational ideology' of Catholic education, along with the model of the school as 'a voluntary community', enables Catholic schools – in the USA at least, to achieve academic results among students from socio-economic backgrounds in excess of those that might otherwise have been predicted, and against a background of modest financial resources.[49] A similar claim is made by the late Dan Murphy who notes that research from a wide range of educationalists including Coleman, Hoffer, Kilgore, Greeley, Rossi, Bryk and Convey (in the USA), Praetz, Parrington, Fahy and Flynn (in Australia), provides compelling and overwhelming evidence 'on the worth of denominational schooling... when judged by the norms of basic educational accountability'.[50] This is true also of Catholic education in Northern Ireland. Some of the achievements of the Catholic sector, despite the relative economic and educational disadvantage of the Catholic population,[51] are, indeed, noteworthy. The Department of Education's statistical bulletin SB2/96 demonstrates the greater presence of relative economic deprivation among the Catholic community in Northern Ireland as compared to its Protestant counterpart, using free meal entitlement as an indicator of relative economic deprivation. More than one third (36.9%) of Catholic children were entitled to free school meals in the academic year 1995/6 while only half that figure (18.8%) of Protestant children qualified for entitlement. The Department notes that research clearly indicates that at this level of socio-economic disadvantage academic results obtained in Catholic schools should be considerably below that of non-Catholic

---

[49] See Bryk, A., 'Lessons from Catholic High Schools on Renewing our Educational Institutions', in ibid., pp. 25–41.

[50] Murphy, D., 'International Trends in Denominational Schooling'. The papers given at the Conference on Denominational Schooling are currently being prepared for publication. Extracts from Murphy's paper have been published in *Parent and Teacher Magazine* (Dublin, October/November 1998), pp. 18–20. I am indebted to Kevin Williams (Mater Dei College, Dublin) for supplying me with a copy of Dan Murphy's paper. All references to Murphy's research are taken from this.

[51] See, for example, Borooah, V., 'Is There a Penalty to Being a Catholic in Northern Ireland? An Econometric Analysis of the Relationship Between Religious Belief and Occupational Success', in *European Journal of Political Economy* (Elsevier, 1999), Vol. 15, pp. 163–192.

schools.[52] Yet the school performance tables, now commonly known as the league tables, year on year, suggest that this is not the case and that Catholic schools, despite higher levels of deprivation, and with modest resources, perform at a level higher than might be expected. In relation to academic results achieved in the selection test taken in the final year of Key Stage Two the Department itself concludes:

> When schools with similar levels of free school meals are compared, pupils from schools under Catholic management were more likely to achieve a grade A than their counterparts in schools under other management.[53]

Furthermore, at the other end of school life, Gallagher notes that since 1973 there has been a marked increase in the proportion of university entrants in Northern Ireland from manual backgrounds and that this appears to interact with religion. He points out that in 1991 more than forty per cent of Catholic university entrants were from working class backgrounds as compared with less than twenty-five per cent of Protestant entrants.[54] As with the case of selection itself, however, this commendable achievement may not be without a cost. Gallagher goes on to point out that the proportion of unqualified leavers is greater in the Catholic sector than in the controlled sector and that this poorer relative performance is greatest among boys in Catholic schools.[55] This may be partially explained by the relative lack of grammar school places in the Catholic sector, nevertheless the relatively poor performance of pupils in the secondary sector illustrates the price that many young people pay under the current system of transfer.

Nor can the issue be fudged. Over the past few years the issue of selection has taken on an air of added importance. The imposition of Direct Rule from Westminster in 1972 effectively 'froze' much debate on educational – and many other – issues for many years. Quite simply, secretaries of state often saw themselves placed in a position of managing social and political issues rather than developing them. Scarce wonder that *laissez-faire* or, more accurately, *laissez-rester* was often employed by those who would be charged with occupying positions of authority without local

[52] On this see an article by Fr Donal McKeown in *The Irish News* (April 17 1997).
[53] DENI, SB2/96, quoted McKeown, ibid.
[54] Gallagher, op. cit., p. 52.
[55] Ibid., p. 36.

accountability. The Good Friday Agreement changed that utterly and radically. Perhaps the most important element of that political development was the establishment of a ministerial executive by which the main political parties would wield real political power for the first time in almost three decades. Under the agreed arrangements those parties which secured sufficient support would be allocated ministerial positions according to the principle of proportionality. The securing of the educational portfolio in the new executive by Sinn Féin has ensured that selection has moved to the top of the political agenda. In Northern Ireland we are now effectively in a process of consultation in relation to this thorny issue. Strong, albeit initial, indications are that the current system may be radically amended if not abolished altogether. Yet, that is not to say that Northern Ireland will witness a comprehensivisation of schooling similar to that which took place in England and Wales during the 1960s and 1970s. The grammar school lobby has many powerful supporters who owe their social and economic position to their grammar school education. Many parents stress the value, at least in academic terms, of the benefits of a grammar school education.

Nor have three decades of comprehensive education in England and Wales realized an equitable and just schooling system. Many of the aspects of the grammar/secondary (or intermediate) divide have resurfaced in the high achieving/underachieving comprehensives with the social class of the catchment area playing an important role. The Catholic authorities in particular will have difficult choices to make. To unilaterally abandon selection and go comprehensive as it could be argued is demanded by the Gospel value of justice may not, in practice, overcome precisely those injustices which such a move would be aimed at achieving. Selection might simply reappear under another guise. Furthermore, such a move would almost certainly accentuate an already growing trend among some Catholic parents, which is that of sending their children to non-Catholic schools, in particular non-Catholic grammar schools. Although almost all Catholic parents in Northern Ireland do send their children to Catholic primary schools, a proportion of these children do not transfer to Catholic post-primary schools. Although no precise figure is available for Catholic students attending non-Catholic post-primary schools, it would appear that approximately five per cent of Catholic pupils do not transfer to Catholic post-primary schools at the end of Key Stage Two, instead going to non-Catholic grammar schools.[56] If the Catholic authorities abandon their grammar

schools without convincing parents that whatever replaces them
will provide for the excellence associated with the grammar sector,
it is feared that many more parents would look favourably at the
non-Catholic grammar sector. There is no easy solution to this
question, yet it is one that must be faced with wisdom and courage.
If the Catholic Church is to be true to its educational mission then
it must be guided by the twin Gospel values of justice and respect
for each person's God-given human dignity. The current competitive model with winners and losers clearly is not in line with these
values and does indeed present all associated with Catholic education with a serious dilemma and challenge, one made all the more
pressing with the recent publication of the long-awaited report
commissioned by the Department of Education on the effects of
selection.[57]

The Gallagher/Smith Report

One of the first actions taken by the Education Minister, Martin
McGuinness, on his appointment to that position in the new
power-sharing Northern Ireland administration was to instruct the
Department of Education to set up a working party 'to investigate
the effects on pupils and their families, teachers, schools and the
community of the existing selective structure of secondary education in Northern Ireland, in order to provide a better basis for
informed debate on the future structure of secondary education'.[58] In addition, the working party was requested to identify
and assess the relative strengths and weaknesses of alternative
models to the current selective system.[59] The project team, chaired
by Tony Gallagher and Alan Smith, published its report in
September 2000. Many of its findings concurred with those made
in previous research and outlined above. On the one hand, the
selective system in Northern Ireland appears to produce higher
academic standards than are achieved in any other region in the
UK. On the other hand, the educational system in Northern
Ireland also produces a longer 'tail', i.e. those who leave school at

---

[56] This figure can be obtained by comparing the number of pupils at Catholic
primary school with the combined Catholic post-primary figures from the
CCMS statistics, *op. cit.*

[57] Gallagher, A. and Smith, A., *The Effects of the Selective System of Secondary Education
in Northern Ireland* (Belfast, DENI, 2000).

[58] ibid., Appendix 3.

[59] See ibid.

the end of Key Stage Three with no GCSE passes at grades A*–C (or equivalent), than in any other part of the UK.[60] In particular, underachievement in the secondary sector is noted.[61] Other negative effects associated with the selective system include distortion of the curriculum, particularly in Key Stage Two, the issue of the self-esteem of those deemed 'failures' and the primacy of quantitative academic results over other crucial areas such as pastoral care. The Report identifies five different models for post-primary education: the current selective system, delayed selection as currently operating in the Craigavon area of Northern Ireland, common primary and lower secondary schools, followed by differentiated upper secondary schools, similar to those which are common in Italy and France, differentiated post-primary schools with distinctive academic and vocational curricula and, finally, a thorough comprehensive system as found in Scotland.[62] Although no system is recommended in the Report, it is clear from the assessment of the relative strengths and weaknesses of the respective systems, and from the initial comments of the Minister, that the status quo is not a long-term solution to the issues of educational disadvantage and polarity in achievement. The Minister of Education has announced the setting up of an independent Review Body, chaired by the former Ombudsman, Gerry Burns, to consider future arrangements for post-primary education, which will have wide-ranging terms of reference and will undertake extensive consultation. The Review Body has been instructed to report to the Minister by the end of May 2001.

Perhaps one of the most disappointing aspects of the Gallagher/Smith Report was the somewhat limited exploration of alternative models to selection. The special and, indeed, unique nature of Northern Irish society may require considerably more imaginative initiatives than are presented in the Report. The importance of 'vision', of what Bryk above calls 'the inspirational ideology', cannot be overstated. Of course, for the vision to become realized in practice there must be a buying into the ethos of the school by all of the partners of the school community, namely, students, teachers, non-teaching staff, parents, governors and trustees. When the vision becomes a living, commonly shared social outlook or set of values, which underpins educational practice and guides and informs relationships within the educational

---

[60] See ibid., Table 4.1 and Figure 4.1.
[61] See ibid., Section 4.
[62] See ibid., 10.1.2.

institutions, the actual educational experience and outcomes of that experience can be altered fundamentally. James Coleman refers to this as 'social capital', and suggests that when social capital is high – i.e., when a community and all its institutions including churches, schools, etc., share core values and virtues – educational achievement can be considerably enhanced.[63] The Church's response to the recently published Gallagher Report on alternatives to selection will provide the Catholic authorities with a unique opportunity to give courageous and visionary leadership in an area that is central to the Church's salvific mission to the young. The Catholic Church should welcome rather than fear the new challenges facing it. The Church's response to the Gallagher/Smith Report should be guided by its unique philosophy and values, especially its long-standing commitment to the common good, solidarity with one's fellow man/woman, the idea of school as a voluntary community and, above all else, its vision of education as a thoroughly spirit-filled and human-defining activity at which justice lies at the centre. Given the Catholic Church's long and wide experience in the educational field throughout the world one would expect that the Church will play an important and vital role in shaping the future of education in Northern Ireland.

The Integrated Sector: a New Challenge to Catholic Education?

If the issue of selection presents the Catholic Church in Northern Ireland with a timely and, indeed, welcome challenge, the current debate concerning integrated education raises other, equally, if not more, serious, issues. In particular, the very *raison d'être* of Catholic schooling is currently being questioned by some powerful voices. Perhaps Professor Julia Neuberger, Chancellor of the University of Ulster who, at the opening of a new integrated school, argued against public funds being made available to non-integrated schools, made the most forthright and spectacular attack on denominational education three ago. The essence of Professor Neuberger's argument was that denominational education – and especially Catholic education – is divisive and

---

[63] See, for example, Coleman, J., Hoffer T., and Kilmore, S., *High School Achievement: Public, Catholic and Private Schools Compared* (New York, Basic Books, 1982).

contributes to the conflict in Northern Ireland.[64] Underpinning
Professor Neuberger's thesis is the commonly held notion that
tolerance, mutual respect and understanding are the sole preserve
of one sector – the integrated system – and that Catholic schools
are, in some sense, less tolerant and divisive.

The Catholic Church's apparent suspicion of a fully integrated
system of schooling is understandable given the rather obvious
attempts at social engineering dating back to the 1831 Stanley
proposals and later by a succession of Unionist governments in
Northern Ireland. Unionist domination ensured that any envisaged 'shared schools' system could only be on the basis of the
Catholic sector transferring to the controlled (*de facto*
Protestant/Unionist) sector.[65] Critics of Catholic education usually
exhibited traditional Unionist suspicion that Catholic schools were
institutions of sedition, citing the Catholic authorities' refusal to
instruct Catholic schools to fly the Union Flag as evidence of disloyalty.[66] Nor was hostility to the Catholic insistence on maintaining
its own educational system limited to those from a Unionist background. The British Home Secretary, James Callaghan, addressing
the Labour Party Conference in 1969, demonstrated a typical
misunderstanding of what Catholic education is about when he
explicitly equated demands for separate education with the authorities' discrimination in the areas of housing and jobs – an
accusation frequently made by Catholics against the Unionist
establishment. According to Callaghan:

> I find it equally offensive if it is separate education that is advanced
> as an unshakeable principle... That is equally as offensive as a deci-
> sion by a group in power which denies a man a house because of his
> religion and because he is in a minority.[67]

In reality the issue of integrated education remained off-stage for
much of the first five decades of the existence of the Northern
Ireland state, with Unionist politicians and some Protestant
spokespersons using the Catholic community's demand for its
own schooling system as evidence of its disloyalty and constantly

---

[64] Professor Neuberger's comments were carried on BBC Radio Ulster's
'Talkback' programme (16 April 1997) and repeated in *The Irish News* (17 April
1997).

[65] On this issue see McGrath, pp. 178–185, 203–218 and 224–227.

[66] See, for example, Captain Robert Mitchell, Unionist MP for North Armagh, NI
Commons LXXVI 114, 1 October 1969.

[67] Quoted *The Belfast Telegraph* (30 September 1969).

offering the controlled sector as a model of an already existent integrated sector – constantly refused by the unwilling and recalcitrant Catholic authorities. The on-set of the 'Troubles' – the civil strife of the past three decades – in 1969, however, gave those who favour integration a much-needed boost and placed education very much at the centre of public debate. The formation of the lobby group All Children Together (ACT) in early 1972 acted as a catalyst for the supporters of integration. Initially set up by a group of parents in North Down who sent their children to controlled schools and who wished to ensure that their children received Catholic religious instruction and sacramental preparation – which in itself presented difficulties for the Catholic hierarchy given its view of the Catholic school as an integral part of parish life and faith formation[68] – this group soon became a vehicle through which demands for the creation of an integrated education sector would be pursued. A number of influential figures in Northern Ireland society who, as the historian Andrew Boyd points out, sought to '[lay] the blame for Northern Ireland's troubles on the schools',[69] attached themselves to ACT and promoted this viewpoint with some success. According to Boyd:

> It was taken up by the Unionist press and then by Terence O'Neill when he was Prime Minister. James Callaghan fell for it when he was Home Secretary and responsible for reforming Northern Ireland in 1969.[70]

What, in fact, many 'fell for' was the theory that denominational education, if not the primary cause of the conflict in Northern Ireland, a major element that exasperates the social and religious divisions there and that the Catholic Church, through its insistence on the right of Catholic parents to have their children educated at Catholic schools, stands accused of barring the way to reconciliation and peace. Gallagher and Worrall point out that the explosion of the conflict onto the streets in 1969 brought with it many supposed 'experts' with their own preconceived solutions. According to Gallagher and Worrall:

> When it came to education, they were like wasps in a honey pot. Supported by a limited number of indigenous reformers they began

[68] On the dispute between ACT and the Church authorities see McGrath, op. cit., pp. 208–209.
[69] Boyd, A., 'Is Integrated Education the Answer?', in *The Irish Weekly*, 4 September 1976.
[70] ibid., p. 4.

almost with one voice to advise British Home secretaries and their successors, the Secretaries of State for Northern Ireland, to look carefully at the education system. It was all so clear to them much of the trouble starts in the schools. The equations were quickly and simplistically stated. Segregated education equals ignorance and strife; integrated education equals understanding and reconcilia- tion; *ergo*, integrate, and the sooner the better.[71]

The first major breakthrough for this lobby, at least in legislative terms, was achieved with the inclusion in the Education (Northern Ireland) Act of 1978 of a clause that mandated the Government 'to facilitate the establishment in Northern Ireland of schools likely to be attended by pupils of different religious affiliations or cultural traditions'.[72] The Catholic authorities mounted a principled defence in support of denominational schools based on parental right to choose and made a plea for equal treatment – a position that they have reiterated time and time again. In their response to the Education Reform Order of 1989 the Northern Bishops state the following:

> We are not contesting the rights of parents to choose schools to which they send their children and to receive adequate Government funding to support their choice. We simply insist that those who choose Catholic schools should not be less favourably treated finan- cially than those who choose integrated schools. We deeply regret that, despite our reasoned objections, the Government should at this time have persisted in pursuing a course that is regarded by the great majority of the Catholic community as inequitable and unjust.[73]

Throughout the 1970s and much of the 1980s successive Governments remained sceptical about the long-term feasibility of the integrated sector attracting large-scale numbers of pupils. The arrival of Mawhinney to office in 1986 led to a change in Government policy in relation to integrated education from one of sceptical support to one of active promotion for integrated educa- tion. The 1988 DENI consultative document, *Education in Northern Ireland – Proposals for Reform*, contained new Government thinking on this matter. Integrated schools were to receive preferential treatment for building projects. The temptation for already

---

[71] Gallagher, E. and Worrall, S., *Christians in Ulster 1968–1980* (Oxford, Oxford University Press, 1982) p. 157.

[72] House of Lords Fifth Series 387 277, 10 November 1977.

[73] Northern Catholic Bishops, *Statement from the Northern Catholic Bishops on the Education Reform (Northern Ireland) Order 1989* (Belfast, Episcopal Diocesan Office, 1989), p. 2.

existing schools to opt for integrated status in order to jump the queue for capital building costs or to remain open in a time of falling school numbers is obvious. The Government's newfound attraction to promoting the integrated sector was not limited to words and platitudes. Since the 1989 Order the British Government has engaged in large-scale capital building projects for the integrated sector. In 1997 the Government dedicated itself to spending twenty-eight million pounds on new integrated schools over the next three years. This has enabled the integrated education sector to grow from slightly under three per cent of the school population to four per cent. This compares with a total annual budget for all maintained and controlled schools of just twenty-seven million pounds.[74] Furthermore, the 1989 Order not only granted integrated schools favoured status for capital building funding and full maintenance costs, it also established and funded an official body – the Northern Ireland Council for Integrated Education (NICIE) – to promote the ideals of integrated education through public information and advice to potential school governors and in the media. The direction taken by Brian Mawhinney in the late 1980s has been consistently followed by subsequent administrations. What is remarkable, however, is that, given the favourable media portrayal, the political support and the economic inducements, the integrated sector has not attracted the numbers that its supporters might have anticipated. Figures in the 1999/2000 school census indicate that in Northern Ireland there are twenty-seven integrated primary schools and sixteen integrated post-primary schools.[75] This compares with more than one thousand primary schools and more than two hundred post-primary schools in the controlled and maintained sectors.[76]

Just how 'integrated' some of the integrated schools are in reality is open to question. The visionaries in ACT and NICIE originally sought to set the balance between Catholic and Protestant pupils within the range sixty/forty per cent. Outside of that band schools might be perceived to be predominantly of one tradition or the other. Yet, in the drive to promote integration this balance has been totally abandoned. Schools simply have to demonstrate that they are capable of attracting pupils from both traditions. While many of the schools do indeed attract a balance of students from both cultural and religious traditions, there seems to be a

[74] UK Commons sixth Series 301 955, 26 November 1997 and 307 439, 2 March 1998.
[75] M. McGuinness, Minister of Education, AQW 476/99.
[76] See Gallagher, op. cit., pp. 4, 22.

serious imbalance in many others. For example, in the academic year 1999/2000, the religious breakdown at Bangor Central Integrated Primary School was twenty-two Catholic and two hundred and sixteen Protestant pupils, while at Annsborough Integrated Primary School the proportions are reversed with four Protestant and forty-one Catholic pupils on the roll. The post-primary sector throws up similar examples. At Priory College, for example, only twenty-five Catholic students are registered out of a total school population of more than three hundred. At Fort Hill College less than seven per cent of the pupils come from one section of the community with forty-eight pupils registered as Catholic and six hundred and fifty denoted as Protestant, surely undermining the integrated nature of the school.

There are a number of factors that account for the slow growth in the integrated sector. One of the major difficulties facing those who support integrated education in Northern Ireland is simply that the divided school system reflects the real life separation of the two communities. The two major communities in Northern Ireland live, to a considerable extent, parallel but separate lives. Exact statistics are difficult to discern, but it is an accepted fact that the overwhelming majority of the population of Northern Ireland live in areas inhabited by their own respective 'tribe', with perhaps as much as eighty per cent of the population of Northern Ireland living in communities which are predominantly (i.e. in excess of eighty per cent) either Catholic or Protestant.[77] Addressing the New Ireland Forum in 1983, Cardinal Daly succinctly emphasised the practical difficulties of large-scale integrated education in a fragmented society such as Northern Ireland:

> Even those who believe in the value of integrated education must recognize that their solution would affect very few. It could not, for long established historical and geographical reasons, be realized between, say, the Falls Road and the Shankill Road other than by some process of bussing which would expose young children to real physical danger, intimidation, threats to which no parents would willingly subject their children.[78]

Unless the Government is going to fund a massive capital building programme either in the housing sector or in the creation of new schools on a scale hitherto unimagined, then the vast majority of

[77] See The Statistics and Research Agency, *The Mid-Year Population Estimates* (Belfast, HMSO, 1999).

[78] *New Ireland Forum: Report of Proceedings*, Vol. 12, p. 31, quoted McGrath, op. cit., p. 207.

students will continue to be educated in the currently denominational sectors.

A second and, perhaps, more significant reason for the apparent
reluctance of parents to embrace the integrated project in greater
numbers is the fact that many parents actually support the denominational system. Northern Ireland is quite unlike any other part of
the United Kingdom or the rest of Ireland for that matter. Many
have deep and strong attachments to their respective churches and
communities. It should be of no surprise that many parents would
support their respective schooling systems to which they feel a
considerable degree of loyalty and identification, and of which
they feel a sense of ownership. More than twenty years ago Lord
Elton, the then Northern Ireland Office Minister of Education,
made precisely this point:

> To the outsider it is a perfectly simple object to integrate education:
> but both in practical and philosophical terms it is anything but a
> simple question. The first thing is that people's emotions and loyal-
> ties are very deeply committed indeed and no solution will work that
> is not accepted.[79]

Conclusion: Catholic Education – a Need for Reappraisal?

The central thesis of this paper is that Catholic education in
Northern Ireland has been unfairly treated and portrayed. Many of
those who favour integrated education appear to suggest that
Catholic schooling is, to some degree, deficient in the areas of the
promotion of tolerance and mutual understanding, or, at least,
that integrated education promotes these better. Those charged
with leadership of Catholic education make no claims of superior-
ity in relation to the promotion of tolerance or the common good.
Nor does the Catholic Church oppose integrated education as is
sometimes suggested. Cardinal Daly concisely put the Church's
position on this issue in 1991 as follows:

> Our case has never been one of opposing integrated education, but
> of saying that it should not be promoted to the detriment of other
> forms of education. And while the Government does encourage
> integrated education, integrated education has an opportunity to
> demonstrate its capacity to deliver its ideals. I'm quite happy to
> await the results.[80]

[79] *Fortnight* (May 1980), No. 176, p. 14.
[80] ibid., (September 1991), No. 298, p. 13.

Furthermore, much of the received wisdom on the issue of Catholic schooling and the common good is open to question. Dan Murphy points out that recent research from the USA and Australia 'suggests that pupils in Catholic schools are *less* prejudiced in religious matters than those who attend public (secular) schools'.[81] It appears from Murphy's findings that much can be achieved through a strong ethico-religious formation that allows Catholic education – at its best and most enlightened – to go beyond the simple and limited goal of tolerance towards a genuine understanding of other traditions, both religious and non-religious. If Murphy is correct, those who espouse integrated education as a panacea for intolerance in Northern Ireland may find their own position compromised. Not that one should be surprised if this were found to be the case. Exclusivity and being inward-looking are not – or, at least, should not be – elements of the Catholic vision of education. Indeed, the Catholic philosophy of education, particularly since Vatican II, has been marked by a critical openness to the modern world, embracing what is positive about modernity and challenging the negative, dehumanising aspects of modern living, as well as making ecumenical activity and inter-Faith dialogue categorical and moral imperatives.[82] At the heart of the Catholic vision of education is the synthesis of faith and life based on the recognition that all people are, as John Paul II points out, 'living images of God, redeemed by the blood of Jesus Christ and placed under the permanent action of the Holy Spirit'.[83] With this vision of humankind, 'reaching out' and other-directedness are intrinsic to Catholic faith and not optional extras. They are also essential tasks in pluralist and increasingly secular society. In the context of a divided society such as Northern Ireland this takes on added importance. A central element – indeed, perhaps the guiding principle – of the Good Friday Agreement is that of parity of esteem, of equality, of respect for all traditions and communities. For the first time since the foundation of Northern Ireland, the equal treatment of all is a distinct possibility and a recognised aim of Government. The litmus test of the attainment of this goal may well be the treatment of the Catholic education sector. Does pluralism also include that sector? We do indeed lie in interesting, turbulent and challenging times.

---

[81] Murphy, *op. cit.*

[82] On this view of Catholic education see D. Lane, *The Future of Religion in Irish Education* (Dublin, Veritas, 1997), pp. 131–7.

[83] John Paul II, *Sollicitudo Rei Socialis*, in O'Brien and Shannon (eds), *Catholic Social Thought* (New York, Orbis, 1992) 38, p. 40.

A recognition of the legitimacy of the right to Catholic schooling should not be just a matter of fairness. If we are to build a peaceful and mutually affirming society we will need Catholic education – at its very best – to play a full role.

Part Two

The Contemporary Catholic School

Chapter 4

The Christian Ministry of Teaching

Michael Holman SJ

In the autumn of 1981, I was a history student at the Jesuit house of studies in Oxford, Campion Hall. I was invited by the Jesuit provincial's delegate for secondary education to attend a meeting, the first in what became a long series, of teachers from Jesuit schools up and down the country. A few of these teachers were themselves Jesuits but the great majority were lay men and women. Attendance at the meeting not only afforded me a welcome break from the study of Anglo-Saxon burial sites, it also shaped significantly my outlook on what it meant to be a teacher in a Catholic school.

This conference, and a number later, took place in what was then the pastoral centre of the Leeds diocese near Wetherby in North Yorkshire. The centre occupied a commanding position in Wharfedale, above the river, in wooded parkland with the trees at their resplendent autumnal best during those three bright days in October. The staff at the centre were an esoteric group and included a prize cook, who made her own significant contribution to the success of that week-end, and one elderly assistant who had spent the previous twenty years in Spain as governess to the King's children.

It was the fate of Jesuit students invited to attend meetings such as this that participation was limited by the need to supply, on behalf of the organiser, the necessities of life for the participants. I became the conference *gofer* running in the minibus into Wetherby to provide razor blades, light bulbs and newspapers. This role, in its own curious way, enabled be to meet more participants and in the process understand more fully how the programme of the week-end affected them.

The meeting had as its focus what still remains central and even urgent in Catholic schools today, the *Ministry of Teaching*.

In the nineteen seventies, a group of Jesuits working in the Jesuit Secondary Education Association (JSEA) in the United States were keen to take up the challenge set all Jesuit schools by our then superior general, Fr Pedro Arrupe SJ. In an address to an international congress of Jesuit alumni, entitled *Men for Others*, Fr Arrupe had challenged secondary schools to examine their very *raison d'être*. It was his concern that many Jesuit schools at that time were *de facto* not serving the mission of the Society and the Church, whatever their stated hopes and aspirations may have been. Some were indeed serving only the wealthy while others had narrowly academic ends. Fr Arrupe challenged those responsible for Jesuit schools world-wide to recognize that their first purpose had to be apostolic and missionary, namely, to promote the Christian faith, a necessary aspect of which was to promote evangelical justice. By serving the rich or by delivering only a narrow set of academic objectives it could be that a school not only did not focus on this objective but was even undermining it either by propping up injustices in society or by providing an education which was too little concerned with the development of students in the image and likeness of Jesus Christ and as agents of change in society.

The JSEA responded to Fr Arrupe's challenge in three interrelated ways. The first was to provide school administrators and staff with the resources needed to engage in a process of school self-evaluation and to identify priorities for development. These priorities for development were arrived at in the light of the second initiative, a process of identifying a new set of school aims, in the spirit of Fr Arrupe's address *Men for Others*, which focussed upon the kind of person the school wanted to see graduate from its high school. In the light of that *Profile of the Student at Graduation*, as it became known, schools were encouraged to identify the experiences the students would need to have and the knowledge and the skills they would need to acquire if they were to become, as the tag went, *men and women of faith who were men and women for others*. The point was not that the secular curriculum would be set aside but that the whole learning experience would become one attuned to the primary apostolic focus of the Jesuit school.

This recognition that the whole curriculum was potentially relevant to the school's religious mission had the consequence of including all teachers, not just those occupied with the religious education and formation of the school, in working to achieve the school's faith purpose. All teachers, religious and lay, were now potentially ministers involved in ministry to the young. To support the development of this new awareness of the significance of teaching in a Jesuit school, the JSEA developed a programme on this theme known as the *Colloquium on the Christian Ministry of Teaching*. It proved a successful instrument of staff development in Catholic schools in America and then spread throughout the 1980s and 1990s to schools not only in other parts of the English speaking world but also to a number of schools in Asia and other parts of Europe. The popularity of the *Colloquium* was in part due to its methodology and in part to the spirituality which was implicit in the programme. Perhaps the major reason for its success, however, lay in the fact that it managed, to an extraordinary degree, to assist teachers in many different schools working in a wide variety of contexts to reclaim the initial inspiration which had brought them into teaching and to recognize their work not only as one job amongst other jobs but as a vocation from God, essential to the future of the children whom they taught and to the welfare of the Kingdom of God.

The methodology of the *Colloquium* consisted in a series of guided reflections, led by those who were themselves teachers. It avoided long input sessions, the graveyard of so many well intentioned training conferences for teachers. The benefits of the programme came from reflecting on experience, sharing that experience with others and in the process learning from their experience too.

Participants were invited to reflect on what had first brought them into teaching, to lay hold once again of the hopes and the dreams they had had when they began at college or when they had received news of their first appointment to their first school. They were asked to identify their role models as teachers: the men and women who had taught them and who had shaped their own self understanding of what it was to be a teacher in a Catholic school. They reflected as well on the low points of their teaching experience and what these had done to them, as well as on the high points and on the enthusiasm and sense of motivation they had derived from these. Jesus was a teacher: what kind of a teacher was he? What was there about his teaching and his way of teaching which particularly appealed? Participants were encouraged to reflect as well on the impact which they, like all teachers, for weal or for woe, had had on their students and on the possibility that any teacher can influence young people for life. Perhaps the most challenging aspect of the entire weekend for many was the invitation to own the strengths and talents which they had as people and as teachers and to understand that in those talents and those strengths there were gifts for those whom they taught.

The hoped for outcomes were not how much more the participating staff would know at the end of the weekend but rather what the formative process of the weekend had done to them and in them. Evaluations of the *Colloquium* might highlight the gratitude felt at the opportunity to meet teachers from other schools; the support they felt from each other and from listening to the experiences of others which paralleled their own experiences; the recognition that their work was not just a job but a source of positive influence on those whom they taught. Others might be thankful that Jesus was not someone far distant from their daily preoccupations but someone alive right in the midst of them.

The *Colloquium* process was an attempt not only to enable teachers to recapture their sense of teaching as a ministry rooted in a vocation but also to provide teachers with a spirituality which would enable them to maintain their lives as ministers in schools.

St Ignatius Loyola, the founder of the Jesuits, understood his relationship with God not in terms of withdrawal from the world, in such a way that God was to be found in a monastery or a church, but in terms of finding God in the midst of the everyday events of life. He and his followers, the first members in the sixteenth century of the Society of Jesus, were men attuned to *finding God in all things* and in particular in their experience together and as individuals in the world. Far from this being an individualistic experience, the task of being Christ's apostle in the midst of life made these men ever more mindful of their need to meet Christ in the Sacraments, in his Word and in the Church which spoke with Christ's authentic voice.

Spirituality has to do with the ways and means of attuning oneself to the presence of Jesus and to make an appropriately generous response to that presence. To the extent that the spirituality of Ignatius attunes people in the middle of life to *find God in all things*, it is a spirituality attuned to the reality and the needs of lay ministers, not least teachers in Catholic schools. Which is why the method of the *Colloquium* emphasized so much the significance of reflection on experience. The method of the *Colloquium* taught a way of becoming attuned to the presence of Jesus in the experience of school. The growing realisation that as teachers they were called to be ministers in the schools in which they worked, to the young people for whom they worked, similarly made these ministers only too mindful of how needful they were for the presence of Christ in their lives.

That the *Colloquium* in its time had an impact is unquestioned. It succeeded best in schools which were committed to supporting those who had undergone the programme in the months and years that followed. Groups met to reflect on the presence of Christ in their lives, in their work and in their students. In many places, the experiment floundered partly because of the lack of support within the institution for the project and partly because of the need to comply with the multiplicity of government initiated changes in the 1980s and 1990s which swallowed up all available time.

Twenty years on from that week-end in Wetherby, the need for Catholic schools in this country to identify themselves first and foremost as instruments of the Church's mission and their teachers as ministers is as relevant now as it was twenty years ago. Indeed, the condition of the Church and society in this country make the discovery or rediscovery of this perspective both an urgent task and an exciting challenge. Why?

Statistics, it is true, can be made to tell any story but the statistics on trends in Mass attendance in the Roman Catholic Church over the past thirty years can tell nothing other than a disturbing story. The numbers attending church on a regular basis are declining and they are declining alarmingly. In an article in *The Tablet* of 19 June 1999, Gordon Heald presented research carried out by *Opinion Research Business* which has concluded that Mass attendance in England and Wales has declined sharply since 1964:

1964	2,114,219
1974	1,752,730
1984	1,512,533
1998	1,086,268

Indeed, this represents a decline of 51% in thirty-four years and this at a time when the Catholic population has remained largely stable:

1964	3,827,000
1974	4,162,942
1984	4,220,262
1998	4,134,000

Put another way, the percentage of Catholics practising with regularity in England and Wales has declined thus:

1964	55%
1974	42%
1984	36%
1998	26%

Statistics such as these need to be handled with care. Some, for example, argue that they are an indication not so much of a decline in attachment to the Church as a decline in weekly Mass attendance. It is the patterns of church going that have changed and weekly church attendance is now replaced with fortnightly or monthly attendance. Be that as it may, there is a trend and it is alarming. Numbers *per se* matter less than the message which the numbers convey: for those who call themselves Catholic, fewer and fewer are sufficiently committed to practise their faith regularly. It would be hard to argue that addressing this task is not the most urgent facing the Catholic Church in the United Kingdom today. It would be hard to argue, as well, that the most urgent task facing Catholic schools, which the Church maintains at such considerable expense, is to bring the faith alive amongst the young people and the families with whom they are in daily contact.

In many ways, Catholic schools are well placed to carry out this mission. Far from witnessing to a decline, Gordon Head's statistics demonstrate that the number of Catholic schools in England and Wales has largely held since 1964:

1964	2,888
1974	3,094
1984	2,790
1996	2,493

In other words, the number of Catholic schools is just 15% below the figure in 1964. Gordon Heald concluded his article with the warning that 'without some reform the downward path will continue'. I would argue that the Church needs to face up to the fact that the parish structure in twenty-first century Britain cannot continue to be regarded as the primary point of contact with Catholic people. It is to the schools that young people and their families continue to flock, not the churches. Those schools are now *de facto* the primary Christian communities for countless people in this country for whom the parish and its church is now regrettably foreign territory.

In other ways, however, Catholic schools have become arguably less well suited to promoting the Church's mission than they were just twenty years ago. The reason for this lies in the response which schools have had to make, or have chosen to make, to the reforms which have come their way since the mid 1980s. The effect of these reforms has been to reduce the independence of all schools, Catholic schools included, over curriculum and management matters. The national curriculum, in so far is it is compulsory in all maintained schools in England and Wales, has promoted a prescriptive curriculum which serves the present and future economic interests of the nation. In this context, the role of the teacher has become more and more tightly focussed on the achievement of pupil progress in terms of adding value from one national curriculum key stage to another. In so far as successive governments have promoted competition between schools for pupils, there has been a tendency for some of our most renowned Catholic maintained schools to seek out the brightest and the best and to shape their ethos in order to be well placed in the market place.

If Catholic schools are to meet the pressing needs of the Church in this country, then the apostolic purpose of these schools needs to be primary, not only in name but in fact. What might that mean?

The starting point needs to be the kind of self-reflection which Fr Arrupe promoted in Jesuit schools in the 1970s. We need to look not only at what we say we do, but also at what we actually do, and at the context in which we do it. If our first aim is to promote faith we need to identify what there may be about us which inhibits that mission. Young people are sensitive above all to double standards. If a school says it lives by the Gospel but does not appear to forgive challenging pupils or appears only to be interested in those students who will make their league table position look favourable then the stated aim of the school in promoting faith, of which a key constituent is justice, will be undermined by its hidden, or not so hidden, curriculum. In other words, the very things which we are told make Catholic schools popular – high standards of discipline and academic results – may or may not be undermining their apostolic purpose. The key thing is to have the freedom at least to pose the question and to search out an honest answer.

Making an effective response to this critical situation means many other things too. To begin with, we need to be clear that Catholic schools are primarily places where ministry to the young and their families takes place and where teachers in this context are seen as and operate as ministers. Which is all very well, we can hear those familiar with Catholic schools today shout, but there are many objections to that view. And indeed there are.

One is the pragmatic view that the Catholic school as a place of ministry of this kind has been weakened over the years by the necessary changes in the composition of our staff rooms. Gone are the days when a Catholic head teacher could advertise for posts in the *Times Educational Supplement* and have a number of fine applications and from that number be able to select a bright Catholic graduate. The staff in many Catholic schools increasingly represent the whole spectrum of religious opinion.

This is the context in which we work and while it provides a challenge to the school leader, it is hardly an insuperable one. The invitation is to discover the call of the Lord in it. A creative response to that call requires a work of imagination. Ministry means many things. There will be those who minister in the context of the religious education class and there will be those who make valuable contributions to the retreat programme of the school. In all likelihood, these will be actively committed to the practice of the Catholic faith or members of another Christian denomination. But there are alternative modes of ministry. The challenge to any Catholic head teacher today is to identify just how an individual can contribute from his or her talents to the ministry of the Church in the school. For a number this may mean opening up the role of the class tutor from checking the register and ministering academic progress to taking the kind of active interest in the day to day welfare of a boy or girl which may be absent in the home. For those of other faiths teaching in a Catholic school, there is the opportunity to share their own religious perspective with the students and the staff in a way which leads them to understand their own faith commitment in a new light. Still others may have one of the most significant ministerial talents of all, that of being able to minister to their own colleagues.

The sceptic will still shout that this is all very well but however much the Catholic Church may say that schools are places of ministry, the real business of school, that which takes up 90% of any day and any school year and that in terms of which we are publicly judged, is the business of pupil achievement at whatever stage of the national curriculum. The fact that our schools are for the most part state funded makes it necessary for us to serve the ends set us by the state and the message received more or less each August as GCSE and A level results come out is that Catholic schools are managing to do this very well.

None of this can be denied. This is the real context again in which we work and the invitation is to discover once again the call of the Lord in it and a creative response again requires a work of imagination. Specifically, we need to be able to focus on two things. The first has to do with the content of the curriculum and the second with methodology.

So far as content is concerned, a key aspect of development in our schools should now be working out how in the teaching of English or Science or History or IT we can introduce the specifically religious or ethical perspective. In one way this is only doing justice to the Catholic understanding of the nature of all knowledge as having its source and origin in God himself. In another more practical way it is providing young people with the clear message that religion is not just about what goes on in church but about what we do with our lives.

Methodology is also significant. Once again the call is to be creative. In the last decade, the JSEA in the United States has developed a pedagogical process, known as the *Ignatian Pedagogy*, for use in the classroom which is designed to create a disposition in the student to be more open to the word of God and to Christian involvement in the world. In other words, the claim would be that certain traditional methods of teaching young people have created passive people more ready to accept the status quo than to become open to new possibilities and to themselves becoming agents of change. This *Ignatian Pedagogy* arose from a study of the pedagogical principles of the Spiritual Exercises of St Ignatius Loyola. This process of guided prayer and reflection has assisted a great many to listen to the call of God in their lives and to make a generous response to that call. This process happens in a specific context which the JSEA sees as having parallels in the classroom: a clearly structured approach to learning, valuing the individual's questioning and encouraging students to reflect on what they are learning in the light of their experience.

Making schools places of ministry capable of responding to the challenge facing the Church today, then, means at least three things. It means developing the ministry of teachers in whatever mode might be identified; it means developing the religious and ethical potential of the subjects of the curriculum and it means developing classroom pedagogy in a way that enables young people to be more open to the call of the Lord and to making a response of generosity. All of which would contribute to developing the ministerial culture of the Catholic school.

In a sense this may seem to be asking yet more of teachers in Catholic schools. In fact it is more like asking them to reflect on what they do already and to consider the ways in which the potential of what they do can be maximized. In some ways asking teachers to change the ways they do things is still more challenging than asking them to do more. The latter asks them to give more time, the former asks them to give more of themselves. Which is why no programme of this kind can be carried through without a significant commitment on the part of the school and the Church to providing support for teachers in their ministry. In part this support would need to be geared to providing knowledge, say about how History at GCSE can contribute to the mission of the school; in part to providing the kind of pedagogical skills identified by the JSEA. Most of all, though, there needs to be a way in which ministers in the classroom can be allowed to develop a spirituality which supports their ministry. In this context, the *Colloquium* still has value.

Some years ago, I remember how shocked I was reading an article about suggestions for reform in the Church. The author suggested that the reforms which had taken place still had not enabled the Church to meet the needs of men and women of the time, they were like moving around the chairs on the deck of the sinking Titanic. Because Catholic schools in this country are in daily contact with the unchurched young people and their families, they are places of great potential. There are many things that can be done, as we have seen, to maximize their potential as places of ministry. But there is a sense in which this still does not go to the heart of the matter.

My experience of working with young people and their families suggests that the crisis facing the Church in this country, so far as the decline in the practice of the faith is concerned, has three causes which together mean that they see no compelling reason to practise the faith.

The first cause has to do with what the great majority find when they do go to church, namely a liturgy that does not engage them in the worship of God. Making liturgy better does not have to do only with better music and better homilies. It has to do with rediscovering what the older forms of liturgy, at their best, did manage to do. Namely, creating a sense of God-among-us by the use of means of communication other than the word. Silence communicates, as does reverence and light and smell and colour and sound. The fact that liturgy has become so wordy has made it less accessible to the majority for whom so much of the vocabulary and so many of the concepts are beyond their understanding. When people have been to Church they want to feel different. That is why evangelical services are increasingly popular. People in our post Christian society are thirsting for the kind of support which provides them each week with a sense of God in their lives and so gives them an inspiration and an encouragement for living the Gospel in a world which now either largely ignores it or is openly hostile to it.

The second cause is that we now live in a culture which is consumerist and which, while it has brought an enviable degree of affluence, proclaims a Gospel of fulfilment in the material things of life and does so in a powerful and a compelling way. Happiness is a matter of an individual having more and looking good. That is the psychological underpinning of the free market economy which over the last twenty years we have made for ourselves. In this context, the message of the Gospel that happiness, new life and fulfilment lie in our following a man who looked after the least in society with a love that was self-sacrificing just makes little sense.

The third cause is that we now live in a culture which values above all toleration. This provides for peaceful co-existence with each other in a multi-cultural society and to that extent has brought great and not to be taken for granted benefits. At the same time, however, it has been bought at a cost. The message that seeps down to young people is that each is as good as the other; one set of beliefs no better than any another, it just depends on your particular outlook. To think any different is not *cool*, and certainly not *PC*, not politically correct. In such a context, the truth of Jesus Christ and of Christianity is no better than any other creed, a result of your upbringing and choice, certainly not to be regarded as the one way of salvation.

Being a minister working with children in a society which sees happiness as a matter of here and now material fulfilment and in a society which values each as good as the other, and no better than any other, is no easy thing. There appears to be no compelling reason to believe and no compelling reason to practise what you believe. And when you do dare to practise it, and for a young person it does involve the risk of standing out and being different, you are too easily disappointed.

The effectiveness of ministry in schools depends in large measure on the ability of the Christian churches, and above all their leaders, to help create a new climate of opinion in this country, one which is prepared to see fulfilment in terms other than material comfort and which sees strongly held beliefs and convictions, mutually respected, as the basis of our pluralist society, not a take it or leave it indifference. Be that as it may, schools which seek to be places of ministry are the kinds of schools which the Church needs now. Teachers in those schools do not just do jobs, they fulfil a ministry and are engaged in a work of far greater significance than government descriptors of their role in schools can ever allow for. It is a ministry founded upon a vocation from God and one that is vital to the future welfare of the community of believers in this country.

Chapter 5

Worship in Catholic Schools

Peter Humfrey

The purpose of this chapter is to plead for a greater sense of unity in Catholic schools between religious education, spiritual forma-tion, worship and mission. It is the belief of the author that formation leads to worship and worship leads to mission. The inte-gration of these aspects of Catholic education permits more freely the flowering of faith and the pursuit of discipleship among young people in our schools.

The Context

The liturgy is the summit toward which the activity of the Church is directed; at the same time it is the fountain from which all her power flows.[1] Wherever the faith is studied and learned, it will only find its true meaning in its celebration and in the living out of the celebration in the mission of the Church. The liturgy, especially the Eucharist, defines and nourishes the Church.

The smallest constituent part of the Church is the family – the so-called domestic church.[2] Here the child is nourished in a living faith by the love of the parents and enters into the communion of the church by the sacraments of Baptism and Eucharist. The parish is the community of communities, of the families and groups in a

---

[1] *Sacrosanctum Concilium* 10 (in The Documents of Vatican II).
[2] Domestic Church – *Lumen Gentium* no 11 (in The Documents of Vatican II): 'The Christian home is the place where children receive the first proclamation of the faith. For this reason the family home is rightly called "the domestic church", a community of grace and prayer, a school of human virtues and of Christian charity.' Cf. CCC1666 (*Catechism of the Catholic Church*).

given area who gather regularly to listen to the word of the Lord and to share in the Eucharist in order to have strength for the mission to which they are called by Christ. The school shares in the mission of the Church by providing the experience of a Christian community in which young people can learn about God, share their faith, worship God and be strengthened in their particular calling. All of this is achieved in a wider environment subject to secular concerns and values.

Each of the partners – home, school and parish – need to try to show as much of the life of the Church which is appropriate to their situation. As we speak of a partnership, no one part has the monopoly of the faith and all are needed for a rounded experience of the Church.

Catholic schools provide a religious education for all students, so that they may be theologically literate in the faith.[3] Some students who have a deep faith will receive religious education as catechesis. It will be for them a rich dialogue with the teacher and other students in which all grow in knowledge and understanding. For other students religious education will be a new message heard for the first time about the love of God in Jesus Christ. This may whet their appetite for knowing more and for thinking about becoming disciples of Jesus. For other students religious education may not be an experience of faith or even lead to faith; but it may be that the seeds of the Gospel have been sown to be harvested in due time.[4]

Religious education prepares for and leads to worship. Deeper knowledge of God leads the disciple to the desire to praise and thank God for his goodness and to seek his help and guidance in daily life. Frequently, more can happen in the context of an act of worship than in any one religious education lesson. The student can experience the power of the spirit of Jesus who is present when two or three gather in his name.[5]

The mission of the Church is accomplished by those who have heard the word of God and take it into their hearts, desiring to yield a rich harvest.[6] Mission springs from knowledge of God and from worship of him through Jesus Christ. It cannot spring from one or the other only. For it is in prayer and worship that we hear the call of God and it is in action (mission) that we respond to this call. The school takes part in the mission of the Church by forming

---

[3] Bishops' Statement on Religious Education in Catholic Schools.
[4] Cf. *General Directory for Catechesis* (GDC) 15.
[5] Cf. Matthew 18.20.
[6] Cf. Mk 4.16 and John 12.24.

community, making disciples and sending them out into the world to announce the good news of Jesus Christ. The mission statement of the school will encompass both religious education and worship in order to achieve its mission.

The Principles

Worship takes place in a school when the community gathers to proclaim the worth of God and the worth of its members. Worship may take place anywhere at any time and be formal or informal. It may be part of a designated prayer time or school assembly or occur on special or important occasions. Liturgy is the public worship of the Church. It has a designated structure and follows recognized and authentic patterns. The elements of liturgy are gathering, listening to the word of God, responding to that word in prayer and symbol and action, and finally taking the meaning of the word out into the wider community.

The Second Vatican Council has been the springboard for the renewal of the liturgy. 'It is through the liturgy, especially the divine Eucharistic sacrifice, that "the work of our redemption is exercised".[7] The liturgy is thus the outstanding means by which the faithful can express in their lives, and manifest to others, the mystery of Christ and the real nature of the true church.'[8] Therefore, for all who are in the Catholic school, liturgy should hold a pre-eminent place. Before they come to liturgy the students (and the teachers) need to be called to faith and conversion. This may be an effect of the religious education programme.[9] After this, the Church calls believers to the sacraments and seeks to win them to all the works of charity, piety and the apostolate.[10] The liturgy inspires the faithful to become 'of one heart in love'[11] when they have tasted to their full of the Paschal Mysteries. From the liturgy we achieve the glorification of God and the sanctification of mankind.[12]

The lectionary is the Church's book of God's Word. It arranges the key texts of the Bible into a sequence which follows the cycle of the Church's year and enables a systematic and ordered under-

[7] Prayer over the offerings for the ninth Sunday after Pentecost.
[8] SC 2.
[9] Cf GDC 75.
[10] Cf SC 9.
[11] Postcommunion Prayer in the Easter Vigil Mass.
[12] Cf SC 10.

standing of the message to take place. As the lectionary is the Church's guide in the parish, so it should be the guide in the school. The Sunday readings need to be unfolded to the students and the weekday cycle of readings may be observed in the celebration of assemblies or other prayer opportunities.

The passing of time in the school should be marked by noting the seasons of the year, but more especially the seasons of the Church's year. In these days when supermarkets have all but eliminated the seasons from our tables, the school can keep the rhythm of nature alive in the hearts of the students. The key seasons of Advent–Christmastide and Lent–Eastertide should be marked in the school's cycle of worship. It is vital too to keep the link with the home and the parish in mind when celebrating, for example, Advent. It is important not to anticipate the celebration of Christmas itself in school, thereby depriving family and parish of their roles. A carefully prepared celebration of Advent in school will enhance the celebrations of home and parish. In Lent due observance can be given to the season and a careful preparation for Easter will ensure that the meaning is not lost during the Easter holy days. The culmination of the season in Pentecost will ensure that and appreciation of the work of the Holy Spirit in the school and in the world will not be lost.

The 'Directory for Masses with Children'[13] gives an outline of ways of celebrating effectively with children. Simplicity, clarity and participation are the key ideas. It is not necessary to celebrate a 'cathedral' liturgy in the school hall. Adaptation of the liturgy will enable young people to appreciate the message of the liturgy. Variety will not only help to avoid boredom but will enable a greater understanding of the various parts of the liturgy and enable greater engagement.

There has been a significant growth in Celebrations of the Word for children particularly in parishes where children have a special place during the Liturgy of the Word.[14] The principle of these celebrations is to recognize the presence of Christ in the word and to respond in prayer and action. These celebrations are not particularly a time for teaching or for catechesis. The elements for celebrations of the Word are the same as for other liturgical celebrations – the gathering, listening to the Word, response in prayer or action (drama, poetry, symbol, song, etc.). It could be that school assemblies should follow the pattern of the Church in celebrating

[13] 'Directory for Masses with Children' in *The Liturgy Documents*.
[14] Cf. the work of Sr Joan Brown in *Welcome the Word* and other publications.

the Liturgy of the Word. Truly then assemblies would also be acts of worship according to the law of the land.

Finally, underpinning all the suppositions outlined above, the question arises of the role of the school in the initiation of the young people into the life of the Church. The sacrament of baptism marks the first stage of initiation. Generally only parents and the parish community are prepared for this sacrament. The child is frequently too young to take an active part. The school may create the opportunity in religious education and in worship to explore the meaning and consequences of this sacrament – the dignity of the baptized, their relationship with God, their relationship with those believers round about and the mission of baptism to grow in faith and Christian living.

When children prepare to receive the Body and Blood of Christ for the first time, the role of the school in affirming the faith of the family and of the wider Church is important. There needs to be a sense in which the school can describe itself as a Eucharistic community. Later, generally, when students are considering their approach to adult life, the school can support and encourage them in the preparation for and the celebration of the sacrament of confirmation. This is an opportunity to recognize the gifts given by God for the good of the Church and the world and for the student to begin to experience in a fresh way the fruits of the Spirit given in the sacrament.

It might need to be emphasized that initiation is only the first stage of the Christian life and no student can be expected to turn out of the Catholic school totally equipped for every eventuality in the faith journey ahead.

The Practice

Worship in schools needs to recognize the cultural reality of the students, their faith disposition and the circumstances under which the school operates.

The cultural reality is that students face a market place which competes for their attention not only in terms of the provision of immediately satisfying goods and services but also in terms of offers of a happiness beyond this world, promised through the medium of the things of this world. The pressures on students to conform to the standards of the world are strong. The pressure caused by the break-up of families and the dispersal of the extended family may diminish the resources available to the student to grow in wisdom and confidence.

The *Rite of Christian Initiation of Adults* (RCIA)[15] invites us to reflect that for many people life might be called a spiritual journey. Faith is a gift and grows from a seed to full maturity. The experience of life and of the Church can nourish this growth. The life-journey is from the cradle to the grave. Its stages are duly marked in the secular world but further and more deeply in the world of faith though baptism, confirmation and Eucharist – the sacraments of initiation. Initiation is into the Paschal Mystery of Christ – his suffering, death and resurrection. These sacraments prepare the student for life in the adult world, for commitment in marriage or other Christian vocation and ultimately for sickness and for death. The school has many opportunities to note and mark the stages of the faith journey of students and their families.

The circumstances of the school are moulded by the schools' mission statement. Out of this flow the religious education, the worship and the mission of the school. The RCIA talks also of community[16] and how important is the building of communities for the Gospel to be preached and for young people to grow into faith. The various ministries are also activated.[17] The ministry of the parent is exercised long before the student comes to school and the ministries of the parish too may nourish the young mind and heart in early days.

The ministry of the teacher is of great importance. In a Catholic school, teachers are appointed by the Bishop and are co-workers with him in the preaching of the Gospel and the teaching of the Catholic faith.[18] They do this by their words and by their example, by participation in the Catholic life of the school, and, if not Catholic themselves, by supporting the mission statement of the school.

In religious education, the national Primary Programme, *Here I Am,*[19] provides a great deal of help and support for the teacher – most class teachers will also teach religion. In addition to a grounding in the foundational truths of the faith and a study of scripture and tradition, the teacher is also enabled to lead the children into worship. In the process of the seven Rs,[20] the Rejoice section draws

---

[15] *The Rite of Christian Initiation of Adults,* p. 5.

[16] See especially RCIA no 9: 'the community must be always fully prepared in the pursuit of its apostolic vocation to give help to those who are searching for Christ.'

[17] See also RCIA pp. 10–16.

[18] Cf. GDC 73.

[19] *Here I Am.*

[20] Recognize, Reflect, Respect, Relate, Rejoice, Remember, Renew.

together the themes and the work of the children in prayer and worship, both in the classroom and in the assembly hall. From this celebration, which should take place as part of every theme, flows the exploration of the mission of the child and of the school community when the class reflects on what it has learned and how it will apply its learning in daily life.

In a more systematic and developed way, the national Religious Education Programme for Secondary Schools, *Icons*,[21] written for 11–14 year olds, helps the student to have a deepening grasp of scripture and the liturgy, in addition to Church teaching and doctrine. All the sacraments are studied through the rites. Many of the students will be able to draw on their personal experience of the rites and deepen their appreciation of them though a guided study.

In addition to assembly as a liturgy, we should consider the role of the celebration of the Eucharist.[22] The Eucharist is the summit and the source of the Church's life. The Eucharistic celebration should take place at appropriate times during the course of the schools' year. Major feasts, events, and special occasions are key opportunities. The Eucharist should never be a routine event. The Eucharist should flow from the spiritual and academic life of the school and contribute to it. The Eucharist may help to celebrate achievement and be a source of help and peace in time of trial and difficulty. The careful preparation of the liturgy should be given the highest priority. Not only may a group of staff and pupils engage in the preparation but the involvement of other skills among staff and students, as well as the resources of departments other than the religious education department, may be engaged. The involvement of staff and pupils actively in the celebration is of critical importance; careful delegation of particular tasks may well lead to the enjoyment of greater imagination and creativity. The environment should assist in the celebration; it may be important to avoid the environment of the assembly or the exam hall or gymnasium in order to create a fresh sense of community. Students need to be able to see and hear effectively in order to participate well. Music and drama both express the spirit of our faith and engage the student in a deeper reflection on and awareness of God's purpose.

The liturgy of the word must not overwhelm the liturgy of the Eucharist. The readings must be carefully chosen and be in a

[21] *Icons.*
[22] Cf. 'Directory for Masses with Children' in *The Liturgy Documents.*

language that the students can readily understand. Time must be given after the Gospel for reflection on the readings and for a response to form in the hearts of the participants. This may be the occasion for a homily, or a reflection or a drama or some other poetic or creative response on the part of some of the participants. The response concludes with prayers (the Intercessions or Bidding Prayers) and these need to be carefully composed for the occasion, not seeming to be perfunctory or too generalized.

The music must be effective and relevant. Modern music with biblical words is a more attractive proposition than long hymns in nineteenth century verse. New texts have the possibility of revitalizing congregational singing. Hymns can hold up the action of the Eucharist or cover some part in which participation might be more important. We need to distinguish *singing at Mass* from *singing the Mass.*

The key musical elements in a school Eucharist would be the gathering song/music (preferably begun before the congregation begin to enter), the Gospel greeting (Alleluia), the Eucharistic Acclamations (Holy Holy; the Memorial Acclamation [Christ has died]; the Great Amen). Any further singing does not have such high priority and needs to be carefully integrated into the celebration. It would be good if one day the students could sing the key congregational pieces without books or music sheets, and the cantor or choir would provide verses for meditation. It is important to continue developing a repertoire of Church music, perhaps also in conjunction with local parishes. Remember that what the child sings in primary school will often be what the adult later requests for a wedding or a funeral!

Every school is helped to plan effectively for worship by the construction of a school liturgical calendar. This will mark the seasons and the feasts and add events of local significance. The calendar might include not only the celebrations of the Eucharist but also the assembly pattern and themes as well as other non-eucharistic celebrations that might take place e.g. Award Evenings, Induction Days or *Taster Days,* Leavers' Celebrations and so on. The calendar would be useful to local clergy who might be involved in the life of the school, both for information and for preparation.

Occasionally it may be appropriate to celebrate a baptism in the school. It is important that the school community is involved in the preparation and not simply spectators at the event. It might be the occasion for a renewal of the faith of those already baptized. Celebrations for those who have received the Body and Blood of Jesus for the first time in Holy Communion in their parishes and for those who have received the sacrament of Confirmation may also be appropriate. Needless to say, the presence of adults other than those belonging to the school community gives a sense of the wider nature of the Church community and can enhance the celebration for all participants.

The celebration of reconciliation has an important place in the life of the school. If the mission of Jesus is to reconcile us to one another and to the Father,[23] then this ministry of reconciliation is an integral part of school life. Reconciliation begins with conversion, so conversion to the way of Christ is a task for both staff and students. This inner conversion is lived out in the events of daily life in the school, in relationships among all the school community. Prophets and peacemakers must be identified and respected. Systems in the school must reflect the Gospel message – rewards and sanctions, inclusion or exclusion, partnership with parents and other outside bodies.

Reconciliation can be celebrated in prayer both in class and in assembly, particularly at the Church's penitential seasons and when occasion demands in the course of school life. Sacramental celebration of reconciliation has its place. Best is a well-prepared service of the Word of God and a prayerful response to his message. Then the opportunity to approach a priest for absolution or possibly a lay member of the chaplaincy team for counsel makes the communal prayer a personal reality in the life of the penitent. Provision in this area in school can greatly assist the spiritual growth of the students in ways that are not otherwise open. The sacrament is enabled to be a source of healing and of hope.

Evaluation of all the activity of the school in the light of the vision and mission statements is now commonplace.[24] It is important that the evaluation of the liturgy is taken equally seriously. Evaluation is not simply or necessarily the marking of mistakes and their correction.[25] It is a genuine attempt to consider the value of the experience to the participants. In the light of observations offered, improvements can be made to the quality of the celebrations. It is then possible to gain a sense of direction and purpose to worship. The Section 23 inspections, carried out by diocesan-appointed Inspectors on behalf of the local bishop, will note not only the achievements of religious education but also the success of worship and the possibility of identifying what is commonly

[23] See the Penitential Rite c iv in the Order Of Mass.
[24] *Evaluating the Distinctive Nature of the Catholic School.*
[25] A liturgy 'planned' can 'go wrong'; a liturgy 'prepared' can 'grow and develop'.

called the Catholic ethos. There are excellent instruments to help
the school's self-evaluation in the publications of the Catholic
Education Service.[26]

Case Study One

In a catholic secondary school in the south of England there was a
great debate about the value of the general RE course offered to
the sixth form. The course was sporadic and disjointed. There was
not a lot of enthusiasm on the part of staff or students. The chaplain and two of the teachers decided on a radical course of action.
The idea was to introduce the experience of the Rite of Christian
Initiation, in an adapted form, to the sixth form.[27] The students
were asked to identify where they felt they were on their spiritual
journey – interested in questions about life and faith (period of
evangelisation), or in questions about God, Jesus and the Gospel
(period of catechesis), or in questions about the Church and its
message and work today (mystagogia). The students divided into
roughly three equal groups.

The staff met to discuss their approach; some were concerned
about the open nature of the questions to be discussed under the
three headings, but in the end were prepared to have a go. They
were initially reluctant to work with no agenda other than the questions raised and with no pre-determined outcome. There were to
the surprise of the staff, and of the students themselves, those who
were convinced and regular Catholics who put themselves in the
questions of life and faith groups, while the non-believers and
unchurched put themselves in the groups to study the Church.
The choices generated dialogue amongst staff and students even
before the course began. The first part ran for a term at one hour
per week. After a review it was decided by staff and students to
continue for another term. Students were given the option of
changing groups and some took the opportunity.

At the end the evaluation showed that staff had a high degree of
satisfaction at the participation of the students and were not afraid
to find themselves challenged by the questions and learn from the
group. The students found the novelty helpful; the topics were of
their own choosing; their opinions were heard; often a consensus

[26] The Catholic Education Service, 39, Eccleston Square, London SW1V 1BX.
[27] For a sympathetic treatment of the introduction of new ways of looking at initiation see *On The Threshold*, a report of a Working Party of the Bishops'
Conference of England and Wales.

was reached. The work in groups was completed by a liturgical celebration at Christmas and before Easter a celebration of the Eucharist requested particularly by the students in which all took part. Certainly the interest and enthusiasm was clear and the students and staff were exposed to a practical experience of a genuine process of initiation as promoted by the liturgical documents of the church.[28] The integration of learning, community building, worship and mission presented a satisfying "package" for all concerned.

Case Study Two

This study reflects the desire in a Primary School to link the religious education programme with worship and mission. The staff, taking part in a trial of the material for the revised *Here I Am* RE programme, were encouraged to see how worship could rise out of the religious education work. Two classes of children aged eight and nine years old joined together for the theme 'Celebrations'.[29] Rather than invent a liturgy for its own sake, the teachers invited the children to choose from the work they had done and bring that together to share. This included a reflection on how the New Year was celebrated in different countries and by people of different world faiths. The celebration coincided with the millennium so that the children had plenty of stories about how they celebrated the millennium with their families and friends. The Gospel passages chosen indicated both the springboard of Christian celebration in the birth of Christ two thousand years ago and the renewal of the Paschal Mystery in our own age. The children concluded by reviewing and praying about what they could do to build community in the school and be more aware of the needs of others outside school. The enthusiasm of the children gave encouragement to the teachers. At the end of the celebration, a teacher turned on a cassette player and all began to dance – children and teachers, even the priest – truly a celebration.

Bibliography
Bishops' Conference of England and Wales, *Evaluating the Distinctive Nature of the Catholic School* (London, Catholic Education Service, revised edition 1999).

---

[28] Cf. RCIA 4.
[29] See the theme for the spring term in *Here I Am*.

Bishops' Conference of England and Wales, *On The Threshold: The Report of the Bishops' Conference Working Party on Sacramental Initiation* (Chelmsford, Matthew James, 2000).

Brown, J., *Welcome the Word* (London, McCrimmon, 1995).

Byrne, A., *Here I Am* (London, Collins revised edition, 2000).

Flannery, A. OP (ed.), *Vatican Council II: The Conciliar and Post-conciliar Documents* (Dublin, Dominican Publications, 1975).

Martin, M.J. et al., *Icons* (London, Collins, 2000).

The Liturgy Documents: a parish resource 3rd edition (Chicago, Liturgy Training Publications, Distributed in UK by McCrimmons, 1991).

Vatican, *Catechism of the Catholic Church* (London, Geoffrey Chapman, 1994).

Vatican, *General Directory for Catechesis* (London, Catholic Truth Society, 1997).

Vatican, *Religious Education in Catholic Schools* (London, Catholic Media Office, 2000).

Vatican, *The Rite of Christian Initiation of Adults* (London, Geoffrey Chapman, 1987).

Chapter 6

Leadership and Management

John Sullivan

In this chapter I distinguish leaders from managers and owners and then relate educational leadership to the notions of steward-ship and vocation. Teaching is treated here as a personal activity in the public arena. The implications of such a view are explored in an examination of school leadership at three different levels. The first of these is the classroom, immediate or micro level. Then the middle management, intermediate or meso level is considered. Finally, management at the whole school or macro level receives attention. At each level it is argued that a pervading feature of educational leadership should be its capacity to promote the kind of learning that transforms our lives.

Introduction

A manager of any enterprise has to have a sense of its main purpose and an appreciation of the principles that should guide its operation and that could serve as criteria in evaluating its outcomes as successful or worthwhile. To be effective the manager must be sensitive to the context of the enterprise and aware of the factors that both help and hinder its progress. Insight into current realities internal to the organisation must be matched by an assess-ment of the external environment together with the capacity to envisage the medium and long-term potential of the work-force and resources available. Purposes, people and procedures must be brought into harmony so that energies are co-ordinated and directed in a constructive manner.

A manager can be distinguished both from a leader and from an owner. A manager tends to work within a system that already exists and seeks to ensure that it functions efficiently and effectively. Managers concern themselves with the practical, the present and the internal: their business is order, predictability, policies and procedures, co-ordination and channels of communication. Leaders, in contrast, concern themselves with the symbolic, the imagined (and ideal) and the future: they focus on inspiring a vision, developing a culture, addressing change and facing both the future and the outside world. The two terms, leader and manager, often overlap; they are used interchangeably by many people and each requires supplementation by the other to be fully effective. Management without leadership is sterile and lifeless and can become mechanistic and bureaucratic. It becomes disconnected from what the institution is *for*. Leadership without management loses touch with reality and dashes the very hopes it arouses. It ultimately frustrates because it is careless about *how* to move towards its espoused goals.

In the school context a manager is rarely the owner. A school does not belong to its leaders or managers. As a teacher I do not own the classroom, the pupils, the resources or the learning, even if, with a due sense of pride and achievement, I sometimes speak of *my* classes or results as if I am pleased to benefit from the reputation of my school. These things are neither possessed by me, as an individual, nor even by any collective body of which I am a member. They are, however, entrusted temporarily to my care and, collectively, to our care. We are stewards of public resources that are put into our hands for particular purposes, on behalf of the wider community. We can rightly be held to account for what we do in school with time, people, buildings, resources and knowledge. These are given to us in order to be given away by us; we are expected to maximise their effectiveness in the service of education.

As stewards we are accountable, in different ways and at different levels, for those things (and people) entrusted to us. Our accountability is to a whole host of 'stakeholders', a term that embraces all those with a legitimate interest in the outcomes of our work. These 'stakeholders' include pupils and their parents, our fellow teachers and other members of staff, whose work we draw upon and contribute to; among them we should also include the head teacher (and senior staff) who are responsible for co-ordinating and directing our efforts. The role of stakeholder is also shared by other groups, for example, the governors who appoint us and who have oversight of the school, the local community and the area education authority, together with the diocese, which forms an extended family in the church. To these must be added the teaching profession as a whole, and, not least in importance for the healthy development of education, ourselves.

As a personal activity in the public arena, teaching depends for its effectiveness on a high degree of commitment and self-involvement from staff. Teachers have to project a considerable 'amount' of their own personality into the job. Their 'presence' in the classroom and around the school cannot afford to be minimal. If it is to be significant, it must be one that is vigorous rather than virtual and substantial rather than superficial. Their exemplary role with children, young people and their colleagues relies upon their deepest values, their integrity, their self-knowledge, their sense of purpose in education, their feelings of worth and confidence. In Christian terms, it requires a vocation: the sense that this is *where* God wants me to be; this is *what* God wants me to do; this is *how* God invites me to share my talents; and, most important of all, this is *who* God calls me to be.

In turn, this sense of personal calling connects up with the public dimension: we are called to account because we work, not only with, but also for others, and not just for ourselves, to earn our bread, or to pay the mortgage. Our work is merely a small part of a bigger picture than the story of my own life. It serves a greater cause than meeting our own needs or developing our own talents. It is played out on a larger stage than just our own life and its particular concerns and goals. Our efforts should be directed outwards, towards particular groups of pupils and, more widely, towards the local, regional, national and universal communities to which we belong. Educational leadership and management ultimately must ensure that both the personal and the public dimensions of teaching and learning are addressed, nurtured, developed, supported and challenged to grow. In this sense we can claim that educational leadership and management are forms of pastoral ministry, ways of looking after God's people and valid arenas for contributing to the kingdom where the more abundant life opened up by the Gospel can be experienced.

1. The micro-level of school management

When teachers first start work in a school their immediate concern is usually to establish themselves, both with their classes and with their new colleagues. A newly appointed teacher hopes to earn credibility, as quickly as possible, with adults and children. This requires a degree of acceptance from and a sense of belonging with the rest of the staff, as well as the security of a feeling of control over classroom activity and the capacity to elicit a positive response from pupils.

Initially, a teacher's confidence can be boosted by the warmth, helpfulness and encouragement of colleagues; but it depends, above all, on a sense from within of a basic competence in the job. Self-confidence is confirmed when a teacher enjoys a healthy rela-tionship with pupils, when disciplinary problems do not loom over-large (though they are unlikely to be completely absent), when evidence begins to emerge that learning that is at least partly attributable to one's efforts has taken place, and when colleagues talk to him/her as an equal, as one who shares the burdens and delights of a typical teacher's day.

In these early stages, it would be understandable if a teacher failed to notice much of the meso and macro (see sections 2 and 3, below) role of school leaders and the management dimension of a teacher's work. Since most of their time is spent with children or young people, usually as the only adult in the midst of (approxi-mately) thirty centres of (sometimes conflicting) energy and extremely diverse personalities, a major priority for teachers is being equipped to survive their daily contact with classes, prefer-ably with the added bonus of feeling that they are getting somewhere, that they are making progress in the art of teaching. They rapidly find that, no matter how good their own education has been, and no matter how well prepared they have tried to be, it is always possible to feel caught out, to be surprised, even exposed by the unexpected question and unpredictable types of behaviour and response. Without even realising it, new teachers have to learn very quickly how to manage several things at once: their own learning, the learning of others, the use of time, accom-modation, resources, group dynamics, and, not least, the emotional climate of the classroom. It is little wonder that what happens elsewhere in the school, either in the staff-room, in the corridors, playground, or in the offices of senior colleagues (if they have such luxuries), might not impinge much on their conscious-ness. They are pre-occupied with being ready to teach: with knowing the subject-matter they have to teach today and tomor-row, with keeping order, with having to hand all the necessary equipment and materials, with keeping up with all the marking of pupils' work. This is the micro dimension of teaching.

At this micro level, the focus is specific, concrete, individualist, practical, with limited time-frames. The teacher is concerned above all with issues of direct relevance to the classroom, and, even more narrowly, with what is perceived to affect his or her own classroom, rather than what happens elsewhere. Attention is directed to what he or she has to do, rather than the duties of others. It is about what can be done in this classroom, with these pupils, with these tables, chairs and equipment, regarding this particular item in the curriculum, using these books and materials and these lesson-times, today or this week. Next week or next month is another country, to which we might never travel. It is sufficient to be concerned for the day; indeed, that is all that is possible. An important piece of advice at this stage is for a teacher to remember to allow the non-teacher part of himself or herself to appear occasionally and to acknowledge the non-pupil part of pupils: both teacher and pupil (rightfully) have a life to lead outside of school.

Even at this early stage of teaching, when our concern is with the micro level of management, it is important to realize a double-sided truth: first, the life led outside school deeply affects what happens inside it, both for teachers and for pupils; second, what happens in the limited world of school should contribute to, even transform, the larger life we engage with outside of it. It is unwise, insensitive and self-defeating for teachers to operate in the classroom without careful consideration of how the context and life-situations of their pupils and also their own circumstances influence what is brought into the classroom – in terms of attitudes, values, pre-occupations, skills, experience, expectations, hopes and fears. Without a connection to the bigger picture, a larger story, a deeper purpose, a wider set of values, the routines and rubrics of school soon become, both for teachers and for pupils, restricting, irrelevant, time-wasting and alienating.

Yet, as disciples of Jesus Christ, in the context of teaching, our vocation is to embody, proclaim and facilitate the more abundant life. The most holy or sacred activity that takes place in school is, simply, teaching. If our teaching contributes to bringing people into close contact with truth, if it releases energy, if it inspires growth, if it prompts reflection, if it elicits compassion, if it gives people the capacity and desire for endless learning, then it is contributing to God's Kingdom as well as to pupils' curriculum vitae. All work in school, even at the micro-level, if it is to be life-giving, needs to be informed by a clear vision, a coherent set of principles and a sense of direction. This lifts efficient and effective management – of time, people, resources and learning – into the realm of leadership.

This is not to decry the technical aspects of management in teaching. Having the right things in place allows everyone to do their job properly. Ensuring that there is an orderly environment gives to everyone the security in which it is possible to be creative. The establishment of ground-rules and policies helps our individual efforts to be mutually reinforcing rather than counter-productive; in this way our messages may come across more clearly rather than jostle for attention in the midst of confusion and chaos. Poor management, at every level, prevents learning; it wastes time, constrains creativity, induces dissatisfaction, lowers morale – and, in so doing, it fails to be life-giving. This is as true at the micro level of the classroom as it is at other levels of school management and leadership. All teachers are managers of the work-force (pupils) in their classrooms. As managers, their goal should be the transformation of life through learning.

Seen in this light, two implications are apparent with regard to teaching and management. First, unless teachers can model the way, their chances of being transformative are extremely limited. That is, without the example, through their words and their behaviour, of how their own lives have been deeply affected by what they are teaching, teachers cannot hope to influence their pupils in any significant way. Somehow the words of a car dealer who tries to sell us a Rover as a highly desirable product resonate less effectively in our minds once we know that he or she always buys a Ford for personal use. We scarcely feel inclined or encouraged to invest much of ourselves in something if the person marketing the product remains carefully removed from any personal commitment to it. Teachers need to exemplify that they have been, and indeed still are, 'switched on' by what they teach; it makes a difference for them, life is better for engaging with it, or it is a necessary stepping stone towards something of value.

Such enthusiasm for and commitment to our work must be tempered by a prudential and protective distancing. There is an appropriate distance to be maintained in the classroom (and in whole-school management), if our leadership is not to be crushing, and if it is to facilitate the development of an hospitable space for learning and growth. We need such distancing for several reasons. We must maintain a sense of direction and a strategic oversight of what is going on, rather than getting bogged down or side-tracked in minutiae. We also need a degree of distance to ensure that we are not vulnerable to accusations of either favouritism or its shadow, treating people in our classrooms (or departments or on the staff) as if their 'face does not fit' in our plans. Some distancing is simply an acknowledgement that teachers and pupils inhabit different worlds and that all teaching is, to some extent at least, a bridging between different outlooks. Teachers have different perceptions, habits and priorities from the pupils they invite (and cajole) into their world. Again, to appear too desperate to receive a positive response can be counter-productive in the dramatic and political arena of the classroom. Despite such a need for distance, this must not be so great as to render our approach impersonal, our message inaudible or the difference the aspect of learning has made in our lives unrecognisable. The 'bite' or purchase on our lives of what is being studied must be conveyed, regardless of which aspect of the curriculum we are involved in.

The second implication of envisaging school teaching, management and leadership as aiming for the transformation of lives through learning is that such transformation requires the willing and active co-operation of learners. They cannot be radically changed if they remain passive recipients of the work of the teacher. Effective leadership on the part of the teacher will result, not in the production of passive clones or of obedient, loyal and faithful followers, but in the maximisation of leaders and in the enhancement of leadership qualities among pupils. They must become centres of initiative in their own right. Their trust in and receptivity toward us as teachers jointly serve as a temporary bridge, allowing a passageway on the journey of transformation. To employ a different metaphor, we need to move beyond preparing pupils to be map-readers of the world, as seen by us; our aim should be to empower them to become map-makers of the constantly changing world they find around them. This will be a world that we cannot predict; it will also be one that they will help to construct, both practically and cognitively.

2. The meso-level of school management

At the micro-level of the classroom, the effective teacher creates the conditions in which pupils can feel secure, lower their defences, be willing to experiment, give of their best and interact fruitfully. So too, at the meso or intermediate level, subject leaders or middle managers should aim to create the right conditions for the release of energy of their colleagues, for the harnessing of individual talents for the good of the team and for cohesive and collaborative joint effort. At this stage of management, teachers are concerned with directing and co-ordinating learning beyond their

own classrooms, with supporting and guiding colleagues in their
area of responsibility, with presenting their 'wares' to a wider
public. They are expected to contribute to the development,
implementation and review of school policies. Not only do they
face their own team of staff; they must collaborate with, and sometimes compete with their peers (for example, for resources) over
aspects of whole-school policy.

Thus they play a 'political' role, as figurehead, ambassador,
representative and advocate in a more public arena than their
own team. They must enter into dialogue with colleagues with
different perceptions, expectations and priorities. They also have
to respond effectively to the pressures and opportunities
presented by the head teacher and senior management. In their
management of learning, people, resources and policy, not to
forget their management of self, they are expected to find ways
to support and implement the school's mission, a statement that
encapsulates the school's interpretation of its *raison d'être*, its
primary and enduring purposes. They find themselves mediating
between, on the one hand, the 'front-line' perspective of the classroom teacher whose main priority is coping with pupils and
survival on a day-to-day basis, and, on the other hand, the whole-
school context and longer-term perspective constantly brought
home to them by senior staff.

In courses for teachers with middle management responsibilities, the following aspects frequently receive attention:

- developing with colleagues a vision and shared aims and
  priorities for one's area of responsibility
- effective, but non-officious, forms of communication
- positive team-work
- clear planning
- reviewing the quality of work
- managing performance
- staff development
- work beyond the team or section and
- the management of resources.

All of these make important contributions to the work of staff in a
school, and therefore indirectly influence the progress of pupils.
However, each of them can also easily be carried out in a way that
slips into a mechanical mode that discourages an outward-looking
and life-giving emphasis. In this context I focus on an often somewhat neglected aspect of the role of middle manager in a school,

one that seeks (gently) to remind colleagues of the bigger picture and larger purposes that we are serving.

We have a duty to keep our area of responsibility 'alive'. This area may be either a curriculum subject, or oversight of a group of pupils from a particular age-group, or leadership of some other grouping of staff, or the direction and co-ordination of an improvement project or a priority from the school's development plan. Keeping an area 'alive' implies injecting into it a sense of direction, of purpose, of energy and enthusiasm. This requires attention to context, awareness of assisting and constraining factors, insight into the different 'readings' of the situation offered by relevant staff, sensitivity to their interaction and support for their needs as individuals. We have to balance the differing requirements of task, team and individuals, inevitably sometimes having to compromise if we are to avoid failing in the task, or disrupting the team or crushing an individual.

Keeping an area alive will entail underlining its importance, emphasising – and where necessary clarifying – the role each person has to play, valuing the contribution of each and connecting with other relevant stakeholders and audiences. We might use carefully selected articles from subject or other professional periodical journals to inform, shape and stimulate team discussion. We could build up a team library, asking for and offering suggestions for items to be included, as well as seeking feedback or comment on the usefulness (and limitations) of what has been ordered. We might use a notice-board as a focal point for displaying relevant current affairs and media items, as well as points of interest for team members. Do we encourage pupils to bring in news items relevant to the courses and topics covered by our team? Do we encourage pupils to write about topics they are learning in our area of responsibility in school or community publications? Do members of our team attend conferences, inservice sessions and report back and share what they have learned? Do we ever invite outsiders (for example, from higher education, from a school in another phase of education, from the local community, from the business world) into a team meeting to offer us a different perspective on what we are doing or to inform us of relevant developments elsewhere? Do members of our team provide inservice sessions for our own school staff or for others?

In promoting our area, we seek to ensure that work done in it is recognized and appreciated and that colleagues feel an appropriate status is attributed to what they do (within the range of school priorities). This is part of protecting their morale. We hope to ensure that pupils adopt a positive attitude towards our area. In this way we can attract more pupils to the school or to our particular area, improve the chances of recruiting high calibre staff and satisfy key groups, like inspectors, senior management and governors.

3. The macro-level of school management

At the level of whole-school leadership and management, a head teacher and senior staff have to establish a balance between the expectations of different constituencies, for example, the pupils, the parents, the teachers and other staff, the governing body, the parish and local community, government policy and the requirements of inspection. They often find themselves operating simultaneously out of several competing metaphors: school as family, as business, as church, as political community and as academy. At the macro-level, leaders and managers have to work with longer time-frames than the immediacy of classroom exchanges or the medium-term perspectives of teams and policies. They have to scan the external environment, bring in new ideas and ensure a balance between realism and idealism. They have to 'sell' the school to outsiders, protect its reputation and fight for its rightful share of resources.

By their very nature, such priorities will seem to some of their colleagues rather distant from the 'real' business of the classroom and of dealing with children and young people. But if senior staff spend all their time 'in the trenches' or 'at the chalk face' then the school will be ill-prepared for what tomorrow will bring; it will find itself constantly the victim of other people's decisions and at the back of the queue for resources. Head teachers and senior staff cannot stay as close to the classroom as they once did, if they are to strive to create the best conditions for transformative learning for pupils and staff. At the macro-level it must be acknowledged that senior managers got to where they are now by doing things they don't have to do now and didn't have to do then. There are several implications of this.

First, they must be psychologically prepared to let go of certain areas of responsibility, even if they feel better equipped than others to tackle these tasks. Without such 'letting go' head teachers will not have the space or time to do what only they can do; nor will others have a chance to learn what they have learned along the way. Second, then, they must delegate, for the sake of their own effectiveness and for the sake of others' learning and growth. Without such delegation a school is over-controlled, fearful and ineffective. Third, head teachers must demonstrate that they are willing to learn the new tasks and skills that are essential to their macro role. Again, they must 'model the way', just as classroom teachers must exemplify what they teach. Once the head teacher has given the impression that she or he has stopped learning or has lost the will and capacity to develop further, the time has come to step down from educational leadership.

However, in leaving behind some of the tasks carried out earlier in their careers, senior staff should never give the impression that they are 'above' that kind of activity, or imply that it is no longer important (or demanding). Some kinds of 'forgetting' by senior managers are inherently threatening to staff morale. A familiarity with and sensitivity to the burdens as well as the joys of the classroom must always be part of the repertoire or armoury of staff working at the macro level, if they wish to carry colleagues with them.

All schools have experienced over the last fifteen years tensions between managerialism and professionalism. The management imperative has emphasized features such as planning and predictability, co-ordination and control, measurement and accountability. The kinds of professionalism apparently subject to attack by such managerialism include an emphasis on freedom and initiative, a reliance on individuality and diversity, and an unthreatened space for trust and flair. As has already been intimated at the start of this chapter, the manager focuses on how things are to be done and assumes that the ends or purposes are agreed and understood. In response to inexorable external scrutiny, both governors and senior staff have increasingly developed a more interventionist role in school life, a fresh opportunity for this being the system of performance management being introduced in the UK in the year 2000.

When interventionist and strong management styles are applied to the notion of an authoritative mission, as in the case of Catholic schools, there is the danger of an organizational culture that is burdensome, constricting and life-diminishing being built up. The 'tools' of management then can slip into ever more subtle forms of control, rather than releasing energy. They can create the impression that school leaders are seeking increased surveillance for increased compliance.

To counter such tendencies it becomes imperative that leaders develop appropriate forms of philosophy and spirituality. These should be of such a kind that they provide foundation, support, guidance, discipline and inspiration for education, work and leadership in the school context. Leaders at the macro level must take great pains to steer a path carefully in their dealing with staff, avoiding the two extremes of indifference and interference. In the need for a new form of spirituality for church school leadership, it will be important to counter-balance the current emphasis on training, targets, efficiency and competence with an equal emphasis on formation, prayer, vulnerability and confidence.

The way we carry out our leadership and management role will depend on many factors. First, there will be the particular tasks to be tackled. What actually has to be achieved? Then there are the people we have to work with. What is their understanding of these tasks and what is their commitment to the overall school mission which provides a framework for all our activity? Third, account has to be taken of the resources that are available to us (and to them). Another consideration is the source, type, authority and urgency of external demands on the school. Fifth, there is the matter of the amount of time that is allowed to us to tackle a priority. Although all these have a bearing on how we manage people and a task, there should still be scope for our educational and management principles to come into operation.

Among these I pick out a few to serve as examples. First, we should seek to promote reciprocity and mutuality in all our dealings, in order to prevent authority becoming dominant. It is helpful to inject into as many professional dialogues as possible the following questions: What am I doing that you find helpful and want me to continue? What am I doing that you don't find helpful and hope that I will stop or modify? What am I not doing that you would find helpful and want me to consider?

Second, if we wish to promote learning at all levels, then people should feel able to take risks and make mistakes without being penalized for honest effort. Sharing vulnerability is a major high road to professional growth. Is our school one where we can admit to one another that we find some things difficult and need help? It is only when we can admit to problems that we can begin to tackle them constructively. Pressure to hide from painful realities prevents growth and learning.

Third, it is crucial to avoid slipping into an 'us and them' syndrome, thereby labelling people as on our side or against us. We are all simultaneously part of each other's problems and solutions. Nobody has a monopoly of insight; no-one is the sole cause of difficulty. There are imperfections and deficits in the work of all of us; yet each of us is capable of improvement and of finding a way forward. Our mutual 'readings' of each other and our 'ratings' and expectations of one another can become self-fulfilling prophecies. Therefore we should be cautious about negative judgements and be willing to err on the side of generosity in imputing motives to others.

Fourth, we all learn through a combination of challenge and support. Too much of one and we retreat; too much of the other and we might become complacent. There is no formula for this, since the particular combination of challenge and support we each need for a particular task varies considerably.

Fifth, we must beware of becoming too performance-oriented. It is important to emphasize at least as much the need for a growing self-knowledge. Such self-knowledge, if backed up by evidence and feedback from others on the effects of our work, reduces the power of subjective perceptions and it helps us to match more closely our role to the needs of others.

Sixth, it is as important in school management as it is in the classroom to ensure that our voice connects with our touch, that is, we model what we advocate that others should do. There should be congruence of tone, style and message between our advice and our actions.

Finally, our main aim as managers should be new levels of life within staff as much as higher levels of performance. In this way there is more chance that the learning promoted within the school will be transformative.

At the macro-level, it is incumbent on leaders in Catholic schools to bring to bear on their work a spiritual interpretation, a dimension that is informed by faith. Not only are they professional, organisational, budget and curriculum managers; they should intentionally exercise a spiritual leadership role, one that includes seeking to promote spiritual development among the adults as well as among the pupils. There are many aspects to this spiritual leadership role.

School leaders must be ready to use every opportunity to articulate the 'story' of Catholic education, its purpose and mission, its central features and constituent elements, its living tradition and culture, its leading principles and how these guide decisions, policies, priorities and practices. Sometimes this articulation will be oral, at other times written; sometimes it will be prepared, in the public domain and for a special occasion; most often it will be 'off-the-cuff', informal and addressed to some immediate and unforeseen issue. In talks to parents, pupils, staff and peers, as well as in their letters, prospectus and school policies Catholic school leaders should find ways to communicate their mission effectively.

Headteachers should use the various stages of staff recruitment, selection and induction as occasions when they can 'set out their stall', that is clarify their expectations of colleagues as regards the Christian mission of the school and how everyone might contribute to its implementation and further development. This deliberate bringing to the forefront of people's thinking the relevance of the mission for daily work should be extended to the questions posed in and the criteria that operate in appraisal, performance management, professional development opportunities and internal promotion.

As spiritual leaders, senior staff in Catholic schools should ensure that Religious Education is given a high priority and that teachers are empowered and equipped to promote the spiritual and moral development of pupils throughout the whole curriculum. Particular care must be taken in planning, resourcing and leading worship and assemblies. These assemblies potentially have an important role. They can

- reveal the purchase that the Gospel has in the lives of school leaders
- engage with the rich diversity of Catholic spirituality
- explore the relationship between the living tradition of the Church and the needs and questions of the contemporary world
- acknowledge the centrality of God in our lives
- articulate key values
- build community
- reach out to the world beyond school
- provide space for prayer and
- stimulate reflection

Another task, at this macro-level of Catholic leadership, is to ensure that, as far as possible, there is a harmonious working relationship between the school and the home and a real partnership between the school and its associated parishes. This will entail keeping open the channels of communication, being sensitive to differing perceptions and needs, making connections, and finding ways to facilitate complementarity rather than competition among the respective roles of school, home and parish.

Two further aspects of the spiritual leadership role can be identified, to bring this brief survey to an end. First, the spiritual development and ongoing formation of the staff must remain among the priorities of the head teacher and senior colleagues in any faith-based school. This does not entail intruding into the private lives of teachers – although that private life may often either enhance or undermine the cogency of their witness in school. Nor does it imply a paternalistic, 'preachy' or didactic approach on the part of Catholic school leaders. It does, however, require that the daily decisions of the school are placed within a prayerful framework. There will be a conscious attempt to feed the faith of staff. Colleagues will be challenged to live out the mission of the school in the context of their various professional responsibilities. Resources of a religious as well as professional nature will be made available to staff, supporting their teaching in its academic and spiritual dimensions, underpinning their pastoral work and inspiring their leadership of worship.

Second, none of this is possible, nor can it be sustained, if the spiritual life of school leaders is neglected. They cannot afford to allow themselves to 'run on empty'. Personal renewal is not a luxury; it is a necessity for Catholic school leaders. Among all the many other duties clamouring for their attention, for example, keeping up with relevant legislation, local authority policies and diocesan guidelines, or responding to inspection reports and governors' committees, or dealing with parental requests, and notwithstanding the pressures coming from pupils and staff, Catholic school leaders must, for the sake of the school as well as that of their own health and happiness, deliberately and regularly attend to their own spiritual development. This has to be 'live' rather than simply accumulated 'capital' from the past. It has to be constantly renewed in order to equip them to witness to the more abundant life in ways that are faithful, creative, inclusive, challenging, supportive and inviting others to share the journey.

Conclusion

Although I have offered three categories for investigating management in a Catholic school, the micro, meso and macro, such divisions have only been for the sake of better understanding; there is no rigid separation between the three. It has become clear that the qualities and skills that are needed at the micro level remain necessary at other levels. The matching of approaches to purposes and to people is a constant at all levels; what changes is the context in which this is played out. At all stages I have striven to underline the importance of ensuring that our management responsibilities and our leadership roles are directed towards learning, the kinds of learning that transform life.

Suggestions for further reading

Conroy, J. (ed.), *Catholic Education Inside Out/Outside In* (Dublin, Veritas/Lindisfarne, 1999).

Dwyer, B., *Catholic Schools: Creating a New Culture* (Brunswick, Victoria, E.J. Dwyer, 1993).

Eaton, M. (ed.), *Commitment to Diversity* (London, Cassell, 2000).

Feheney, M. (ed.), *From Ideal to Action* (Dublin, Veritas, 1998).

Grace, G., *School Leadership* (London, Falmer, 2000).

Groome, T., *Educating for Life* (Allen, Texas, Thomas More Press, 1998).

Hunt, T. (ed.), *Catholic School Leadership* (London, Falmer, 2000).

Keane, R. and Riley, D. (eds), *Quality Catholic Schools* (Archdiocese of Brisbane, 1997).

Lombaerts, H. (tr. T. Collins), *The Management and Leadership of Christian Schools* (Groot Bijgaaden, Belgium, Vlaams Lasalliaans Perspectief, 1998).

McLaughlin, D. (ed.), *The Catholic School: Paradoxes and Challenges*, (Strathfield, New South Wales, St Pauls Publications, 2000).

Sullivan, J., *Catholic Schools in Contention* (Dublin, Veritas/Lindisfarne, 2000).

Sullivan, J., *Catholic Education: Distinctive and Inclusive* (Dordrecht, Kluwer Academic Publishing, 2001).

Tuohy, D., *The Inner World of Teaching* (London, Falmer, 1999).

Treston, K., *Creative Christian Leadership* (Mystic, Ct, Twenty-Third Publications, 1995).

Treston, K., *Choosing Life: Pastoral Care for School Communities* (Brisbane, Creation Enterprises, 1997).

Wadman, D. (ed.), *What is different about being a middle manager in a Catholic School?* (London, Catholic Education Service, 1999).

Chapter 7

Governance

Christopher Storr

Introduction

The purpose of this chapter is to describe the main tasks of governing bodies of Catholic schools in England and Wales and to discuss some of the problems they are facing at the beginning of the twenty-first century.

Concentration on a list of problems carries with it the very real risk of presenting a distorted view of the situation. Although governors have problems to address (they always have done) the reader needs to bear in mind that, in general terms, the story of Catholic education in England and Wales in recent years has been one of outstanding success: most schools are popular with both Catholic and non Catholic parents and perform very well in all areas of activity.

An Historical Overview: 1944–1998

English schools seem always to have had a body of lay people overseeing their operation, but only in recent years have they had much to do. Indeed, until recently, only secondary schools had people called governors; primary schools, for the first thirty five years of their existence, were not allowed to have governors at all. They had managers, with very restricted terms of reference. The 1944 Education Act provided that the local education authority (LEA) had control over the 'secular' curriculum of the school and also had the right to veto the appointment of the head teacher, though this was subsequently challenged and eventually became a dead letter. Secondary school governors had wider powers – they did, for example, 'have the general direction of the conduct and curriculum of the school' – but in practice the running of the school was a partnership between the head teacher and the LEA.

Just how little influence early managing and governing bodies had is easily demonstrated. In 1982, a mother complained about the refusal of an inner London primary school to admit her daughter. When enquiry was made, it was revealed that the managing/governing body had not met for seven years. The head teacher and parish priest had got along very nicely without it and no one had noticed either in the Inner London Education Authority or at the diocese. In a nearby county, the Borough Education Committee appointed itself the governing body for all its county secondary schools. Once a term it met to carry out its schools' duties, and, after a short break, reconvened as the Borough Education Committee to receive the resolutions and recommendations it had just passed to itself.

As there was little work to do, there was no particular need for bodies to be either large or representative. A Catholic primary school managing body typically consisted of just six people: four appointed by the 'foundation' (the foundation is the body that originally established the school – usually the diocese, but it might be a religious order) and two by the local authorities. A secondary governing body had ten or twelve members. Head teachers could not be managers or governors of their schools and there was no provision for elected teachers or parents, nor was there any restriction on the number of managing or governing bodies to which a person could be appointed. There were instances where the priest who ran the Diocesan Schools' Commission was chairman of half a dozen schools and clerk to very many more. Disputes rarely arose and when they did, they could be quickly and easily resolved.

This is not the place to describe in detail the transformation that has occurred in school governance following a national enquiry undertaken by Lord Taylor between 1975 and 1977, but I will outline very quickly the key stages.

The first faltering steps were taken in 1980, when primary school managers were re-designated governors and governing bodies increased considerably in size. Elected parent and teacher governors made their appearance for the first time and head teachers obtained the right to be governors of their schools if they wished. Provision was made for the election of non-teacher governors, but this facility was taken up in only a small number of schools. Most primary school governing bodies doubled in size overnight, and

secondary school bodies increased to twenty. The number of
governing bodies of which anyone could be a member was limited
for the first time to five. At a stroke therefore, large numbers of
new people had to be found to undertake the work, and in every
school, for the first time, the parental voice had a right to be heard.

Other changes at that time were relatively limited: governing
bodies were given the duty to publish their admission arrangements and to give parents the right to appeal when a request for a
place for their child at the school was turned down.

It was the 1986 (No. 2) Education Act that firmly established for
the first time the new partnership between parents, teachers and
the churches. It also began the rapid shift of power from LEAs to
schools. Responsibility for the conduct of every school in the
country was given to the governing body. It was the 1986 Act that
introduced the much unloved requirement for governors to hold
an annual meeting for parents at which a report had to be
presented about the way in which they had conducted the school
in the previous twelve months. Any sex education had to be given
'in such a manner as to encourage pupils to have due regard to
moral considerations and the value of family life'. Corporal
punishment was abolished and LEAs were given the duty to
provide free training for governors. From now on at least one foundation governor had to be the parent of a pupil at the school.
Regulations further restricted the number of governing bodies to
which an individual could be appointed to two.

The 1986 Act was quickly followed by Lord Baker's 1988
Education Reform Act which extended the concept of governors'
financial responsibilities by requiring that all but the smallest
schools had to have a budget delegated to them by the LEA. This
was the Act that established, for the first time, the national curriculum, with programmes of study, key stages and attainment targets
in all subjects. Schools had to admit pupils up to an agreed standard number which could be reduced only with the consent of the
Secretary of State.

The 1990s saw an avalanche of legislation. The Schools Act of
1992 established Ofsted (The Office for Standards in Education)
and the Further and Higher Education Act of the same year
removed sixth form colleges (including the Catholic ones) from
LEA maintenance, transferring them to the newly established
Further Education Funding Council. The 1996 Act consolidated
all education legislation for the first time since 1944. Finally in
1998 came the Schools Standards and Framework Act, which rein-
forced the position of school governors, mainly at the expense of

LEAs, and enhanced the position of parents on the governing body. Church schools now had to have two or three parents appointed as foundation governors in addition to those elected by the parental body.

It will be clear from this brief survey, just how much the nature and purpose of school governance has changed in under twenty years.

School Governance Today

Catholic school governors today, both primary and secondary, have six main tasks:

- managing the budget
- the admission of pupils
- the maintenance of the buildings
- the employment of the staff
- responsibility for the curriculum and
- conducting the school in accordance with the trust deed of the founding body.

It has been the practice for many years that governing bodies do their detailed work through a number of committees: The 1998 Act requires schools to have a number of statutory committees. These are:

- staff dismissals committee and dismissal appeal committee
- pupils discipline committee
- pupils admissions committee
- head teacher's appraisal committee.

They are, of course, free to appoint whatever other panels and committees they think fit, provided they do not try to delegate functions that are expressly forbidden.

I will now examine the main tasks and describe some of the problems that are being encountered.

Budget

Catholic school governors have the same responsibilities as their non-Catholic colleagues to manage the budget delegated to them by their local education authority, so there is nothing particularly special about this area of activity, except that, since religious education forms a much greater part of the activities of a Catholic school, money to fund it properly has to be found from other areas of the school's activities. Where there is a difference is that every Catholic school has to run a voluntary fund in parallel with the main school budget. Income for this derives from parental contributions and social activities and may be used to help finance the school's chaplaincy arrangements, any governors' contribution to building work and a salary for the clerk to the governing body.

Pupil Admissions

Decisions about which pupils are to be admitted to the school have to be made in accordance with the school's admissions policy. This policy has to be reviewed annually and, since the 1998 Schools Standards and Framework Act, every Catholic school is required to consult all other admissions authorities in the area (i.e. its own LEA and any relevant neighbouring LEAs, together with the governing bodies of all other aided and foundation schools) before it determines its arrangements. Any disputes that arise at this stage have to be taken to a Local Admissions Forum, which is made up of representatives of the admissions authorities for the area. Forums are only advisory: they have no power to require any of their members to modify a proposed policy.[*] However, any unresolved dispute has to be remitted to an official newly created by the 1998 Act – the Schools' Adjudicator – unless it concerns any matter to do with the religious character of the school, when it has to go to the Secretary of State. About one year into the implementation of the 1998 Act, many Catholic schools have been involved in references to the Adjudicator, either as complainants or subjects of complaint, but at the time of writing there have been only two references to the Secretary of State.

Admissions policies have to be clear, unambiguous and objective, so that parents can easily assess their chances of securing a place for their children. Just how technical these simple requirements make the policy may be understood by studying the following model issued by the Catholic Education Service:

[*]Changes are proposed in the 2002 Education Bill.

Admission Arrangements and Criteria for Catholic Primary Schools.

Basic Information

1   .... (name) Catholic Primary School is situ-
         ated in the Diocese of .... And is maintained by
         the .... Local Education Authority.

2   The governing body of the school is responsible for deter-
         mining and administering the policy relating to the
         admission of pupils to the school. It is guided in that respon-
         sibility by the requirement of the law, by the advice of the
         Diocesan Trustees, and its duty to the school and the
         Catholic community.

3   The   school   primarily   serves   the   parish(es)   of
         ....

4   Having consulted the LEA and others in accord with the
         requirements of the law, the governing body has set as its
         planned admissions number .... pupils for the
         school year commencing ....

5(a)   Parents wishing to apply for a place in the school for their
         child in the school year .... must complete the
         attached/enclosed application form and return the same to
         the school by no later than .... It should be
         carefully noted that all applications must be submitted on
         that form and all applications will be considered at the same
         time.

5(b)   [In accord with the provisions of Regulation 49 of the
         Education (School Government) Regulations 1999, the
         governing body has delegated responsibility for determining
         admissions to its Admissions Committee.]

6   Pupils who are admitted to the school will enter the recep-
         tion   class(es)   on   ....   (or   ....),   or
         (..................).

As required by law, the governing body will not admit more than
30 pupils to any one reception or infants class.

Criteria

> [The school's admissions policy should reflect its purpose of serving the relevant Catholic community or communities. The following criteria are designed to acknowledge that responsibility of the governing body. Therefore, the (Admissions Committee) may apply the following criteria in order of priority:]

(A)   (Baptised) (Roman) (Catholic) children

> [Although Diocesan practice and advice do differ, some would give especial priority to those Catholic children whose parents regularly attend Mass on Sundays and Holy Days of Obligation and verification of the same, if required, would be provided for on the application form duly signed by the priest of the Church normally attended by the family.]

(B)   In the event of any over-subscription in the number of applications made under (a) above, then the [Admissions Committee] will offer places in the following order of priority:

(Baptised) (Roman) (Catholic) children

   (i)   whose families (regularly attend Mass at) or (are resident in the parishes of) .... Catholic Church or ....;

   (ii)   who have a brother or a sister at the school at the time of likely admission;

   (iii) those living nearest to the school, measured by (the shortest walking distance using public highway) (as the crow flies).

(C)   In the event of there being under-subscription for places in the school, then the [Admissions Committee] will admit (Baptised) (Roman) Catholic children whose parents are resident in other parishes at the time of application in the following order of priority;

   (i)   the presence of a brother or sister in the school;

      (ii)   those living nearest to the school as described in (b) (iii) above.

(D)   Notwithstanding all of that above, the [Admissions Committee] shall always give especial consideration to an application made for a place in the school from the parents of a child with special educational needs, medical problems or exceptional domestic or social problems, provided that such application is submitted with appropriate evidence or reports.

(E)   If, after considering applications made which meet any of the above criteria or a combination of one or more of the same and that there remains a shortfall in the planned admissions number, then the [Admissions Committee] may consider applications made by parents of other Christian denominations desirous of obtaining a Christian education for their child provided that such application is supported, in writing, by the appropriate Minister of Religion.

(F)   [The governing body have entered into an arrangement with the .... LEA, under the provisions of S.91 of the School Standards and Framework Act, whereby in the event of the school being under-subscribed in applications submitted which qualify under (A), (B) and (C) above the [Admissions Committee] may admit up to (................) pupils who qualify under (E) above.]

All Catholic schools are established in accordance with the trust deed of the founding diocese or religious order. As indicated above, they therefore have to give first priority to Catholic children. Many are oversubscribed by Catholic children. How, then, are governing bodies to differentiate between competing claims? Some schools operate an elastic catchment area which enables them to expand or contract the boundaries in accordance with the best guess about the number of children likely to be seeking admission. The problem with this is that, at the margins, those living in a road or part of a road may be successful one year but unsuccessful the next. In practice, it is hard to persuade the unlucky ones of the fairness of decisions made in this way, logical though they may be. An alternative approach is to make decisions without regard to geography but on the basis of Catholic commitment. The difficulty then is in deciding what criteria are to be adopted. Is it frequency

of Mass attendance? If so, over what period? Is it commitment to
the life of the parish? If so, whose – the parents' or the children's?
In a recent decision, the Commissioner for Local Administration
(the Ombudsman) held that it was quite in order for a Catholic
governing body to call into question the commitment of a divorced
mother who was living with a partner and therefore to refuse to
admit her daughter to its heavily over-subscribed school. In less
extreme terms, how do you compare membership of the Guild of
St Stephen in one parish with that of the music group in another?
Some governing bodies seek to overcome the difficulty by inter-
viewing prospective pupils but this is a course fraught with
difficulty. For, quite apart from the suspicion that covert selection
by academic ability or social class is being carried out, coaching
applicants will certainly take place if the same questions are asked
of them all and it is impossible to prove a fair process has been
undertaken if different questions are asked of different candidates.

The position is particularly acute in oversubscribed primary
schools. The 1998 Act has put an almost total ban on admissions
that would have led to infant classes having more than 30 children
and in many areas the number of Catholic children having to be
refused a place has therefore increased. It can be expected that
this limit will be extended to junior age classes at some future date,
thus exacerbating the situation.

What is to be done when, as sometimes happens, a school wishes
to offer places to children from practising and committed non-
Catholic Christian families – particularly members of the free
churches, who generally speaking, have no schools of their own –
or even children of other faiths, in preference to Catholic children
from non-practising families? It is easy to see the arguments in
favour, from the school's point-of-view, but what of the trust deed
on which the school was founded, which will usually refer to the
school's work in furthering the work of the Roman Catholic
Church? And are not baptized but non-practising Catholic children even more deserving of the nurture of the Church, through
the medium of the school, than children whose families practise
regularly?

Catholic schools that are under-subscribed also face problems.
In law, like all other schools, they have to accede to parental preference except in certain tightly prescribed circumstances. These
require the agreement of the local education authority to restrict
admission in order to preserve the religious character of the
school. This produces a nice conundrum for governors. The more
non-Catholics that are admitted to the school, the more risk there

is that its distinctive ethos is going to be changed and the less acceptable it is likely to be to Catholic parents, thereby exacerbating the problem that already exists. On the other hand, if the numbers on roll are deliberately kept down, the more the school's budget is going to be adversely affected and the more difficulty it is likely to experience in delivering a broad and balanced curriculum with adequate differentiation to meet the needs of all pupils.

Buildings Matters

Till recently, governors' responsibility for buildings was straightforward: the LEA looked after the inside and governors the outside. In practice, many dioceses looked after major items of governors' maintenance expenditure, leaving the schools themselves to deal with day-to-day repairs and small maintenance jobs. All that has been, and is being, changed. LEAs have been compelled by legislation to delegate their building maintenance money to schools and with it responsibility for deciding what work should be done. Schools have almost universally welcomed this additional freedom, though there have been almost equally universal complaints about the lack of resources that LEAs have delegated. New procedures are currently being introduced by the DfEE which will similarly delegate maintenance money for the exterior of the building to governing bodies with, again, responsibility for deciding what should be done. There are two problems here. First, how is a school to fund maintenance work if it does not have enough money in its budget? At the time of writing a one form entry primary school could expect to receive about £3,000 a year for external maintenance and could aggregate two years' budgets. But the cost of scaffolding required by Health and Safety legislation to facilitate the exterior redecoration of a three story inner city building was in the region of £10,000. The sums clearly do not add up. Large roof repairs pose similar problems. Which other spending are head teachers to cut to make up any deficit? – staffing? books, stationery and apparatus? cleaning? heating and lighting? There are no easy answers. This is a matter of concern to the schools' Trustees (the diocese or religious order), because it is they who own the building, not the governors, and it is they who have obligations to the Charity Commission for the proper safeguarding of the assets of their trust. It is not clear what the Trustees can do, in practice, if they find that some of their school buildings are being neglected.

Employment of Teaching Staff

Catholic school governors have always employed a majority of the staff. At the moment they face a number of problems in the employment of teachers. First, they share in the general shortage that has been common to all schools for many years. More importantly, it is increasingly difficult to recruit practising Catholics. Thirty years ago, the position was very different. The Catholic Church, like the Church of England, had a network of teacher training colleges whose overriding responsibility was the training of committed Catholics for work in Catholic primary and secondary schools. In addition, many religious orders saw their role not only in running their own schools but also in providing members to work in diocesan schools. The abolition of the teacher training colleges and the widespread closure of many church ones, coinciding as it did with the beginning of the long decline in vocations to the priesthood and religious life has changed the situation beyond recognition. Only three free standing Catholic higher education institutions now remain: Newman, Birmingham, St Mary's, Strawberry Hill and Trinity and All Saints, Leeds. Two others – Digby Stuart, Roehampton and Notre Dame, Liverpool both form parts of ecumenical ventures. For this and other reasons, the majority of Catholic young people who are interested in teaching attend a secular higher education institution either for their first degree or their post graduate certificate in education or both. It is increasingly common, therefore, that those beginning a career in a Catholic school have had no specific training to prepare them for the work. Dioceses have responded by providing study courses leading to the Certificate in Religious Studies on a part-time or distance learning basis, but young teachers who may have family commitments have problems finding both the money and the time to avail themselves of these opportunities.

There is, too, difficulty in recruiting Catholics to the most senior positions in schools – headship and deputy headship. School leadership is a very onerous task in any school these days. The church links that all Catholic schools are expected to have, coupled with the need to give Religious Education an adequate place in a highly structured and overloaded curriculum, impose additional burdens which many Catholic teachers simply do not wish to undertake.

The Catholic Bishops have issued guidance to governors in this matter. This is the most recent version and stresses that head teachers, deputies and heads of RE must be practising Catholics.

Memorandum on the Appointment
of Teachers to Catholic Schools

1 PURPOSE OF MEMORANDUM

This memorandum is addressed on behalf of the Bishops of England and Wales to the governors of Catholic schools. Its purpose is to help and guide governors to fulfil their responsibilities concerning the appointment of teachers.

2 ESSENTIAL QUALITIES OF CATHOLIC TEACHERS

The preservation and development of the quality and distinctive nature of Catholic schools depends essentially on the faith, practice and standards of the teachers in the schools:

'Modern man listens more willingly to witnesses than to teachers and, if he does listen to teachers, it is because they are witnesses.' (Pope Paul VI, 1974)

Governors of Roman Catholic voluntary aided and independent schools are the employers of the teachers, to whom they should give clear guidelines about the Catholic character, education and life of their school.

As the employers of the teachers in the school the governors should issue the appropriate contract of employment and associated documentation as provided by the Catholic Education Service.

3 THE IDEAL FOR WHICH WE SHOULD AIM

Everyone should appreciate the need to staff Catholic schools as far as possible with practising and well qualified Catholic teachers.

To find a Catholic teacher who combines personal conviction and practice of the faith with the required professional qualifications and experience, especially in specialist subjects, is therefore the ideal for which we aim.

Nevertheless, we acknowledge with gratitude the devotion and service given by many teachers in our schools who are not themselves Catholics and we recognize our obligations to them.

4 IMPLEMENTING THE IDEAL

Where no acceptable Catholic teacher, such as one who is Catholic only in name, has applied for a vacant post, it is often necessary or appropriate to re-advertise more widely. Only where an appointment cannot be delayed and there is no suitable Catholic applicant will governors seek to appoint good qualified teachers of other faiths whose personal and professional standards come nearest to the ideal.

Governors should, of course, be careful not to appoint any teacher who is not in sympathy with or who does not respect the aims and objectives of a Catholic school, much less one who is hostile to the Catholic faith.

5 POSTS TO BE HELD ONLY BY CATHOLIC TEACHERS

The posts of head, deputy head and head or co-ordinator of Religious Education must be reserved for practising Catholics. Other senior pastoral posts, e.g. in secondary schools, heads of upper, middle or lower school, pupil counsellors or co-ordinators and teacher mentors and in primary schools, heads of infant or junior departments, pastoral counsellors or co-ordinators and teacher mentors, should wherever possible be held by practising Catholics. Advertisements for these posts should make clear from the outset that applications are invited in accordance with these requirements.

6 RELIGIOUS EDUCATION DEPARTMENT

Secondary: The Religious Education departments in our secondary schools are of particular importance and should have at least parity of esteem with any other subject department. Governors are urged, in consultation with the head teacher, to give the highest possible status to the department and highest possible points to its head or co-ordinator. This will encourage Catholic teachers to specialize in religious education and attract the best candidates. It is better to defer an appointment to the department if, initially, a suitable applicant does not apply.

Primary: While the structures for the provision and organization or Religious Education in our primary schools will be different from those of our secondary schools, governors of primary schools must have the same concern for Religious Education, ensuring that it is properly organized, co-ordinated and taught. Its co-ordinator should again therefore have at least parity in status and remuneration with those of other curriculum areas.

7 REPRESENTATION AT SHORT LISTING AND INTERVIEWING

At a meeting of the governors held to consider the short listing or appointment of head teacher, or heads of RE, a representative of the Bishop must always be invited to be present. A representative may be invited whenever senior posts with pastoral responsibility are being considered. (As is provided for at Schedule 17, Paragraph 28 (2) of the Schools Standards and Framework Act, 1998, such advisory rights must be granted where the governing body has afforded such rights to the chief education officer of the LEA in these or all teaching appointments.)

8 DELEGATION OF POWER OF APPOINTMENT

In the case of voluntary aided schools, when governors delegate to a committee of the governing body and/or head teacher their power and right of appointment of teachers, it is essential that the terms of reference for such delegation, and the circumstances in which it may be exercised, are made explicit.

Where the power of appointment is delegated to a committee, this should normally have at least three members of whom two should be foundation governors. Appointment to the most senior posts should usually be reserved to the full governing body, as is provided for at paragraph 30 of Schedule 17 of the School Standards and Framework Act.

Problems also arise because the culture of the Catholic school which appears to make it so popular – particularly with non-Catholic parents – from time to time seems to be out of step with what contemporary British society finds acceptable. Teachers working in Catholic schools in nearly all cases sign an employment contract that they will 'have regard to the Roman Catholic character of the school and not ... do anything in any way detrimental or prejudicial to the interests of the same'. Difficulties arise when Catholic teachers want to co-habit, when divorcees remarry without annulment and occasionally from pressure to acknowledge and accept homosexual relationships. The paradox is that parents who have very often chosen a Catholic school because of its strong ethos object when action needs to be taken against popular teachers whose conduct is putting the ethos at risk. However, education law has recently strengthened the position of governors. Section 60 (5) (b) of the Schools Standards and Framework Act says about voluntary aided schools: 'Regard may be had in connection with the termination of the employment of any teacher at the school to any conduct on his part which is incompatible with the precepts, or with the upholding of the tenets, of the religion or religious denomination so specified.'

There has been speculation that the implementation of the European Union Draft Directive on Equal Treatment in Employment would restrict the authority of Church schools to discriminate in favour of their own adherents in the matter of appointment of teaching staff, but at the time of writing this chapter, Baroness Blackstone made the following statement in the House of Lords:

> We agree that it should be acceptable for a Church school to be able to require a teacher to be an active member of the Church in question. We shall press for amendments to the directive to ensure that there is no question of a religious organization being forced to employ people who are not members of the relevant faith, because that would dilute the maintenance of a distinctive religious ethos. This is not a matter of the UK versus the European Commission or the rest of Europe. This was always the intention behind the proposals and I am sure that many other member states have similar views. ... I return to the concern that the employment directive might require religious organizations that believe that homosexual activity is wrong to open all jobs to practising homosexuals. The Government accept that difference in treatment in such circumstances may be justifiable. It would be unacceptable, for example, for a teacher in a Catholic school to challenge openly the teachings of the Church on homosexuality. We shall continue negotiating on that point to ensure that the directive is clear. We are also concerned to ensure that the employment directive will permit Section 60 of the School Standards and Framework Act 1998 to be maintained.

Curriculum and Ethos

Finally, we come to the most important task of the governing body of a Catholic school – its responsibility for the conduct of the school and the curriculum. The Church has always been clear that its schools have a distinctive character. The Sacred Congregation for Catholic Education published in 1977 a pamphlet 'The Catholic School'. 'The Catholic School'[1] has much to say on this subject:

[1] 'The Catholic School' (London, Catholic Truth Society, 1977).

Christ is the foundation of the whole educational enterprise in a Catholic school;

the Catholic school forms part of the saving mission of the Church, especially for education in the faith;

its task is fundamentally a synthesis of culture and faith and a synthesis of faith and life;

the specific mission of the school, then, is a critical systematic transmission of culture in the light of faith and the bringing forth of the power of Christian virtue by the integration of culture with faith and of faith with living.

Clearly, according to this, the Catholic school's business is something very different from that of its neighbouring community schools.

How far Catholic schools were alert to these insights in the past is an interesting question. But the issue has become much more significant since the 1988 Education Reform Act. As indicated above, it was this piece of legislation that introduced, for the first time, the notion of a national curriculum. At the same time, governing bodies of aided schools were required to draw up a curriculum policy statement and, in doing so, to have regard to their LEA's curriculum policy statement. In practice, many schools simply adopted without comment or amendment the LEA's curriculum policy statement with a distinctive Religious Education element grafted on to it. The schools therefore found themselves in the awkward position of having an explicitly Catholic mission statement and a list of detailed aims and objectives that were similarly distinctive, but a curriculum policy statement and development plan that in most cases were not distinct at all, except with regard to Religious Education and worship. Given the many pressures on schools at that time, it is hardly surprising that in many cases the problem was simply not recognised. But advice has been available for the whole of the period. The Sacred Congregation document *The Religious Dimension of Education in the Catholic school* which was coincidentally first published also in 1988, has a lot to say about matters of this kind:

In a number of countries, renewal in school programming has given increased attention to science and technology. Those teaching these subject areas must not ignore the religious dimension. They should help their students to understand that positive science, and the technology allied to it, is a part of the universe created by God.

The wonder that past ages felt when contemplating this universe, recorded by the Biblical authors is still valid for students today; ... there can be no conflict between faith and true scientific knowledge; both find their source in God.

Teachers should guide the students' work in such a way that they would be able to discover a religious dimension in the world of human history.... Schools should 'help students see history as something real: the drama a human grandeur and human misery'.

The protagonist of history is the human person, who projects onto the world, on a larger scale, the good and the evil that is within each individual. History is, then, a monumental struggle between these two fundamental realities, and is subject to moral judgements.

Literary and artistic works depict the struggles of societies, of families, and individuals. They spring from the depths of the human heart revealing its lights and its shadows, its hope and its despair. The Christian perspective goes beyond the merely human, and offers more penetrating criteria for understanding the human struggle and mysteries of the human spirit.[2]

If the national curriculum is approached with insights such as these in mind, its delivery in Catholic schools is going to be very different from that in other schools.

It follows from this that foundation governors need to understand that their role is apostolic. They are their Bishops' representatives in taking the Church's mission to the community served by their school. They therefore have a personal relationship with the Bishop which is qualitatively unlike anything within the job description of the governor of a community school. This is why the commissioning ceremonies that several dioceses now organize at the beginning of governors' terms of office are so important.

The Catholic Education Service and individual dioceses have done much to help raise awareness, but the structure of the system does not help. The Catholic Education Service has, for very many years, produced valuable guides to the successive Education Acts, drawing out those changes that particularly affect Catholic schools. Then, in 1992, 1994 and 1998 it produced comprehensive in-service training packs based on videos specially prepared for Catholic schools. These packs were possible because of grant aid from the Department for Education and Employment's predecessor

---

[2] *The Religious Dimension of Education in a Catholic School* (London, Catholic Truth Society, 1988).

organizations. As with many specific grants, however, funding has been reduced over the years and is now substantially in the hands of the LEAs and the schools themselves. It is therefore difficult for either the central Catholic Education Service or dioceses to promote the legitimate interests of Catholic school governors as they would wish. On the one hand, the dioceses do not have the resources either in terms of money or manpower to deal comprehensively with all the issues that require attention and on the other, many local education authorities, who in law have responsibility for governor training, do not accept that they have a requirement to fund distinctive support in the way that is required for Catholic schools.

As has been indicated, governors are now responsible not only for the conduct of the school but also for the curriculum. They have always shown understandable reluctance to become too deeply involved in matters to do with the curriculum, but now they cannot avoid them. They have to have a policy which requires that the performance of every teacher in the school is reviewed on an annual basis against previously defined objectives. Although the implementation of the policy is in the hands of the head teacher, the performance of the head teacher has to be similarly reviewed by a committee of the governors with the help of an independent external advisor. In the light of what has been said earlier in this chapter it must be right that the criteria to be adopted in performance management have distinctive Catholic references.

The two major issues surrounding the governance of Catholic schools are the recruitment of suitable people to serve as foundation governors and their training. They must have a proper understanding of the nature and purpose of the Catholic school as an environment 'permeated with the Gospel spirit of love and freedom' where everyone is 'aware of the living presence of Jesus the "Master" and where men and women are guided "to human and Christian perfection"'.

If these challenges can be successfully met, together with the need to promote the concept of teaching as a vocation, the future for Catholic schools will indeed be bright.

Extracts from CES and CTS documents are reproduced here with permission.

Chapter 8

The Disposition of the Chaplain

Michael A. Hayes

Introduction

Some years ago a colleague who was visiting Rome sent me a post-card of what was obviously a section of a large mosaic. The description of the reverse read: *Roma: Basilica of St Clement – Mosaic of the Apse (12th Cent.) Chaplain.* My curiosity about the character described as Chaplain on this picture post-card led me to visit the *Basilica di San Clemente* which is just some three hundred yards from the Colosseum in Rome and to make my own study of the larger mosaic. The fruit of that study is the setting for this reflection on chaplaincy.

For over twenty years I have worked as a Chaplain in nursery, infant, junior, and secondary schools, and for eight years as a full-time Chaplain in Higher Education. My experience, therefore, encourages me to offer the following reflection which is primarily focused in chaplaincy in an educational context. I have purposely chosen to give the chapter the title 'The Disposition of the Chaplain' – partly because it seems to me a key issue – especially as the question of the 'role' of the Chaplain can be so diffuse. When I began my ministry in Higher Education I was very anxious to answer 'What does a Chaplain do?' I soon realized that I needed to carry out the role of Chaplain as the person I am, to 'play to my own strengths'. There is no single blueprint for work in chaplaincy. What a Chaplain does will for the most part be quite specific to the individual and to the context and circumstance of the appointment. For some, chaplaincy will be engaged in what is very much a part-time basis in a very busy parish, for others it will be a full-time ministry of a lay Catholic, with perhaps, appropriate remuneration.

The ministry will always have some liturgical aspect, will be concerned with prayer, spirituality, guidance and offering vision, will involve listening skills, and be affirming and supportive of colleagues and students and of others. The *what* of chaplaincy will always be the desire and call to carry out these aspects of ministry. The *how* of chaplaincy in the way that these are expressed and achieved will always be determined by the person. This chapter explores, by way of reflection on a mosaic in a church in Rome, the *disposition* of the Chaplain, that is the basic attitudes and qualities that are brought to the specific context of ministry.

There will always be a specific context within which the Chaplain recognizes his or her place in the larger framework of the institution, but it is also important to place the role of the institution within the wider context of the Christian faith-story. The Christian framework offers a meta-story or meta-narrative in the exploration of the relationship between human experience and knowledge of a Self-communicating God.

Put more simply the Christian story offers a perspective on what it means to be human. This story understands that we are made in the image and likeness of God, that God's desire is that we might share God's life, that this same God has communicated to us in Christ. This same Christ has entrusted within the Church a ministry of service that enables individuals and communities to deepen their relationship with a God who desires nothing more than their salvation. It is this understanding of the human person, shared by a community of believers, that underpins Catholic education and offers its distinctive contribution. The life of an educational establishment is varied and rich. The Chaplain to such an institution – and indeed to non-educational institutions – can make a significant contribution in the building and developing of a notion of Christian community within that institution. In order for that contribution to be as effective as possible, it seems to me that the Chaplain needs consciously to carry out his or her ministry within the context of the meta-narrative.

The Mosaic at San Clemente

G.K. Chesterton described San Clemente:

> [h]ere is an older type of symbolism in which the real nature of the triumph of Christian things is traced in mosaic in the apse of the ancient church of St Clement, one of the most remarkable and yet one of the most Roman of churches. The old decoration of the apse

expresses the idea with a symmetry that is almost startling. The apse is a half-moon of gold on the usual pattern; but at the top there is a cloud out of which comes the hand of God above the crucifix. It does not merely bless it or even rest on it. It seems to take the cross as if by the cross-hilt and thrust it like a sword into the earth below. Yet in one sense it is the very reverse of a sword, since its touch is not death but life; life springing and sprouting and shooting into the air, that the world may have life, and that it may have it more abundantly... The very disproportion between the long loops and circles sprawling everywhere and the slender cross at whose touch they have leapt into life, emphasizes with energy the power of that magic wand. Curled inside each of the circles, as in something that is at once a nest and a new separate world, is a bird, to express the universal birth of life; and each bird is different in species or colour. No one but a madman could stand before it and say that our faith is anti-vital or a creed of death. And there is one last touch, which has already been remarked by many, that the face of the Crucified, which in most images is naturally tragic, is in this case radiant and like the sun at noon; or like the works that have no need to be written here in any motto or inscription: 'I am the Resurrection and the Life'.[1]

The Basilica of San Clemente in Rome takes its name from Pope St Clement who died around 100 CE. The present Basilica is built on layers of three earlier buildings. There is evidence of Christian worship taking place there since the end of the first century or the beginning of the second. The present Basilica dates to 1100. There are many fascinating elements in this building but the mosaic in the Apse overshadows them all. The symbolism in the mosaic is early Christian in a medieval setting. It portrays a depth of theological reflection centred on the Incarnation and the redeeming sacrifice of the Cross. A theme that runs through Christian liturgy is that of the Cross as the throne from which Christ reigns and is glorified. The Cross is the central motif of this mosaic, out of which flows a vine in encircling branches. Within these encircling branches there are men and women engaged in work: the prophets are depicted foretelling the saving Word; the four evangelists; Mary the mother of Jesus with St John; there are twelve doves on the extremities of the cross, symbols of the Apostles who brought the 'good news'; and the Bishops and Doctors of the Church representing the preaching of that 'good news' are present. The Church has become in the mosaic the vineyard of the Lord. The inscription at the bottom states 'We have likened the Church to this vine; the Law made it

---

[1] Chesterton, G.K., *The Resurrection of Rome* (London, Hodder & Stoughton, 1930), pp. 340–42.

wither but the Cross causes it to bloom. . .' Other symbols include a peacock, a symbol of the resurrection and immortality, while two thirsty deer can be seen drinking from the rivers of salvation symbolising the desire of the faithful to be united with God. At the foot of the Cross are the four great doctors of the Church, St Ambrose, St Gregory, St Augustine and St Jerome.

It is interesting to note that between St Gregory and St Ambrose there is a tonsured figure giving food and drink to a brightly coloured bird. This figure has been identified as the feudal lord's Chaplain (the feudal lord and his family are represented in another section of the mosaic and may represent the artist's patrons). It would be easy to miss the bent figure, engaged in what might seem an unimportant domestic task.

What this mosaic offers to our consideration of the disposition of the Chaplain is the sense of a larger picture: a great framework which is unmistakably focused on the central figure of the life-giving Christ. The fact that this figure of the Chaplain is posed between Gregory and Ambrose is worth reflecting upon. They are both Doctors of the Church; both were great teachers and great pastors. This medieval setting can perhaps suggest that the Chaplain needs to be conscious that he or she stands within a living teaching tradition that is pastoral in its concern and is a ministry based on service of others. Both of these great Doctors of the Church engaged in the theological task of exploring the dialectic between human experience and knowledge of a Self-communicating God: that the source of their service of others is rooted in the redemption of Christ, that all ministries in the Church will be refreshed and kept alive by a conscious alignment with Christ as the vine. Two further points can also help our reflection. It was Gregory who sent Augustine to England in 597 while Ambrose was called to be bishop while still a catechumen. The ministry of Chaplain is indeed a ministry of being sent to others; it is a ministry entrusted by the Church for its upbringing. Yet the Chaplain must also recognize that he or she is on a journey of faith like Ambrose as, of course, are those to whom he or she is sent to serve. Chaplaincy has a context and a dynamic, and these lie at the heart of the disposition that the Chaplain brings to that ministry.

A starting point – a ministry of witnessing

In pursuing this ministry one could start by arguing that the Chaplain needs to begin with a willingness to witness to what is a serious personal faith. This is a very important starting point. An inspiration for this witness lies at the heart of Pope Paul VI's exhortation on *Evangelisation Today*:

> Above all the Gospel must be proclaimed by witness. Take a Christian or handful of Christians who, in the midst of their own community, show their capacity for understanding and acceptance, their sharing of life and destiny with other people, their solidarity with the efforts of all for whatever is noble and good. Let us suppose that, in addition they radiate in an all together simple and unaffected way their faith in values that go beyond current values, and their hope in something that is not seen and that one would not dare to imagine. Through this wordless witness these Christians stir up irresistible questions in the hearts of those who see how they live. Why are they like this? Why do they live in this way? What or who is it that inspires them? Why are they in our midst? ... Let us therefore preserve our fervour of spirit. Let us preserve the delight and comforting joy of evangelising, even when it is in tears that we must sow. May it mean for us an interior enthusiasm that nobody and nothing can quench.[2]

Witnessing to the presence of God in the world begins with witnessing to the presence of God in one's own life. The innumerable personal relationships that comprise a Chaplain's work will only be life-giving if he or she witnesses to the reality of the life-giving presence of the Christ, the fruitful vine of the mosaic. The witness of the Chaplain will always be founded on recognizing that it is not simply the quantity and quality of relationships that are established in the institution where the chaplaincy is carried out, rather it is whether those who encounter the Chaplain encounter Christ. A disposition to present Christ in word and action is therefore key to the process of evangelising. The Chaplain's role must be one of witnessing, be that at the student bar or over endless cups of coffee in the staff room.

Other key aspects of this disposition

Chaplaincy, like all Christian ministry, includes aspects of formation. In writing about the spirituality of the religious educator, Groome[3] wrote some years ago that such a person needed to have four qualities: a passion for people; a love of tradition; the gift of

[2] *Evangelii Nuntiand* (Evangelisation in the modern world) Pope Paul VI, 8 December 1975.
[3] Groome, T., 'The Spirituality of the Religious Educator' in *Journal of Religious Education*, vol. 88, no. 1, Winter 1988, pp. 9–44.

hospitality; and a willingness to educate for God's reign. These four aspects are also a valuable way of exploring the disposition that goes with the ministry of Chaplain.

Chaplaincy by its very nature is focused on people and indeed is one of the areas of any institution where the structures and systems are often deliberately at a minimum, precisely so that the Chaplain can have access to people as and when it is most helpful. The Chaplain will always be part of the structure and the systems of the institution, but only because that will facilitate access to people to whom one seeks to be the pastor. A 'passion for people' reminds us that in any assessment or evaluation, the commitment to the people one serves is the primary measure of chaplaincy. There may well be constant temptation to be part of the 'system'. There will be certainly opportunities and invitations to enter into the 'politics' of the institution; a 'passion for people' will be an invaluable grounding that will reinforce the disposition that will always call us to the service of people.

The Chaplain in the *San Clemente* mosaic who is engaged in feeding the birds – exotic, colourful birds like so many of those whom we encounter in chaplaincy – is found between Ambrose and Gregory. We always work in the context of faith that has been explored, elaborated and reflected on within a great tradition. The passing on of faith and making it real in every generation, this is our task too. The Chaplain does not simply try to 'solve' people's problems, 'fix' things that have gone wrong. What the Chaplain is called to do is to try to help the individual to integrate their own story into the Christian story – the meta-narrative. To some extent we are in line with the great teachers and thinkers of the Christian tradition, and it is our own sense – and understanding – of the great tradition which helps us assist others in belonging to the body of Christ. Because every situation and pastoral experience is unique, there will always be the temptation to suggest that we need to 'invent' a new response in each situation. A sense of tradition and belonging to the wider Church will always help us to ponder the new event within the context of that which we have received and hope to hand on – the tradition.

Hospitality

Godfrey[4] writing on hospitality states 'the word *hospitality* (Latin

---

[4] Godfrey, K., 'Hospitality' in M. Downey (ed.), *The New Dictionary of Catholic Spirituality* (Collegeville, Minnesota, The Liturgical Press, 1993), pp. 515–516.

hospitium) derives from *hospes*, meaning both "guest" and "host". Behind this dual connotation lies the Greek concept *xenos*, a stranger who receives a welcome or who welcomes. Hospitality implies mutuality and is characterized by sincere graciousness between strangers. Hospitality is a constituent of the Judeo-Christian tradition. In the Old Testament God is identified in the duality of guest and host, for example in the encounter at the oak of Mamre (Gen. 18.1–15). This theme is continued in the New Testament with Jesus' concern for the needs of the poor, the marginalised, the sinner, etc.[5] He is the supreme host who washes the feet of the guests at the Last Supper.[6] Nouwen describes hospitality as 'the creation of space where the stranger can enter and become a friend instead of an enemy'.[7] Hospitality is placing at the heart of ministry a mindfulness in treating others as the body of Christ. Every encounter, therefore, is an encounter with Christ.

This vision of hospitality can seem a bit removed from our own experience and yet, in practical terms, is it not true that so many of our significant encounters where we feel our chaplaincy is truly life-giving, are over tea or coffee, or a late evening drink? Is it not the case that the endless coffee mugs, packets of biscuits, the some-times banal conversations, are the immediate context of so much of our ministry? In seeking to be hospitable we are recognizing that the person who came with question, or difficulty, is the stranger Christ came to encounter and be encountered by.

A local context

Some chaplaincy work will be carried out within a specific Christian or Catholic context – some schools, colleges, and hospitals. Other Chaplains will serve in a context that does not specifically embrace a Christian ethos. In both cases the burden of the ethos cannot be left to the Chaplain alone. In specifically Christian institutions, the role of the Chaplain will be within a stated ethos, and will be a significant person in trying to ensure that the ethos is clear and acknowledged. At times this will call for a critical stance – the Chaplain must be prepared to challenge if necessary – that is part of the calling. In institutions which do not have a specifically Christian ethos – prisons, universities,

[5] Mt. 8.20, 9.10, Mark 7.24, 14.3; Luke 7.36; 8.3; 9.53, 10.38, 14.1, 19.5; John 12.2.
[6] Mark 6.41–45, 8.6–9, 14.22; Luke 22.27; John 13.1–7.
[7] Nouwen, H., 'Hospitality', *Monastic Studies* 10 (1974), pp. 1–28.

hospitals and others – the Chaplain will also be called to be a prophetic voice working within the community, again a call that will be challenging.

Developing a disposition

To be really effective, chaplaincy cannot be a ministry that is simply dumped on the 'young priest' or a religious who is available. The growing number of paid, lay Chaplains is a real encouragement in the ensuring that willingness and energy and purpose are key factors underlying the disposition of the Chaplain. But this does raise questions of selection, training, induction, support, and ongoing appraisal – issues that are going to become more urgent as so many institutions conduct themselves in an increasingly professional manner with clear lines of accountability. I am convinced that it is not just the consideration of role and place within an institution that will help the development of chaplaincy, but a greater reflection on underlying values and attitudes, which can be seen in terms of disposition.

Experience of chaplaincy, like all ministries is as much about learning to 'fail' as learning to 'succeed'. We are all greatly blessed when things that we have carefully planned and arranged back fire, and when caught totally off-guard we surprisingly find ourselves uttering words of pure wisdom and power. These experiences tell me that it really is God's work and not mine, that Christ is truly the life-giving heart of the great mosaic of our lives and relationships, who gives us a natural propensity for humility, which is a key element in the disposition of the Chaplain.

This is the importance of the great willingness to be humbled by the experienced. Shannon describes humility as 'rooted in the truth of reality. Grounded in a deep awareness of our limitations and shortcomings in the presence of the divine perfection, and of our sinfulness in the presence of the all-holy God, it leads us to a profound sense of total dependence on God and to an ardent desire to do God's will in all things. It means, therefore, grasping the truth about ourselves and about God.'[8]

The word 'humility' is a derivative of the Latin, *humus,* which means ground or soil. Its use in biblical literature gives insight into it as a virtue. In the Old Testament is the attitude of the *'anawim,*

[8] Shannon, W., 'Humility' in M. Downey (ed.), *The New Dictionary of Catholic Spirituality* (Collegeville, Minnesota, The Liturgical Press, 1993), pp. 516–518.

the poor of Yahweh', who hears the cry of the poor who rely totally in gratitude on God.

After Christianity became established the first great spiritual movement, monasticism, which began with the Desert tradition in the fourth century saw humility as an important virtue, as the *Sayings of the Desert Fathers* indicate:

> A brother questioned Abba Motius, saying, 'If I go to dwell some-where, how do you want me to live? The old man said to him, 'If you live somewhere, do not seek to be known for anything special' ... The brother said to him, 'What shall I do, then?' The old man said, 'Wherever you live, follow the same manner of life as everyone else and if you see devout men who you trust doing something, do the same and you will be at peace. For this is humility: to see yourself to be the same as the rest.'[9]

We have already mentioned St Pope Gregory I. In *The Pastoral Office* he wrote that those who have authority in the Church should always be aware of their own frailty. He describes humility as 'the mistress and mother of all the virtues' (*Moralia*, xxiii, 13, 24; PL 76:265b). He also calls the humility of human persons 'true wisdom' and the humility of God 'the instrument of our redemption'.

Like Thomas Aquinas, who linked humility with magnanimity Thomas Merton identifies the humble person as 'living no longer for himself ... the spirit is delivered of all the limitations and vicis-situdes of creaturehood and contingency, and swims in the attributes of God, whose power, magnificence, greatness and eter-nity have, through love, through humility, become our own'.[10] The virtue of humility enables the Chaplain to keep focused on the task of serving others, for humility is the opposite of pride.[11]

Conclusion

The day to day exercise of the ministry of Chaplain will be specific to the strengths of the individual and the circumstance of the appointment. This chapter has explored the overall disposition of the Chaplain and some of the qualities that the holder of such a

---

[9] Motius, quoted in B. Ward (trans.) *The Sayings of the Desert Fathers: The Alphabetical Collection* (Kalamazoo, Michigan, Cistercian Publications Inc, 1984), p. 148, n. 1.

[10] Merton, T., *New Seeds of Contemplation* (New York, New Directions, 1961), p. 181.

[11] Exercise number 146 in Ganess, G. (trans.) *The Spiritual Exercises of Saint Ignatius* (Chicago, Loyola Press, 1992), pp. 66–67.

ministry might be expected to hold. These qualities include:

- an awareness that the Chaplain does not have sole responsibility of the ethos of the institution; the Chaplain has a specific role, sometimes that role will include the need to challenge the institution or its ethos. This is part of the prophetic call common to all Christians through their baptism. The Chaplain will discover his or her reality in the day to day dealings within an institution where other values than the Christian are significant.
- an awareness that this is a ministry within the Church; that it takes place within the teaching and pastoral mission of the Church. The system of school in this country is in the main a 'dual-system'.[12] This recognizes that there is inevitably a sense of dual belonging. It is often the secular authority that raises the finances and determines the legal constraints of the institution. While the Church is happy to work alongside secular authorities for the promotion of common values, as Christians we can never abdicate our belonging to the Kingdom.
- an understanding that at the heart of ministry is service of the people of God, which means having a passion for people. This mission of the Church is always to people – the lost and the found, those wishing to belong and those who simply need help. Service for the Christian is always to our brothers and sisters, never to 'Big-Brother'!
- an understanding and living out of Christian hospitality. It is not inappropriate that at the heart of the sacramental life of the Catholic Church is the altar, where we are served and nourished by one who came 'to serve and not to be served'.
- a willingness to be humbled by the experience, because the ministry of Chaplain – like all Christian ministry – is really only discovered in practice. It is within the encounter with brothers and sisters that the Lord teaches and guides us that we may know – often through failure – to what we are called.
- an awareness of his or her own journey of faith and an ability to affirm others in their journey. This is such a danger – especially but not uniquely within an educational establishment – of the culture of the 'expert'. The Chaplain is called to be one who can only show the way by walking along with those to whom they minister. There is no blue-print or plan that is

[12] Of the approximately 2500 Catholic schools in England and Wales, 140 are private schools.

true for each and every one. There has to be the humility of
offering what one can and the disposition to be able to let
the other go and perhaps – God willing – find another who
will offer the guidance that they might need for their own
unique journey and unique call.

Boland points out that for Thomas Aquinas the notion a disposition or *habitus* is important 'for his understanding of the human
being as a moral agent as well as for his account of grace, and in
particular of those gifts of faith, hope and charity which Christian
tradition calls "theological virtues"'.[13] Disposition for Aquinas
involves some form of self-possession and is directed toward action.
It is an awareness of the habit of action. To return to the mosaic of
San Clemente, here the Chaplain is not the focus of the mosaic,
the Chaplain has a place within the whole picture. The focus is the
life-giving Christ on the cross. The Chaplain is called to be consistent, realistic and audacious in his or her sharing in the life-giving
ministry of Christ. Underlying this call is not a programme of work,
a simple job description, but a habitus, a disposition, foundational
attitudes and qualities. These enable the Chaplain to minister with
a consistency – constant fidelity to the tradition, with realism –
recognizing the constraints and specific nature of institutions, situations, and people, and audacity – the fixed vision that all life is
focused on the life-giving cross of Christ.

---

[13] Boland, V. 'Aquinas and Simplicius on Dispositions – A Question in
Fundamental Moral Theory' in *New Blackfriars*, Vol. 82, No. 968, October 2001,
pp. 467–478.

Part Three

Challenges in Catholic Education

Chapter 9

Continuing Professional Development

Muriel Robinson

'I have no doubt that lives are being changed by this course.' This was the verdict of our external examiner at a recent examination board for the Diploma in Religious Education at the University of Brighton, a part-time course for teachers, catechists and those involved in other aspects of formation work in parishes which includes simultaneous study for the CCRS (Catholic Certificate in Religious Studies). This was the view he had reached after four years of contact with the programme, reading essays and journals and meeting staff and students. It goes without saying that we were glad to receive such a confirmation of the value of this programme, yet after the meeting I found myself wondering, not for the first time, whether the CCRS alone would be receiving the same accolade, and whether the lives being changed were as a result leading to any real impact on Catholic schooling locally.

We have been running the programme at Brighton for eight years; around 225 students have so far started on the programme. As a secular university we may seem like strange bedfellows for the Roman Catholic Church, but the partnership has worked remarkably well since each half brings something to the relationship which the other side cannot offer. With no remaining Catholic institute of higher education[1] south of London, the University of Brighton offers a contact with higher education which has given the course a high degree of objectivity and a thorough understanding of the academic health process necessary for good quality assurance. By utilising the university's part-time student funding

---

[1] Excluding St John's Seminary at Wonersh which cannot award British university degrees in its own right.

from HEFCE we escape the funding issues which seem to exist for other diocesan centres, since the course is properly funded and lecturers are contracted and paid by the university. The contact with the diocese has helped the university too, both by adding a valuable extra dimension to its part-time provision which has led to a revival of interest in religious studies within the university and by offering a productive route to meeting its aim of widening participation. Many of the catechists who come on the programme have few formal academic qualifications, if any, yet some are now enrolled on a part-time degree route designed especially to offer progression from the Diploma in Religious Education.

So what's the problem?

This, then, sounds like a real success story, yet in terms of meeting the needs of local Catholic schools, the picture is more complex. I want to argue in this chapter both for the necessity of teachers in the Catholic sector having opportunities for continuing professional development related to the nature of Catholic education, and for a need for a reconsideration of how best this can be provided and viewed as valuable by teachers. To do this I will consider the nature of and need for lifelong professional learning and the difficulties around encouraging teachers to share our view that such learning is essential. But first, what are the factors leading to my unease?

I need to start by affirming my belief that for many of our students the experience of studying at Brighton has indeed been life-changing. As a former course leader and tutor on the programme I have witnessed this regularly both in student journals and in discussion as well as in watching students as they set out with renewed enthusiasm and increased knowledge to work in their parishes and deaneries. This is not to suggest that the process is a smooth and easy one. For many students the course asks for an element of reshaping of personal beliefs and schemata through its exploration of such matters as scriptural study and Church doctrine. As we warn students at interview, the experience of studying one's own belief systems can be disturbing and even disorienting. It can happen that students on the course discover that what they believe is not necessarily paralleled by current church doctrine and that they then have to do some hard thinking to reconsider their faith in the light of new knowledge. Indeed, this is one reason for the journals, which offer a space where such exploration and reflection can happen throughout the two years of the course. For many students, as the external examiner discovered, the experience is truly formative and leads to a much greater depth of understanding and a renewed and more mature faith life-changing indeed.

In terms of change then leading to changes in schools, though, there is a problem related to recruitment patterns. It is sadly the case that although our original aim was to recruit around 50% of each intake from the teaching profession, this is a target we have rarely met, and even some of those who are teachers who come on the course are drawn to it because they are also parish catechists and feel the need for support in this role. So although we may be changing lives, we are not always changing schools in the way we had hoped. This failure to convince teachers to enrol, despite diocesan figures which suggest many teachers in local Catholic schools do not have either the older Catholic Teachers' Certificate or the CCRS, constitutes one of the threads leading to my concerns.

Another anxiety, as hinted above, comes from a concern that the particular model at Brighton might have something to do with the quality of the provision. I have already said that the CCRS is embedded within a diploma structure at Brighton. The six core and a range of approved professional modules of the CCRS (including some designed specifically for teachers) are taught in line with the national pattern in terms of taught hours and assignment length, with no academic requirements for entry; instead, all applicants are interviewed to ensure they understand what they are taking on and to enable us to judge their readiness for both the academic aspects of the course and for the possible disruption to their world view. The diploma elements are wrapped around the CCRS modules to offer what we perceive to be complementary experiences. These include some support for students in study skills and some optional liturgical and pastoral experiences, but in academic terms the most important element is the action learning set which runs throughout each year. Action learning will be discussed more fully below but in brief this means that each student is in a small group of around six people who meet regularly (about once a month) to discuss how they are making sense of the course and what impact it is having on their professional or voluntary roles. These action learning sets are assessed by means of the response journals mentioned above, which can be most easily described as a two-way written conversation between the student and the action set facilitator. The action sets run throughout the two years of the course and offer an opportunity for reflection and synthesis of the separate CCRS modules which seems to us to be essential if students are to gain the maximum benefit from this programme. As one student said of her journal,

> The journal was crucial for me. I don't think I would have been able to stay with the course without the encouragement I had from [tutor's name] through the journal. When I felt stupid, ignorant, incapable, doubtful, misunderstood and misunderstanding, she was there, standing beside me. When I needed a push she gave it, when I needed to look at another aspect of a thing she pointed me in the right direction, when I wanted to give up she gave me inspiration.[2]

Much of the process of change, then, is made explicit through the discussions in journals and action sets, and one point I shall be making below is that the articulation of tacit knowledge and understanding is a key element in effective professional lifelong learning. Without such opportunities as these, there is a question as to how effective the CCRS alone would be for our students.

So on the one hand there is an issue related to the limited enthusiasm displayed by teachers for undertaking this qualification, and on the other a question about the current shape of the CCRS and its potential for offering really worthwhile professional development opportunities. Each of these will be examined below, but first it is important to consider why teachers in Catholic schools need continuing professional development related to the particular nature of Catholic education.

The Nature of the Catholic School

Other chapters in this book explore in more depth the particular nature of the Catholic school. Key issues which emerge from such discussions tend to stress the ethos of the school as a Christian community which nurtures both learning and faith development. Sullivan[3] has presented five potential models of school, rejecting models based on family, business, church, and political community in favour of academy, which he defines as 'an ordered and hospitable space for learning'. What would distinguish a Catholic school from its secular equivalent might thus be the ordering of

---

[2] Quoted from a student interview carried out as part of research into the programme in 1994.
[3] Sullivan, J., *Catholic Schools in Contention* (Dublin, Veritas Publications, 2000).

the space, the nature of the hospitality and the range of learning. Within the ordered space one might expect to find symbols which present the outward and visible signs of the Catholic faith, but also evidence of Gospel values; such values would also inform both the hospitality and the learning both within and beyond the formal curriculum.

Obviously this series of assertions could be debated at greater length, but since that debate is happening elsewhere in this volume I want to ask what such a model might imply about the teachers required by Catholic schools. Archbishop Vincent Nichols recently spoke of the Catholic school as a '"catechetical community" with responsibility for living and sharing faith'.[4] It has long been acknowledged, too, that teachers need explicit preparation for their role in this catechetical community:

> But let teachers recognize that the Catholic school depends upon them almost entirely for the accomplishment of its goals and programs. They should therefore be very carefully prepared so that both in secular and religious knowledge they are equipped with suitable qualifications and also with a pedagogical skill that is in keeping with the findings of the contemporary world.[5]

This model of a body of teachers able to draw on sound religious knowledge and understanding reappears in more recent statements such as this view from the Congregation for Catholic Education:

> It is from its Catholic identity that the school derives its original characteristics and its 'structure' as a genuine instrument of the Church, a place of real and specific pastoral ministry. The Catholic school participates in the evangelising mission of the Church and is the privileged environment in which Christian education is carried out.[6]

It is important to be clear that these views do not relate solely to formal religious education sessions. There is a clear emphasis on the need for all teachers to share in this pastoral and catechetical

---

[4] Archbishop Vincent Nichols, Address to the Catholic Association of Schools and Colleges, Harrogate, 4 March 2000 (available at http://www.tasc.ac.uk/cc/CN/00/00306c.htm).

[5] *Declaration on Christian Education: Gravissimum Educationis*, Vatican Council II, Oct 1965, section 8.

[6] *The Catholic School on the Threshold of the Third Millennium*, Congregation for Catholic Education, April 1998, Para. 11.

ministry if school life as a whole is to offer this 'privileged environment'. This means that ideally every teacher in a Catholic school needs a clear understanding of the belief systems of Catholicism and a well-developed awareness of their own stance in relation to these belief systems. If, as Louise Moore argues, 'it is important for teachers [in a Catholic school] themselves to be models of Christian thought and action',[7] there are implications for both pre-service and in-service education for teachers.

This is particularly so since for a variety of reasons it cannot be assumed that all those teaching in Catholic schools in the UK already have sufficient grounding in the Catholic faith. The increasing laicisation of the teaching force has played a part here, as has the increasing need to employ non-Catholics to ensure an adequate staffing base in most Catholic schools.[8] In addition those Catholics who are teaching in the Catholic sector are increasingly unlikely to have trained at Catholic colleges of higher education after the series of closure and amalgamations and are thus likely to have had little chance to take the CCRS as students; those who follow a PGCE route cannot complete the two years of the CCRS during their one-year course. It is worth bearing in mind, too, that the vast majority of teachers in schools today have been educated since the Second Vatican Council. One reason for the introduction of the CCRS in England was an awareness by Roman Catholic authorities of a gap in the knowledge base of current Church members, born of the swing from a traditional catechism-based approach of rote learning to a post-Vatican II emphasis on personal experience and faith journeys often not rooted in any connection to theology. Thus even those who have attended Catholic churches and schools throughout their lives may begin initial teacher education with little explicit understanding of their faith.

If, then, the nature of the Catholic school is so dependent upon the ability of those working in the school to carry out their pastoral and catechetical ministry in every aspect of their working lives, and if a significant number of them are not ready to do so when taking

---

[7] Moore, L., 'Staff Development in the Catholic School', in T. Hunt, T. Oldenski and T. Wallace (eds), *Catholic School Leadership: An Invitation to Lead* (London, Falmer, 2000, p. 96).

[8] For research evidence on the difficulties in appointing Catholic teachers see O'Keefe, J. and O'Keeffe, B., 'Directions for Research in Catholic Education in the USA and the UK', in T. McLaughlin, J. O'Keefe and B. O'Keeffe (eds), *The Contemporary Catholic School: Context, Identity and Diversity* (London, Falmer, 1996, pp. 300–302).

up their posts, there is a clear need both for initial teacher education to offer those wishing to work in the Catholic sector adequate
preparation and for in-service opportunities for both Catholics and
others working in Catholic schools. The CCRS was set up in recognition of that and it is one of the reasons why we at Brighton are
also involved in this enterprise. But given what we know about
adult learning and the ways in which continuing professional
development can contribute to this, is the CCRS the right answer,
or even one right answer among many possibilities? To begin to
answer this question I need to turn to explore what we know about
lifelong professional learning and how we apply this knowledge at
Brighton.

Continuing Professional Development: the nature of adult learning

This is not the place to debate at great length all the existing learning theories, a task ably fulfilled in many other places,[9] but I do
need to identify some of the key themes which we regard as central
to our work at Brighton and which have contributed to the success
of our courses.

Paulo Freire's work has become a significant model for many
adult education programmes. In brief, he argued against what he
called the 'banking' model of study, where students are treated as
empty deposit accounts to be filled up with deposits of knowledge
selected for them by others, and in favour of conscientization, a
process whereby the learners themselves identify what they need to
know in order to become more in control of their world.[10] This
view has been highly influential at Brighton, where we work to
ensure a close fit between the needs articulated by those on our
CPD programmes and the content of those programmes. However,
for us conscientization also has to include an awareness of the relevance of professional experience as a source of understanding.
Schön[11] has emphasized how crucial it is to reflect on professional

---

[9] See for example Savage, M., 'Adult Learning and the Churches' and Astley, J.,
'Dimensions of Christian Education', in J. Astley (ed.), *Learning in the Way:
Research and Reflection on Adult Christian Education* (Leominster, Gracewing,
2000).

[10] See for example Freire, P., *Pedagogy of the Oppressed* (Harmondsworth, Penguin,
1972).

[11] Schön, D., *The Reflective Practitioner: How Professionals Think In Action* (New York,
Basic Books, 1983).

practice in a way which will allow growth and development to emerge from that reflection. Coining the notion of the reflective practitioner, he argues that for any professional there is a need to continue to develop by cultivating a habitually reflective stance to practice which continually questions assumptions in the light of new evidence. Such reflection requires an uncovering of tacit knowledge, the knowledge about how to operate in any situation which we have acquired through practice and which we need to make explicit to allow a proper reflection on our understanding.

Such models might imply an emphasis on the learner's prior experience at the expense of other knowledge and an adoption of a Piagetian view of the learner as independently rediscovering the way the world is. Bruner, one of the notable early exponents of this Piagetian approach, has since argued for a more mediated stance[12] which requires intervention by teacher, parent or significant other in the learning process, drawing on Vygotsky's model of learning as apprenticeship.[13] Here existing knowledge from the world interacts with personal experience in a dialectic relationship so that each is adjusted in the light of the other. The individual both shapes and is shaped by society.

Our concern to offer adults continuing professional development which allows interaction between prior experience and new knowledge has led to our use of action learning principles in many of our courses, including the Diploma in Religious Education. Action learning can be traced back to the 1920s, when Revans, the first person to use the term, was a physicist, working with eight Nobel prizewinners at the Cavendish Laboratory in Cambridge. Revans and the others would meet each week to discuss their work and support each other in exploring the difficulties they were having. The learning within action learning has been explained by Revans as '$L=P+Q$'.[14] In this equation, P is programmed knowledge, which Revans calls 'the stuff of traditional instruction',[15] the knowledge that already appears in books on a subject or which would constitute the canon. Q is 'questioning insight', the ability to test programmed knowledge by asking questions which will lead us forward to new lines of enquiry.

In the context of the Diploma in Religious Education, then,

[12] Bruner, J., *Actual Minds, Possible Worlds* (Cambridge, Massachusetts, Harvard University Press, 1986).
[13] Vygotsky, L., *Mind in Society: the Development of Higher Psychological Processes* (Cambridge, Massachusetts, Harvard University Press, 1978).
[14] Revans, R., *The ABC of Action Learning* (Kent, Chartwell-Bratt, 1983).
[15] Ibid.

action learning principles are applied through the action learning sets which offer an explicit opportunity for students to reflect on the programmed knowledge being explored in the core modules and an opportunity to consider how this interacts with their lived professional experience. Although a tutor is present, this person has the role of facilitating and does not offer expert advice on the content of the programme; such discussion and support is contained within the CCRS modules. An action set is not a seminar but a situation where the onus is on each participant to set out their current course of action with regard to the course and to explore difficulties together to generate ways forward. Nor is this a group therapy session or faith-sharing group, and one of the facilitator's roles is to ensure a properly professional approach which avoids too much personal revelation or soul-searching at the expense of reflection on the process of continuing professional development.

So far I have argued that there is a need for continuing professional development for teachers in Catholic schools and that for this to be effective it needs to allow for teachers to reflect on their experience in the light of new knowledge whilst also testing that knowledge against their lived experience. Such a view is supported by Lacey when she argues that:

> Teachers begin the process of creating rather than reproducing culture when they bring their own professional knowledge into articulate form and interpret its meaning with others in a community of inquiry.[16]

Given that this is the case, it is important to consider why it might be that at least in the case of the Brighton programme we have failed to persuade schools and teachers that the CCRS is a worthwhile and important course which would enrich Catholic education and which is needed by all those teaching in the Catholic sector. This might be a local situation reflecting on the provision at Brighton; this might be a more general issue related to the current state of the teaching profession; or it might be that the actuality of the CCRS does not provide an appropriate experience for serving teachers. Each of these possibilities will be examined below before I conclude by suggesting some ways forward.

[16] Lacey, C., 'Renewing Teaching: Building Professional Communities of Hope and Inquiry', in T. McLaughlin, J. O'Keefe and B. O'Keeffe (eds), *The Contemporary Catholic School: Context, Identity and Diversity* (London, Falmer,1996, p. 259).

Issues related to the provision at Brighton

It might be argued that this is a problem unique to Brighton and that it is some weakness in our provision which discourages teachers from enrolling. There may be an element of suspicion among some teachers about the credibility of a course run by a secular university, but since the diocese has been explicitly supportive of the programme in many arenas this seems unlikely. Many of the local Catholic schools know us well through working in partnership with us in initial teacher training and staff from these schools show little reluctance to access other aspects of our in-service provision such as our MA Ed. The CCRS modules are taught by well-known local experts and the programme is run by a member of staff of the university who is a respected figure in the diocese and deanery. Credibility thus seems an unlikely reason for the reluctance of teachers to enrol for the programme, especially since the teachers who do enrol value the experience.

There could be an issue related to publicity. Is the course suffering from a lack of awareness on the part of schools and governors? Again this seems unlikely. Not only do schools regularly receive specific publicity about our provision, but the programme leader has also spent a significant amount of time visiting heads of the local Catholic schools to discuss the programme and its relevance for all teachers in the Catholic sector. The diocesan advisory staff have a long-standing connection with the programme and teach on it where appropriate. The course is also regularly advertized in parish newsletters (with good response from catechists and other parish workers). Again, then, ignorance of the existence of the programme seems an unlikely cause of the low numbers of teachers enrolling.

Some might suggest that because the CCRS at Brighton is wrapped up in the Diploma in Religious Education this might be a deterrent. I shall discuss the level of the CCRS below and show why it may be that this itself is a problem, but in terms of the Brighton model it needs to be borne in mind that the extra elements required for the Diploma are both concurrent and optional. It takes no longer to complete the Diploma than to study for the CCRS anywhere else. If the Diploma were truly an inhibiting factor one might expect this to affect recruitment across all groups, yet the overall recruitment is strong and this is a programme which regularly meets its targets more easily than other aspects of our provision.

Obviously we need to reflect carefully and regularly on the nature of provision at Brighton and to be ready to adjust what we do to meet needs more effectively; our whole philosophy of continuing professional development depends on this. But it does seem as though there may be other factors operating to dissuade teachers from taking on the CCRS which also need to be taken into account.

Teachers and Continuing Professional Development

My role at Brighton takes me regularly to meetings with colleagues from other institutions and the issue of declining recruitment for all continuing professional development programmes for teachers is often raised. Nationally recent reforms and changes in the education structure seem to have resulted in a reluctance by teachers to take on any form of continuing professional development and a national consultation by the government is looking at ways to reform provision. Courses which continue to attract teachers include those with a specific focus on new initiatives such as the national numeracy and literacy strategies and those which are seen as necessary for promotion such as masters programmes. Our own needs analysis work reveals that many teachers feel undervalued and overworked at present and so are reluctant to take on extra commitments outside school time, especially where there is little financial support from schools to pay fees and little chance of any extra free time in school to support study. To hard-pressed teachers already in post, the CCRS may well be a very low priority, and all the time that governors neither require it from applicants nor require teachers to take the course after appointment this situation is unlikely to change.[17]

One reason why the CCRS might be so particularly vulnerable to this situation derives from its status as an entry level course (a concept which in itself has yet to be articulated clearly and which is interpreted differently in different regions as a result). We have taken this to mean HE level 1. Increasingly teaching is becoming a graduate profession; even those who did start teaching without a degree have often already increased their qualification level by taking either a part-time in-service BEd or Open University degree.

[17] Recent moves by the diocese have increased the pressure on governors to ensure that all those appointed to senior posts either have or enrol for the CCRS; however, this has resulted in some less than enthusiastic students arriving feeling compelled to take what they see as a low level course.

Even the Cert Ed qualified teachers could hardly see the CCRS as a hierarchical progression since the Cert Ed is also rated as a Level 1 course. For any teacher, then to register for the CCRS is a sideways move. It will give breadth but not an advanced level of qualification.

Of itself this should not be a dissuading factor, but our experience over the past few years has been that although our other non-postgraduate courses do attract teachers, these teachers often come to the course for its practical benefit but do not want the credit from it and thus are reluctant to complete the assessment element of the programme. The courses which they choose are almost always relatively short (one term or less) and very focused (for example, we run popular Level 2 programmes on such topics as behaviour management and the numeracy and literacy strategies).

As a result, we have recognized that two-year diploma level courses are not in general attractive to teachers and have discontinued other diploma-level awards for teachers. Where teachers are prepared to commit to a longer programme, they are more likely to be drawn to the masters level awards. Our MA Ed is fairly typical nationally in being a two-year part-time award, or in other words the same length as the CCRS. Teachers looking for career development and promotion are very likely to reason that a masters degree is a more universally recognised advantage on an application form than the CCRS and, if both take the same amount of time, the MA Ed is likely to be more appealing. At a time when pressures on teachers are perceived to be so great it is hardly surprising that such decisions are made, particularly in the southeast region where teachers are relatively likely to stay in post for some time and where Catholic schools are finding it increasingly difficult to attract good Catholic candidates to vacancies, particularly at a senior level.

Possible deterrent factors within the current CCRS

One issue which may limit recruitment, then, stems in part from the decision to develop the CCRS as a course which can be accessed by a wide range of people:

> Any person who is or wishes to be involved in Catholic education and formation may apply for this course. This includes those involved in Religious Education in schools, Parish catechesis and

other ministries in the Church and anyone who wishes to follow the
course for faith development or personal interest.[18]

In many ways this is a strength of the CCRS and we have found
great benefits at Brighton from the different insights brought by
those with different roles. Teachers and catechists are equally
likely in our experience to be starting from a point where they may
need an entry level encounter with existing knowledge and to
bring a wealth of personal experience to bear on this knowledge.
However, the lack of any higher level award and the lack of a more
precise audit of existing strengths and needs at entry may well be a
deterrent factor for teachers, who may not recognize that the
CCRS is at an appropriate level for them as a result.

Another issue is the legacy of former programmes. Whatever the
truth of the public image of the old Catholic Teachers' Certificate,
there are many teachers who claim to have been given this at college
almost as a matter of course ('with the cornflakes'). This can either
lead to those who do not have the older qualification assuming the
CCRS is an equally soft option and therefore not worth the effort, or
to their being reluctant to have to study seriously to acquire what
their colleagues seem to have collected almost automatically. And
of course this may also be one factor in the reluctance of governing
bodies to require the CCRS either at appointment or as a condition
of appointment, especially as it becomes harder for schools to
appoint Catholic teachers with or without the CCRS. This will take
time to change, and will ultimately rely upon a critical mass of teachers with the CCRS who can witness for its value.

The last and most difficult issue which may inhibit teacher
recruitment is the actual structure of the programme, which may
well be a deterrent to those teachers who enquire but do not apply.
First, there seems to be a mismatch between the aims of the
programme and its syllabus and structure. In particular, the
emphasis on a 'banking' or transmission model displayed in the
learning outcomes and syllabus outlines for each CCRS module is
out of step with the more general aims and the prescribed learning
process. Not only is there a conflict of pedagogy, the limit of ten
hours per module to cover transmission of knowledge, discussion
and reflection on the relationship between such knowledge and
the students' experience can only result in a superficiality of
approach and limited time for discussion.

---

[18] CCRS Course Handbook, Bishops' Conference of England and Wales Board of
Religious Studies, 1996.

The tensions over content and time also work against the principles for good adult learning set out earlier. As already mentioned, there is no opportunity for students to start by auditing their existing knowledge and experience and then develop a programme of study which will address specific needs; there is little opportunity to relate theory and experience and thus explore tacit knowledge; there is no time to become a reflective practitioner; and the CCRS (as opposed to the Brighton diploma) offers limited opportunities for action learning so that Q can work on P, especially given that CCRS students may not have any current professional or voluntary teaching or formation role or any experience of such a role to bring to the situation.

The choice of core modules may also be a part of the problem. The CCRS offers what appears to be a watered-down version of the seminary syllabus, with some surprising gaps. In a time when the secular national curriculum for schools stresses the importance of children's spiritual development,[19] it seems odd to find no required module on spirituality; it is certainly much requested by students who are baffled by its exclusion. It is equally surprising that there is no core module addressing systematic theology more generally, given the kinds of questions which would seem to arise naturally in many Religious Education or formation situations. This is in contrast with other current approaches to adult education within the Christian Church:

> I shall begin this search for a theology by trying to articulate the theological premises implicit in my own involvement in adult learning. At the heart of this articulation is a sense of Christian adult education ... as 'faith seeking understanding' – as itself a kind of doing theology.[20]

Although individual modules may address some theological issues there is no cohesive synthesis of this idea in the CCRS. The lack of attention to other world religions is another limiting factor when we consider the needs of teachers in Catholic schools today. It is possible that some of the teachers who initially express interest in

[19] 'Foremost is a belief in education, at home and at school, as a route to the spiritual, moral, social, cultural, physical and mental development, and thus the well-being, of the individual.' From the general introduction to the values and purposes underpinning the school curriculum, as set out on the national curriculum website (http://www.nc.uk.net/about/values_aims_purposes.html).

[20] Watkins, C., 'A Christian theology of models of education', in I. Cundy et al., *Tomorrow Is Another Country: Education In A Post-Modern World* (London, Church House Publishing, 1996, p.39).

the course perceive the content as too far from their own needs and experiences to be relevant and I return to this in my suggested ways forward.

Ways forward

The reluctance of teachers in Arundel and Brighton to undertake the CCRS may then stem from a range of factors, including some local issues but more particularly related both to the current realities of classroom life and to views of the CCRS as non-essential and possibly inadequate. Given the importance for Catholic education of ensuring a well-educated teaching force, and given the limitations of the current model in providing genuine opportunities for high quality staff development for teachers, what can be done? In this concluding section I offer some suggestions for ways forward.

First, it would seem timely to review the current structure of the CCRS and to reconsider how best it can be reshaped to provide a better fit with the needs of all those for whom it is designed. Although there are undoubted attractions in the principle of an inclusive course which brings together pre-service and in-service teachers and parish catechists, it may be that the losses entailed in such a universality are too great to be balanced out by the gains. In particular, I would suggest that the needs of those who are not yet engaged in teaching or parish catechesis are very different from those of serving teachers and experienced parish workers. The emphasis on a transmission model displayed in the learning outcomes and syllabus outlines for each CCRS module could also usefully be reconfigured to allow more space for the learner's experience to be an explicitly recognized part of the learning situation. We need to consider a more flexible approach which might include more precise needs analysis, extra time for discussion, different level outcomes, and more emphasis on applied knowledge for those actively involved in teaching and formation.

At the same time, we need to find ways to make it desirable for teachers to prioritize the CCRS or its successor, and to help governors and senior management understand the importance of continuing professional development in this area for all staff whatever their subject background. This would entail considerable work by the Board of Religious Studies and by the diocesan centres and Catholic colleges, but seems an essential step if serving teachers are to become more aware of the need for and benefits of this kind of professional development. One factor here which may need further thought is that of accreditation. All the time that the CCRS sits outside both FE and HE structures it lacks a currency for those within the education sector and a clarity of focus, and it is good to hear of recent discussions about such issues. Diocese and schools need to consider a package of incentives such as some release of time for study, fees being paid in part or full, books bought, and opportunities provided to feed back to colleagues and develop school-based in-service for colleagues to share experiences and knowledge from the programme.

Finally, if this is truly to be continuing professional development, which entails lifelong learning, it is not enough to see the CCRS as a one-off finite event which once completed will be sufficient for all time. There is a need for a much more flexible programme of renewal, with other short courses and study opportunities (including action learning and school-based research) and with a hierarchy of awards beyond the CCRS at least as far as masters level. It needs to be a normal part of every Catholic school's development plan to include in-service for all staff in this central area which links with award-bearing work and which values the achievement of colleagues who undertake such awards and the contribution they can then make to school-based professional development.

Conclusion

I began this chapter by asking whether the changed lives at Brighton are leading to changed schools. For those teachers who do undertake the Diploma in Religious Education, I would argue that the answer is yes. However, the reasons for this may in part be to do with the action learning dimension in the Diploma, and the scale of change is limited by the low numbers of teachers on the programme. There is a real need for this work to continue, but I suspect that without a reconsideration of the kind suggested above this will not happen at Brighton. If we are to encourage more teachers onto the programme here and elsewhere then the way in which we seek to change lives and thus schools must itself be changed.

Chapter 10

Educating to Challenge:
Discovering the Alternatives

Moyra J. Healy

The history behind the thinking.

'I have come that they may have life, and have it in all its fullness.'[1]

Our chaplain uses these words at the end-of-placement Mass we hold to celebrate the success of ten pupils who have emotional and behavioural difficulties. They will have just completed a four-week course designed to help them to make the right choices in their lives, so that they can return to their own schools successfully.

The Zacchaeus Centre opened for its first group in October 1995. It is the first Catholic Behaviour Support Centre in the country and the first centre designed exclusively to be inclusive. In other words, it was planned as a preventative measure rather than along the lines of the Pupil Referral Units (PRUs), whose main role is to manage pupils who have already been permanently excluded from their mainstream schools. It has been designed in order to reduce the number of permanent exclusions in Catholic schools in Birmingham, which, at the time, reflected the then growing trend across all schools in Britain. Its name was chosen because Zacchaeus,[2] though rich in material wealth (as indeed are many of our children), was spiritually poor, and only when he had been forgiven by Jesus, was he able to reform and change.

In order for us to understand how this centre differs from the PRUs, let us look first of all at the historical role and function of the latter.

[1] John 10.10.
[2] The rich man mentioned in Luke19.1–10.

Pupil Referral Units were set up in order to ensure that the Education Act of 1944 was fulfilled. This Act of Parliament states that: 'under Section 36 of the Education Act of 1944 parents of children of compulsory school age (5–16) are required to ensure that they receive a suitable education by regular attendance at school or otherwise. Failure to comply with this duty can lead to prosecution. By law schools are required to take attendance registers twice a day. This is done at the beginning of the morning and afternoon sessions.... Local education authorities (LEAs) are responsible in law for making sure that pupils attend school'[3] (in 1973 the school leaving age was raised to the age of 16, introducing the infamous 'ROSLA'[4] year).

When a pupil displays serious anti-social behaviour, a school may be forced, in order to protect other pupils and/or the staff, into permanently excluding a pupil. No school uses permanent exclusion lightly – in fact it is one of the hardest decisions a head teacher has to make. If that exclusion is upheld, after the statutory appeals have taken place, the local education authority is obliged to provide a minimum educational provision and the pupil is sent to the local PRU.

In the past, the child was placed at the unit into a small group of usually no more than eight pupils. Since PRUs are open-ended, the group might change from week to week, with some children moving on and others joining, so each child would be given individual work to do. Teachers in the PRUs were under tremendous pressure. Not only were they expected to bring their pupils' behaviour up to a satisfactory standard so that a new school could be approached to give the pupil a second chance, but they were also expected to support pupils once they had moved into that new school, and often were also called upon to try to support pupils who were seen by the home school to be on their way towards permanent exclusion.

There were too few teachers and too few PRUs and too many pupils being excluded – with the numbers increasing each year. Many PRUs resolved the problem in the only way they could manage and that was to reduce the amount of time each pupil had at the unit, staggering the day so that pupils came and went at various times. As one group left, another came in to take its place.

---

[3] D/EE *Education Act 1944*.

[4] ROSLA was the acronym for Raising of the School Leaving Age. Many new initiatives were introduced at this time, some, admittedly, as panic measures to provide some kind of alternative education for pupils who had previously left school before the public examination year.

This was seen as useful for two reasons. Firstly, it meant the maximum use of teacher time with the maximum number of pupils and secondly, it meant that the real recidivists could not 'infect' those who were not too far down the road towards anti-social behaviour.

Although there was a common policy to have PRUs across the country, each LEA set them up in its own way. Some were excellent, others far from being so.

The attitudes of many people both within and outwith the Education Service were negative. Unwittingly, people saw these pupils as failures – as indeed they did themselves. There was a strong feeling that such pupils needed to be punished further for what they had done to cause their exclusion. Some even saw them as uneducable, so made little effort to do so. Conversely, teachers who worked in units often felt marginalized and, like their pupils, had low self-worth. There was an attitude that seemed to be saying 'Put rubbish kids with rubbish teachers and keep them out of the fold – it's not our problem if we can't see what's happening.' Thus (at its worst), teachers who felt rejected might say to the school 'failures', 'Never mind, everyone else is rejecting you, but we won't. There's where you can play pool, that's where you can smoke your cigarettes, and don't worry, we won't make you do what everyone else wants you to do.' And so the image of rough centres with rough pupils came into being.

Realistically, very few were in this mould. Most teachers tried very hard to work positively with their pupils, but the success rates were still low. Mainstream schools, understandably, did not want to take on too many excluded pupils since knowledge that they had would affect the reputation of the school. Parents might well remove their children from the school until it gradually became a 'sink' school.

The situation was based on crisis management. Multi-agency approaches were rare, and many pupils voted with their feet and refused to attend the units. Educational Welfare Officers would visit homes and find the family had fled or the pupil had done so with parents unaware of where they had gone. We had a whole sub-group of the disappeared in our society. It was unsatisfactory and we could see that later our prisons were being filled with people who had failed at school and at their education.

Too many children have become part of the 'lost generation', disappearing from school rolls, and appearing later as part of the criminal statistics. This costs the state a great deal of money, so anything that stops this from happening has got to be good.

There are many factors that cause a child to be permanently excluded from school. It would be naive to blame one element. Poverty in all its forms, lack of parenting skills, the breakdown of family life, the rush of life in our technological world contribute, but so do constraints in the national curriculum, league tables, and the fear of schools closing because of a 'bad' reputation. Competition has meant that the very children who would benefit most from a broad education, leading them out into the light of knowledge, are losing out. They have been marginalized; their needs often pushed under the carpet.

In 1988 the ten Catholic secondary schools in the city of Birmingham set up a partnership, whereby staffs meet regularly sharing expertise and experience. More recently, the feeder Catholic primary schools set one up too.

Some years after its inception, the Secondary Partnership recognized a singular gap in its educational provision. Children recognized as having emotional and behavioural difficulties were not being catered for within the Catholic ethos.

How could we hold our heads up high if we continued in this vein? Jesus came to call those on the margins of society. He spent time with ordinary people, many of whom made errors and sinned against God and humankind. We are all made in the image and likeness of the Father who loves us as we are. By permanently excluding pupils with challenging behaviour was the message they were receiving 'I am not good enough to stay in a Catholic school'? Might we not have been accused of failing to fulfil the inclusivity of Jesus' Gospel teaching?

It was decided, therefore, to open a Behaviour Support Centre of our own, in which we would be able to maintain that certain uniqueness which is true of most Catholic schools. Difficult to identify and even more so to write about, there is something which is special about the Catholic system. Is it the feeling that we are all one family? Is it that we are more aware of the spirituality inherent in each one of us? Is it (more likely), that we allow each other to be spiritual and encourage everyone to be open about our need to express love in its true meaning, as taught by Jesus Christ?

In order to help my training, I was seconded to one of the city's Behaviour Support Centres, the Bridge Centre, part of Birmingham's PRU. I worked with a number of superb teachers and under the leadership of an inspirational Head of Centre. Whilst there, I was able to see how stretched the staff was in its efforts to do everything it could for pupils who had often completely lost heart, because they felt rejected as failures once they had been permanently excluded. I also learnt many skills there to help support all pupils.

I have always found that children, especially those written off by the great majority, have a deep inner awareness. They are often harder on themselves than everyone else. They believe that life is an all or nothing affair, one is either perfect or one is a walking disaster. There are no shades of grey and no allowance for even the smallest failure or weakness can be tolerated. They also believe everyone else thinks this way. That is why they are so hard on other people. It is almost as if they think they missed out on the 'behaviour lesson' everyone else learnt when they were two years old. Once we convince ourselves that we cannot do something, it will take someone with a very strong will to change our thinking. If I am ferociously angry with someone, it will do me no good to hear the words 'Just ignore it'. That will only make things worse, and yet we say it to children who have no inner resources to cope. Their negativity rubs off on us. We allow them to suck us into the state of treating them the way they have always been treated, so that they can say 'I knew I was no good, I told you so!' Children with behavioural difficulties have to live with themselves for twenty-four hours a day – we only have to live with them for six. We need to hear what they are saying to us. It is very difficult in the 'busyness' of mainstream schools to devote the time required to listen actively, but that is part of the solution to the problems we are facing.

If we are to be truly inclusive there is a huge leap we must take. We must learn to accept that it is not the child but the behaviour that is wrong. There is no point in endlessly punishing children with behavioural difficulties. 'Sin-bins' have never and will never resolve the issues. Only education can do that.

Zacchaeus Centre's beginnings

In 1995 the parish priest of a central inner-city parish offered accommodation to the Zacchaeus project. In the September of that year my colleague John Manion and I met to prepare and plan the centre for its opening. It is perfect for our needs and central for the pupils who travel from all quarters of our city. It consists of a large 'L' shaped room, warm in winter and cool in summer, a bright and airy space where no one can hide and where we all feel safe.

We had a bare canvas on which to work, and the planning stages were exciting. Who were to be helped, how were they to be helped, what would our criteria for referral be and how was it to be run?

It seemed most appropriate to assist pupils who were not yet at the end of the road for exclusion, but whom teachers, within their professional remit, knew were well on the way. Realizing that experts recognized that once pupils have been permanently excluded it is very difficult to help them back to the solid ground of a mainstream education, we decided the preventative approach would be best. To use a rather simplistic analogy – if I am suffering from a bacterial infection, it is better that I am treated early rather than wait until it has overwhelmed my system and I find I am at death's door. It may well be in such circumstances that the skill of the doctor, the efficacy of the medication and my own body's resources all help me to recover, but this is not guaranteed. Early intervention is much more likely to effect the cure.

Pupils who have emotional and behavioural difficulties (EBD), demand the attention they crave. They may display inappropriate behaviour toward both adults and peers; they may seem rude, vulgar and domineering. They may be classified as bullies and have a record for fighting, or have a poor punctuality and attendance record, linked to challenging behaviour. They may appear to be very anti-authority or have switched-off from school. Most will be under-achieving. There could be difficulties outside the classroom, at breaktimes and lunchtimes, when discipline is freer. At the other end of the scale they may be school-refusers, the bullied, the lonely – the children instinctively rejected by others because they don't fit in.

We limited our places to pupils in Years 7, 8 and 9, at Key Stage Three. Once up and running, it was hoped that pupils in Years 10 and 11, at Key Stage Four, would no longer need us. The developmental gap between an 11-year-old pupil and a 16-year-old one is much greater than that between an 11-year-old and a 14-year-old. We were intending to teach the pupils together in class and felt that trying to be all things to everyone would be a recipe for disaster. After five years experience, we are still comfortable with that assumption. That is not to say that the process would not work at Key Stage Four – it would translate very well, and indeed some of the Transactional Analysis lessons could be done in greater depth and be understood at a deeper level by more mature students. There is also a strong argument for providing something similar for younger pupils at Key Stage Two or even Key Stage One.

The Programme

The Centre runs a five-week cycle. The first week is set aside for Centre staff to interview the pupils designated for the following cycle, with the parent/carer. Each school is sent a calendar and various programmes relating to the Centre at the start of each academic year. The school has the responsibility for setting up the interview at the stated time with the parent and pupil. Pupils come to us for a four-week block and each school may take one placement in each cycle, thus we have a maximum of ten pupils at any one time and each school can send seven pupils each academic year.

Schools prioritize which pupils they want us to work with. We have a very close relationship with our mainstream colleagues and feel that we should be of service to them, hence our only criteria for referral are:

- pupils should be on roll
- pupils must be at Key Stage Three
- pupils will be at risk of permanent exclusion.

We interview in the home school so that pupils and parents will see that we are members of the school's staff offering a specialist course in behaviour management. The only difference for the pupil is that the classes take place in a classroom 'down the road' in the City Centre.

The course is a definitive 'closed-end' programme. It is much more effective for being so. There is a precise beginning, middle and end. The programme is planned with exact objectives, and the group dynamics can be determined and engineered to provide the most favourable conditions for pupils' success.

In general, pupils fall into one of two categories. Either they display reactive behaviour, caused by some traumatic incident in their lives, or they display poor behaviour that has been learnt. In the former situation, the one place the pupils feel that they can express their feelings is at school, since it is somewhere they know and are known and mostly, they feel safe there. Staff and fellow pupils may well be subjected to some fairly difficult and anti-social reactions from them. In the latter case, school will be experiencing almost constant low to middle level disruption from these pupils, which has a negative effect on other pupils and on the ability of the teacher to teach appropriately.

The Centre's aims are simple. These are:

- to practise acceptable classroom behaviour so that it becomes second nature
- to help our charges to discover why they choose to behave inappropriately so frequently when the rest of the class does not
- to give our pupils strategies for managing their behaviour so that they will no longer bear serious consequences for inappropriate responses.

Each day begins with an assembly in our small chapel, a corner of the large classroom specifically designated and recognized as a 'quiet' area. We often include children's personal prayers in these assemblies.

There are four lessons per day, and we disapply pupils from the national curriculum during their stay with us. This is done by the Governing Bodies of our ten feeder schools including a statement in their official documentation to the effect that 'Whilst on a four-week placement at the Zacchaeus Centre, a pupil will be disapplied from the national curriculum.' We include special lessons on behaviour management and also on anger management. We use Circle Time as an effective methodology.

Each pupil has a notice board with name, school and photograph on it. It is theirs to display items of work of which they are especially proud. Every day pupils are issued with a Daily Progress Record, which records grades they have maintained for appropriate behaviour during the day. These they take home for their parents to see and praise.

At the end of the week, the grades are percentaged, and pupils are given a Weekly Progress Record to take home for their parents to sign and return. Grades above 80% earn a Bronze Certificate. Those pupils who have tried exceptionally hard are also awarded a Silver Certificate. All pupils work toward earning a Gold Certificate and a Platinum Progress Award, with which they are honoured at the end of the placement.

In 1999 we were able to appoint a third permanent member of staff. This helped considerably in the smooth running of the Centre and also in liaising with schools. Also appointed at this time was a part-time teacher. There are many other people who work on a voluntary part-time basis: retired teachers, a psychotherapist, and a volunteer from the Human City Institute.[5] We also offer on site

---

[5] A group set up across the whole of Industry and Business in Birmingham whose aim is to make the City more human in its treatment of and dealings with its people.

training to students from Teacher Training Colleges, students on work experience placements, seminarians and novices, youth workers and professional colleagues.

Our latest development is to have a full-time Chaplain. He is a priest in the Religious Congregation of the *Oblates of Mary Immaculate*, and his Provincial Council agreed that the ministry of the Zacchaeus Centre fulfilled the charism of its Order 'to bring the Good News to the poor'.[6] His role is threefold:

- He provides the very necessary link between home, school, the Church and the Centre.
- He celebrates Mass; in particular the 'graduation' Mass at the end of each cycle and any other liturgies and assemblies as appropriate.
- He shows our pupils that the Church, in its official capacity, welcomes them as members of its family and wants them to feel included.

At all times we are positive with our charges. We have a simple 'Code of Conduct' which when obeyed, brings the reward of maintaining their grades which leads to the weekly certificates. There are consequences for breaking the code, but they are not harsh. They consist of the pupil losing a grade if he or she wilfully chooses to continue with the inappropriate behaviour after being formally warned.

We tell each pupil before they come to the Centre that their teachers have especially selected them because the school knows they can make a success of it. We constantly praise our children – all have a low sense of self-worth. They may have the feeling that the world has given up on them and so they give up on themselves. Pupils are taught that only they can change themselves – we merely show them the way. We tell them they are worth it. We remind them of the love of God as manifested by Jesus Christ and that they are never alone.

We talk, we listen, we support. At all times we find the good side to praise, rather than the negative to condemn. We negotiate targets with the pupils that they will set themselves to achieve on return to the home school, which can form the basis of an Individual Behaviour Plan. These are done in a one-to-one interview in order to protect each pupil's privacy and dignity. We negotiate with the school what it can put in place for the pupil –

---

[6] Luke 4.18.

this could be along the lines of moving a pupil from one set to another or arranging for the pupil to be given a mentor who will be a mediator and supporter. We laugh a lot. We develop a secure, safe and loving environment, an incubator for pupils' embryonic self-esteem.

At the end of the four-week cycle, we celebrate with a Mass. This acts as a sort of graduation ceremony, a rite of passage, whereby pupils know they have achieved their worth. Parents, teachers and friends are invited to share their success, and for many parents it is an emotional occasion. It may well be the first time in a long time that they have been invited to school to celebrate something worthy. The children are proud too, to show what they have achieved. During the Mass, they are presented with the certificates they have earned, and a few words are said about each child.

On the Monday after, pupils return to their home school to be welcomed by a senior member of staff in a specially arranged reintegration interview. They receive weekly in-school support from one of the Centre's staff. Most important, they know that any mistakes they may have made in the past have been forgiven. This is their new start, now they can 'have life, and have it in all its fullness'.[7]

Strategies for managing pupils with challenging behaviour

Teaching is a skilled craft. It is not true that anyone can teach and, although some people are incredibly knowledgeable and intelligent, it does not follow that they will have the gift of imparting that knowledge or the gift of encouraging people to learn. In teaching, particularly children with behavioural difficulties, we must forget the 'Mussolini stance' and the 'death stare', the 'don't smile until Christmas' approaches[8] – as they just do not work. In fact they are actively provocative to a damaged pupil. Instead, good teachers develop a positive approach to behaviour management and most pupils respond positively most of the time.

The first factor of which to be aware is that we cannot be in total control of other people's behaviour. They are in control of it and will make choices as to how it will manifest itself. Our pupils' choices will be based on how I, as the teacher, approach them as

[7] Ibid.
[8] These destructive pieces of advice are regularly given to student teachers and teachers at the Newly Qualified Teacher status, by long serving practitioners. Most of us have experienced this in our early years of teaching.

pupils. Therefore I must be in control of myself, aware of my expectations in the classroom, unafraid of what is going to happen in the lesson because I have prepared the content, the class and myself for what is to come. Pupils must feel secure that firstly, I know what I am doing, secondly, that they will be safe, and thirdly that what we are to do is going to be purposeful, relevant and interesting.

Good teachers are benevolent dictators. For instance, they decide when the windows are opened or the lights are switched on. They check that all pupils are ready to begin learning and are equipped to do so. They come prepared to resolve difficulties quickly and effortlessly (e.g. they carry spare pens and pencils with them). They are comfortable in postponing the resolution until later, (e.g. 'I know that you are worried about the pen you have lost, John. I will deal with it later in the lesson, but for now I'd be grateful if you would use this one'), so as not to waste the majority of the pupils' time. Being responsible for small decisions shows children that the teacher cares about the minutiae of the classroom – it gives a subliminal message that everyone will be safe, that they as learners can forget all outside distractions and carry on with the objectives of the lesson. (The good teacher remembers later to solve the problem of the pen!)

Teaching is concerned with rewarding appropriate behaviour, regularly and fairly. All pupils should be getting some rewards every lesson. In the secondary school especially, where pupils have to learn the expectations of at least ten different teachers and switch from one response to another every hour, it is vital to explain clearly when one meets a class for the first time, what is expected from the class and what they can expect. Good teachers set standards as soon as they enter the room by explaining their code of conduct. Achieving appropriate behaviour is active not passive.

All teachers must be sincere – children see through hypocrisy in a matter of minutes. If we are to teach in a Catholic environment it is imperative that we have forgiveness as the norm in our classroom. Forgiveness does not mean 'giving in' and excusing poor behaviour. It means issuing consequences dispassionately, fairly and consistently and then getting on with the rest of the lesson. It means not referring to the incident again, but dealing with every incident individually.

Children should be treated as we want them to be rather than as they actually are. They will live up to our hopes. One of our pupils related an incident where he had been told by a teacher, in a corridor, in front of a great many other people, adults and children alike, that he was 'one of the worst five pupils in the school'. He said he felt very 'disappointed' that he was only 'Number Five' and determined to try to reach 'Number One' as soon as possible. It is very tempting at times to tell children what their faults are, but they do not need to hear them. They know only too well where they are going wrong. What they are unsure about is where they are doing things correctly.

'I just want to teach!' is the cry often heard from teachers experiencing difficulties. Unless the behaviour is taught first, we cannot teach the subject. I cannot expect others to have taught my behavioural standards. Each of us is unique and has personal expectations.

Most schools now have a Code of Conduct. Some are overly detailed and therefore difficult to maintain. If I as the teacher cannot remember it, my pupils will not be able to do so either.

Here is a possible Code of Conduct that could be used either throughout a whole school or by an individual classroom teacher:

Our target is to show respect for others

- by never using 'put-downs'
- by being prepared to begin work promptly
- by listening to the teacher
- by raising our hand to speak
- by avoiding distractions
- by working hard.

Good teachers teach by example. They never use sarcasm, and we, especially in our Catholic environment, should avoid such an easy tool as a management technique. It sends a message that it is okay to put other people down, and yet that one habit probably creates more disharmony and difficulties in schools than any other does.

By concentrating on praise, children learn what teachers find acceptable rather than learning what they find inappropriate, which can be used against them by pupils who have learnt to play the game of 'bait the teacher'. If I say to you, 'Don't think about bananas', what picture immediately comes into your head?

Endeavour should be praised as well as achievement. Good teachers are not mean with rewards. They know they are not devalued by regular use. Keeping rewards simple allows the teacher not to feel harassed by a complicated system, so they will feel happier about issuing them. Having a stack of photocopied 'Congratulations' notes in one's desk to be issued to pupils to take home is easy and achieves a positive feedback.

It is interesting that in our wonderfully expressive language, the word 'just' means both 'fair' and 'only'. As a young teacher I often heard more experienced colleagues stating that a pupil was 'just an attention seeker'. This sent me the message that because the child was 'only' an attention seeker, my best course of action was to ignore her! Let us turn that suggestion around and state that it is 'fair' for that child to be an attention seeker, and is in fact an attention 'needer', and the situation immediately becomes manageable. Giving the disparagingly known 'attention-seekers' attention fixes stops difficulties occurring. Teachers should not judge, they should react as positively as possible in each situation.

Using sanctions sparingly makes sense. Keep them simple, too. A one-minute detention at the end of the lesson works because the child knows you will do it. It will delay them significantly enough to be late for the next class, or last in the tuck or dinner queue.

The better teachers avoid shouting, other than to get attention in the first place. Speaking assertively rather than aggressively, gets the desired response. Reminding pupils that they are choosing to behave in a certain manner can be useful, but so can affirming to the pupil that the teacher understands the difficulty. 'I see that you are finding it hard to concentrate at the moment, Jane, what do you need me to do for you?', can instantly help a pupil put things right.

Speaking to pupils with behavioural difficulties at times when it is not expected shows that you value them as human beings, and they will respond accordingly (e.g. asking after their interests, when passing them on the stairs).

Poor teaching will be a contributory factor in children's poor behaviour, but when a teacher is in control of himself and is well-prepared and a child still misbehaves, then the teacher can reassure himself that the cause has come from elsewhere. Having tried to identify the problem, the teacher may still eventually have to resort to the consequence procedure. Reminding pupils they have a choice and do they really want to bring a sanction on themselves can be very effective. Making them aware that they are responsible for their actions and the consequence is equally effective. Issuing the 'suspended sentence' is often as effective as carrying it out. 'If you choose to behave like that again, you will have forced me to inform your parents about both incidents.' Many pupils see this as a more fair and just way of dealing with them, because it shows the teacher has acknowledged the wrong-doing, but is making allowances for human nature.

The teacher becomes the referee of the code of conduct; behaviour management is therefore depersonalized. Using this system, all children, including the quiet 'middle' group of pupils, are rewarded too. Good schools are consistent, because all teachers give out rewards and sanctions in the same way as each other. Just as loving parents will show a united face to their children, so that the children cannot manipulate them, so should a school set up its behaviour plan similarly. We should never hear, 'Miss so-and-so doesn't make us do that!' in a school.

Most children want to please their teachers, even those children with behavioural problems. They do not always know how to please us, so the trick is to tell them. If teachers are calm, honest, generous and sincere, children will appreciate their efforts and work for them. Gradually, as young people mature, the good teacher will empower pupils to work for themselves. Ruling by fear is not successful. A class of children sitting in petrified silence is not learning, the only skill it learns is how to avoid that teacher's tongue-lashing. Being polite teaches by example, barking orders suits the barrack room not the classroom. If teachers don't nag, pupils won't ignore.

Learning pupils' names as quickly as possible shows a powerful measure of respect and helps teachers to be in control. Saying, 'You, at the back there, you, the one with the dark hair, no, not you, him!' hardly engenders trust. Devising a seating plan makes tons of sense. The teacher can learn the names even more quickly. Pupils don't have to be separated from their friends, as separating them later can be a simple sanction if they can't maintain the teacher's standards.

Teachers should watch out for the manipulators. They are more devious than the boisterous. Their sanction should be more serious than that of the hapless perpetrator.

Children accept that teachers may treat one person differently from another, they are more adult and emotionally can understand more than we give them credit for. They will support the actions of their teacher if the potential situations and their solutions are explained in advance. Apologies when in the wrong put teachers high in pupils' estimation. As soon as possible after delivering a sanction, a good teacher gives the child praise. They are seen as fair. Speaking non-threateningly and being assertive is not a sign of weakness, but of strength. Predictability makes for security; at Zacchaeus Centre, pupils are told each week and then reminded each day of what they can expect.

Using a phrase like 'I need you to. . .' creates a sense of urgency and importance. It is much more effective than 'You must...'. It also strengthens the times when a teacher needs to say, 'No, on this issue I will not compromise, as it would not be good for any of us.' Pupils should know that the teacher has standards that no amount of cajoling, whining or threats can lower. A sense of humour solves many potential difficulties.

Giving pupils a specific time frame in which to complete set pieces of work is good because it is purposeful and then giving warnings when the time is nearly up is helpful. Open-ended tasks are an uphill struggle for pupils with behavioural difficulties, they are too vague and provide opportunities for misbehaviour.

Setting 'quizzes' rather than tests is positive as it makes learning fun, but pupils are still gaining the skills of recall and understanding and how to revise, so that when it becomes really important for them, those skills will be second nature.

One of our 'graduates' left a note for future pupils. It says, 'It is good to be here at Zacchaeus and to be given the chance to start again. They teach you that only you can change yourself, but that you can do it.'

So, what are the alternatives we have discovered in educating to challenge our young people? I believe that good teachers (a phrase I have used a great deal in this chapter), show care, concern and consistency towards their charges. If 'catholic' means universal, then we as Catholic educators have a responsibility towards all our pupils, especially those who may not be receiving appropriate care, concern and consistency elsewhere. If we do not do this, whose responsibility is it? And, most worrying, what will happen in society if we claim that it is not our problem? Teachers are the second most important influence on children after their families, and they do help to shape future society. It is a very serious responsibility indeed. Jesus was known as 'Rabbi' which means 'teacher'. Let us mould our professional conduct in our Catholic schools on Jesus; we can do no better. May God bless all our endeavours.

Chapter 11

Nurture, Commitment and Curriculum

David Hay

> Primary words do not signify things, but they intimate relations.
>
> Martin Buber

Mission Territory

If one of the tasks of Catholic schools is to nurture commitment, then in many cases they appear to have lost their way. According to the UK Christian Handbook for 1999/2000[1] there has been a decline in Mass attendance in mainland Britain over the past twenty years of approximately 35%. Two thirds of that drop has taken place in the last ten years[2] and young people, many of whom have been through a Catholic education, make up a large proportion of those who have lapsed. The point can be made by glancing round at the age structure of the congregation at most Sunday Masses. This is in spite of the popularity and academic success of Catholic schools, and the prayers, energy and money that are poured into maintaining the national system.

Catholic schools in Britain have become mission territory and I suspect the same is true for much of Western Europe. In 1988 the Sacred Congregation for Catholic Education recognized the crisis in its document *The Religious Dimension of Education in a Catholic School:*

[1] Brierley, P. (ed.), *Religious Trends 1999/2000* (Carlisle, Paternoster Publishing, 2000).

[2] Over the same period in Northern Ireland, Mass attendance has increased by almost 4%, suggesting that the social and political factors influencing Church adherence are rather different from those in mainland Britain.

For some of today's youth, the years spent in a Catholic school seem to have scarcely any effect. They seem to have a negative attitude toward all the various ways in which a Christian life is expressed – prayer, participation in the Mass, or the frequenting of the Sacraments. Some even reject these expressions outright, especially those associated with an institutional Church.

What underlies this crisis? To begin with we need to look at the social context with which religious commitment has to contend. A year or so ago my colleague Rebecca Nye and I published the results of a study of the spiritual life of children in state (i.e. non-church) primary schools in Nottingham and Birmingham.[3] The two groups of children we studied were six and ten year olds and the great majority of them came from non-churchgoing home backgrounds. In spite of that, we found an easily recognizable spirituality in all of the children. But there was a clear difference between the six year olds and the ten year olds in how they handled it. On the whole the younger children, even those from a secularized environment, spoke easily and unselfconsciously about religious matters. The ten year olds were much more likely to be reticent. We got the impression that religion had begun to be something of an embarrassment for many of them. One of the more uncomfortable findings was to do with the suppression of their spiritual lives. Even children who quite evidently had a rich spirituality (they spoke freely to us about it) said they would make fun of other children who were foolish enough to raise the subject in public. Evidently Rebecca and I had found ourselves in the presence of a taboo.

The fact is that in contemporary Britain, claiming formal allegiance to a Christian institution is increasingly becoming a countercultural act. Leading a religious life that contradicts the secular norm (if it is not due merely to obliviousness of the surrounding milieu) requires the kind of strength of character that can only come from personal commitment. We chose to do our research in state schools because we wanted to study the spirituality of children who were at a distance from a religious environment. But the pressures of mainstream society do not stop at the doors of the church or the devout home. However carefully children have been nurtured in the faith at home, in the parish and in the Catholic school, they cannot fail to encounter the dominant assumptions of society unless they are enclosed in a ghetto. Modern media pressure and the ubiquity of electronic communications have seen to that. The secular *mores* of pupils in the local state

---

[3]   Hay, D. with Nye, R., *The Spirit of the Child* (London, HarperCollins, 1998).

Comprehensive are on the whole as likely to have been encountered by the children in St Mary's Catholic Comprehensive down
the road. Consequently the natural questioning that is a feature of
adolescence will quite often have just as sharply a sceptical edge in
St Mary's as in the state school.

This raises an uncomfortable dilemma. In its 1997 document *The
Catholic School on the Threshold of the Third Millennium*, the Sacred
Congregation for Catholic education stated:

> From the nature of the Catholic school ... stems one of the most
> significant elements of its educational project: the synthesis between
> culture and faith.

But as Pope Paul VI stated in 1967 in his Apostolic Exhortation on
the mission of the Church, *Evangelii nuntiandi*, 'the split between
the Gospel and culture is without a doubt the drama of our time.'

Children discover this to be so, as they become inducted into the
adult world. Serious tensions are set up which in many cases are
resolved by the decision to lapse from the practice of faith. So how
can teachers help to make a connection between contemporary
culture and religion? Some people think we shouldn't bother.
From their perspective the most important educational tactic is to
ensure that pupils are presented with a crystal clear and dogmatic
statement of the major elements of the deposit of faith. Once they
know their faith, so it is believed, they will be able to stick to it. To
my eye this stance often conveys a sense of closing the doors on the
outside world. I do not believe that this is an effective way of
nurturing a mature faith.

A more liberal approach by no means sets aside the importance
of doctrine. But it accepts the complexity of the world in which all
children grow up, surrounded by the sophisticated modes of
communication that mark the computer age. More stress is therefore laid on the inevitability of dialogue. It is believed that a
confident faith emerges, not in isolation, but in the process of
pondering the realities of secular and multicultural Britain as they
impinge on one's religious life. One so to speak moves towards a
mature understanding of and commitment to the wisdom of
Christian doctrine through reflection on praxis.[4]

By temperament I am in tune with this latter approach. Yet I find
myself doubtful of the effectiveness of such a strategy if it remains
at the level of intellectual debate. Catholic education has to be still

---

[4] See Groome, T., *Christian Religious Education: Sharing our Story and Vision* (San
Francisco, Harper and Row, 1980).

more radical if it is to be truly countercultural and permit the awakening of the spiritual awareness that underpins genuine religious commitment. The clash between religious and secular ways of understanding reality takes place at a much deeper level than the cut and thrust of everyday debate. We Europeans are all of us, whether or not we are religious believers, inheritors of an extremely powerful and all pervasive secular narrative. It claims to explain to us how human beings have become progressively freed from the errors of religion following the Enlightenment in the sixteenth and seventeenth centuries.[5] But a postmodern understanding of the power of social construction suggests that secular accounts of reality are no different from any other kinds of meta-narrative in their power to direct our awareness. As Catholics we need to be aware not only of secular ideas as such, but of their constricting effects on human perception even to the extent of putting religious belief beyond the pale of rational debate. This is a taboo that Catholic teachers need to learn to transcend.

Relational Consciousness

My evidence for this is based on the empirical research I have been doing over the past twenty-five years on the nature of human spirituality. These investigations took their origin from the work of the zoologist Alister Hardy.[6] Hardy believed that our religious experience – by which he typically meant an awareness of the presence of God – is not illusory as numerous critics of religion have alleged, but is based on a predisposition that has evolved during the process of natural selection because it has survival value.[7] Hardy also differed from many more benevolently inclined students of religious experience (for example William James and Rudolf Otto)

---

[5] The American Jesuit scholar Michael Buckley suggests that the turn away from religious experience during the seventeenth century was colluded with by theologians. See his fine book *At the Origins of Modern Atheism* (New Haven, Yale University Press, 1987).

[6] Sir Alister Hardy FRS was Linacre Professor of Zoology in the University of Oxford from 1946 to 1961.

[7] Religious believers are not always happy with an account of the spiritual life that connects it to something as earthbound as our biological nature. But this is to misunderstand Hardy's intentions. He was personally a devout man, well aware of the reductionist critique of religion and wanted to offer a scientific account of what it is in our human nature that allows us to be religious in the first place (see Hardy, A.C., *The Divine Flame*, London, Collins, 1966; also, *The Spiritual Nature of Man*, Oxford, The Clarendon Press, 1979).

in suggesting that when it has not been suppressed, spiritual awareness is commonplace and not confined to the relatively rare
ecstatic experiences that interested James and Otto.

If Hardy is right, then everyone, whatever their religious beliefs
or lack of them, has this predisposition. But what happens to it in
a cultural milieu such as our own, that is inclined to be dismissive
of religion? How does a secularized human being deal with this
aspect of their humanity? One suggestion[8] is that it becomes an
embarrassment and therefore a private matter, ignored and often
forgotten, or perhaps even repressed. The consequence of this
secrecy is that spirituality ceases to express itself publicly in recognizable ways, though it may frequently appear unexpectedly,
wrapped in non-religious forms of language.

Is this happening in our Catholic schools and if so, how could we
leap over the barrier? In our work with young children, Rebecca
Nye and I were faced with the problem of inviting the youngsters
to talk about their spirituality, whilst being aware that very few of
them came from formally practising religious backgrounds. We felt
it necessary to devise a way of introducing the theme without
employing the religious language of which they were likely to be
unaware or from which they were alienated. We did this by identifying a set of three areas of human experience where we might
expect spiritual awareness to arise. They were:

(a) awareness of the here-and-now – characteristically a require-
     ment for genuine prayer, in which one consciously places
     oneself in the presence of God. This here-and-nowness or as
     the child psychologist Margaret Donaldson calls it, the 'point
     mode'[9] is also the normal mode of awareness in very young
     children, only gradually replaced for most of the time in adult
     life by the 'line mode', a dwelling in the past or the future.

(b) awareness of mystery – commonplace in childhood where the
     simplest phenomena (water coming out of a tap, a light
     coming on when a switch is tripped) are matter for awe. The
     mysterious nature of reality becomes largely covered over in
     adult life by scientific explanation. In fact of course at the
     profoundest level the mystery doesn't go away (i.e. why is
     there something rather than nothing?)

[8] See Hay, D., *Exploring Inner Space* (London, Penguin Books, 1982), also *Religious
     Experience Today* (London, Cassell, 1990).
[9] See Donaldson, M., *Human Minds* (London, Allen Lane, 1992).

(c) awareness of value – as Donaldson[10] points out, intensity of feeling is a measure of how much we value something. Since religion is concerned with what matters most of all to us – the meaning and destiny of our lives – it is also the source of particularly strong feeling. Socialization into adult life tends to flatten out the intensity of feeling in young children. They are much more likely to be emotionally in touch with what matters to them, and this includes spiritual awareness.

One of the main ways that these themes could be explored with the children without bringing religious language was by inviting them to reflect on a set of photographs of children in situations where spiritual awareness might be expected to arise. For example one photograph was of a little girl staring into the fire, another was of a boy looking out of the window at the stars, a third was of a girl crying when she saw her pet gerbil lying dead in its cage.

The outcome of the research conversations was over a thousand pages of transcribed text relating to the children's spirituality. We wanted to see if there was some overall theme connecting all the children's talk and we used a computer programme to help us identify it. Rebecca labelled the common ground that emerged 'relational consciousness', in order to emphasize its two components:

- an unusual level of *consciousness* or perceptiveness, relative to other passages of conversation spoken by that child
- conversation expressed in a context of how the child *related* to things, other people, him/herself, and God.[11]

'Relational consciousness' is a useful term to refer to the biologically determined predisposition that permits us to have a spiritual life in the first place. In our reflections on the functions of relational consciousness it also became clear that there is a further way in which it is a crucial component of our human make-up. It underlies the ethical impulse. Research over the past decade into the communication that goes on between newborn infants and their mothers[12] shows that reciprocal awareness of relationship

[10] Ibid.

[11] Hay with Nye, op. cit., p. 113.

[12] See Nagy, E. and Molnar, P., 'Homo imitans or Homo provocans? In search of the mechanism of inborn social competence', *International Journal of Psychophysiology* 18, 1994, 128. Also see Murray, L. and Andrews, L., *The Social Baby* (The Children's Project Ltd., 2000).

commences at birth and is associated with intense emotion. It is prior to all social construction or philosophical speculation, as a primary aspect of what it is to be human. It can be seen as the basis for a holistic understanding of our relationship to other people, to our material environment and to God.[13] People talk about the insight that comes to them at times of spiritual awareness as having the effect of shortening the psychological distance not only between themselves and God but also in relation to other people and the environment. But the cultural assumptions of post-Enlightenment Europe have a powerful effect in suppressing or even repressing such insight.

The attach on relational consciousness

This sense of relationship, present in all children, is absolutely fundamental for the construction of genuine human community.[14] Yet in every society it quickly has to contend with the process of socialization. Paradoxically, learning how to survive as a social being goes hand in hand with the discovery of one's individuality. In the historical circumstances in Europe following the Reformation it has also led rather more ominously to the isolation of the individual through the development of extreme forms of individualism. I am suggesting that in certain circumstances this process of cultural construction limits or blots out natural rela- tional consciousness, and therefore spirituality. That is to say it cripples people's awareness, narrowing their vision and preventing them from becoming whole human beings.

The empirical evidence for such a process has become increas- ingly clear in recent decades. Nevertheless the beginnings of the sequence, perfectly benign and extremely valuable in themselves, can be traced back to the moment when the skills of reading and writing are acquired. The effect of the coming of literacy on self awareness was particularly vividly demonstrated nearly seventy years ago in the work of the eminent Soviet psychologist Alexander

[13] Incidentally once we accept this point of view, the ancient intuition that morals and religion are closely interconnected is given strong support. I need to add however that since on this argument the ethical impulse arises from the common precursor of both religion and morality, it is logically perfectly possi- ble for secularists to be in touch with their relational consciousness but without accepting a religious interpretation of life.

[14] For a fine exposition of this point see Macmurray, J., *The Self as Agent and Persons in Relation* (London, Faber & Faber (reissued, 1995).

Luria.[15] During the early part of the 1930s Luria began a two-year study of illiterate peasants living in the remote republics of Uzbekistan and Kyrgystan. At the time Stalin was introducing collective farming in the region and with it the literacy necessary to manage the farms. Luria wanted to use this large scale social experiment to find out how the ability to read and write affected the thought processes of people who were hitherto completely illiterate. There were vivid differences between illiterate people and those who had begun to be literate. Most crucially in relation to the present argument, he was able to show that literacy allows us to have a private world, different in character from the collective consciousness that is characteristic of oral societies. It massively facilitates our withdrawal from the here-and-now immediacy of direct personal relationship.

Most of us would see this development entirely positively, especially as we ourselves are part of that literate world. It is what allows us to accumulate the store of knowledge necessary for scientific and technical progress. It also allows us to have much greater individuality by creating a clearer boundary between the self and the constraints of the surrounding community. But there is a down side. The Jesuit scholar Walter Ong[16] offers a simple illustration of the effect of literacy on the sense of here-and-now immediacy in genuine relationship. Suppose a teacher is working on some problem with a class of students. They get on well together and there is a sense of communal achievement. Then the teacher asks the class to turn to a page in a textbook. What was a community a moment before becomes a set of isolates, separately absorbed in the text they are reading. The power of this phenomenon is incalculably great in a culture where the great majority of our processing of reality is via text (as is the case at this moment, as you read the text I have written). Over and above that, the invention of the internet determined how I prepared this text and communicated it to my editor. These most recent developments have been critiqued by John L. Locke[17] as the basis for the creation of a world of strangers.

It may rightly be pointed out that all large-scale religious cultures, including Catholicism, have been spread through

---

[15] See Luria, A.R., *Cognitive Development: Its Cultural and Social Foundations* (Harvard University Press, 1976).

[16] See Ong, W.J., SJ, *Orality and Literacy: The Technologizing of the Word* (London and New York, Methuen, 1982).

[17] See Locke, J.L., *Why we Don't Talk to Each Other any More: the Devoicing of Society* (New York, Simon & Schuster Inc., 1998).

reading and writing. Reference is often made to the three great Western monotheisms (Judaism, Christianity and Islam) as religions of the Book. What we also find in these religions is a vast and extremely sophisticated literature on meditation, contemplation, prayer and devotion, specifically designed to protect the point mode, the here-and-now context of relational consciousness. The loss of this sophistication as the result of secularization is another source of the inner loneliness that besets modern society.

The solitariness of the inhabitants of post-Enlightenment European culture, their distancing from their relational consciousness, has a still more radical source through the emergence of individualism. Individualism is a pivotal characteristic of Western modernity.[18] It is also multifaceted and I do not have the space to enter into a discussion of this, but I do want to make a brief reference to one of its more destructive aspects by mentioning the influence of Thomas Hobbes. Most of us know of him because of his masterwork *Leviathan*, published in 1651 where he states his famous conclusion that human life in the state of nature is 'solitary, nasty, brutish and short'. His materialist interpretation led him to the view that life is fundamentally warfare of all against all. The notion of the individual as isolated continues as a central philosophical assumption through the theoreticians of the Social Contract in the eighteenth century, the extreme egoism of, for example, Friedrich Neitzsche and Max Stirner in the nineteenth century, and the rugged individualism much admired in modern America. This kind of assumption about our human nature continues to underlie mainstream political theory in our own day, as has been convincingly argued by C.B. MacPherson, who first labelled it as the 'theory of possessive individualism'.[19] The assumptions of individualism, at least in the form to which I have adverted, are totally at odds with relational consciousness.

Relational Consciousness and Catholic Education

Those assumptions also utterly contradict the central Christian understanding of our purposes in life: to love God and to love our

[18] See for example, Lukes, S., *Individualism*, (Oxford, Basil Blackwell, 1973); Bellah, R.M. et al. *Habits of the Heart: Individualism and Commitment in American Life* (New York, Harper & Row, 1985); Dumont, R., *Essays on Individualism* (Chicago University Press, 1986).

[19] MacPherson, C.B., *The Political Theory of Possessive Individualism: From Hobbes to Locke* (Oxford, The Clarendon Press, 1962).

neighbour as ourselves. My argument is that the individualistic ideology that has become increasingly dominant in European influenced societies over the past three hundred years often has the literal effect of crippling our ability to perceive this. We learn a set of intellectual priorities which discourage attention and can perhaps even obliterate relational consciousness. To close it off is to shut down the natural capacity that allows us to have a spiritual life in the first place. The fundamental implausibility that many people find in relation to faith is much more likely to lie in that blindness than in the rational arguments put forward against religious belief. As I mentioned earlier, I am also convinced that this impoverishment is a major source of the difficulties we face in the creation of a coherent and morally responsible human community. Once relational consciousness is submerged, the voluntary sustaining of communal moral values can no longer be relied upon. The maintenance of law and order comes more and more to depend on techniques that threaten civil liberties: electronic surveillance, the creation of detailed data banks, street corner video-cameras, a huge increase in bureaucratic procedures for ensuring accountability.

What sort of educational response is appropriate in facing up to these difficulties? How do we go about nurturing religious commitment in the missionary environment of the modern Catholic school? The Jesuit theologian Jon Sobrino[20] has offered an interesting commentary on *Evangelii Nuntiandi*, discussing the three major hindrances to the nurture of religious commitment identified by Paul VI. Each of them has an application in the school classroom.

The first hindrance is the pervasive culture of atheism to which I have already referred at some length. The second impediment is related to inculturation, the problem caused by the imposition of forms of expression of the Christian faith that are alien to the people on whom they are imposed. It is important to note that this is nothing to do with the truth or falsity of Christian beliefs, but with the gulf that Paul VI noted between faith and culture. Here I think modern communication theory can help us. The Japanese scholar Muneo Jay Yoshikawa[21] has written particularly illuminatingly on the problems confronting those who are attempting to

[20] Sobrino, J., SJ, *The True Church and the Poor* (Maryknoll, New York, Orbis Books, 1984).
[21] Yoshikawa, M.J., 'The double-swing model of intercultural communication between the East and the West', in D.L. Kincaid (ed.), *Communication Theory: Eastern and Western Perspectives* (San Diego, Academic Press Inc., 1987).

engage in dialogue across cultural boundaries, in this case European and Far Eastern traditions. These are analogies between such a dialogue and the encounter that perhaps often takes place between teachers and alienated pupils in Catholic schools. Yoshikawa identifies four modes of intercultural encounter and communication:

(a) The *ethnocentric* mode is where I perceive the people I am encountering entirely through my own frame of reference. Whatever thoughts and ideas they may have are mere shadows to me and I ignore them. The communication is one-sided and I am deaf to attempts they may make to present their point of view. One might link this mode with an old-fashioned catechism class in which the only purpose is to ensure the successful rote learning of Catholic beliefs.

(b) The *control* mode is where I scrutinize quite carefully the cultural realities of the people I am encountering. My purpose in taking account of their perspective is however entirely manipulative in that I use the information to control and guide them into accepting my point of view. I suspect that the teaching that goes on in most school classrooms (Catholic or state) is often in this mode.

(c) The *dialectical* mode is where my aim is to achieve a 'fusion' that transcends the differences between myself and those with whom I am in conversation. According to Yoshikawa, in practice such an ideal fusion tends to degenerate into pseudo-dialectic in one of two ways. Either my devotion to the people with whom I am speaking leads me to lose my cultural identity and my beliefs disappear into theirs, or they submerge their identities into mine through a kind of hidden coercion. One can imagine apparently liberal religious discussions in the Church school classroom quite often turning into pseudo-dialectic of this kind.

(d) The *dialogical* mode of encounter requires me to recognize the primacy of relationship between myself and those with whom I am in communication. Whilst it is true that we are separate and independent, we are also simultaneously interdependent. Yoshikawa puts it thus:

The cultural integrity of A and B and the differences and similarities

of A and B are recognized and respected. The emphasis is on whole-
ness, mutuality and dynamic meeting of A and B. Even in their
union, A and B each maintains a separate identity.[22]

Notice that Yoshikawa is referring here to the individuality of A
and B, not to individualism. The more we believe that God the
Holy Spirit speaks to everyone, the more we are likely to feel that
Yoshikawa's dialogical mode is an appropriate one for the
Religious Education classroom. We need to be alert for the ways in
which spiritual awareness expresses itself in our pupils and, as my
work with Rebecca Nye has shown, this will very often be in
languages and cultural modes quite remote from Christian ortho-
doxy. Our acceptance of the genuineness of such spirituality does
not imply any dilution of our Catholic beliefs; that would be a
retreat to the kind of pseudo-dialectic where we allow our own
perspectives to be submerged. But authentic nurture does require
us to honour the stances of our pupils, many of them looking at us
suspiciously across an increasingly wide cultural divide. Ideally
what will happen is a moving together of understanding without
the disappearance of the individuality of either teacher or pupils.

This brings us to the third crisis of evangelization noted in
Evangelii nuntiandi, the tragedy that occurs when evangelization is
seen as mere proclamation, that is, as in Yoshikawa's modes (a)
and (b). Sobrino remarks that:

> When Jesus says, for example, that 'the kingdom of God is at hand'
> or that 'whoever would save his life will lose it' or that 'greater love
> has no man than this, than a man lay down his life for his friends',
> he is not simply making statements to be registered and reflected on
> by the mind.[23]

And later:

> In regard to 'the intersubjective character of Christian faith', the
> New Testament makes it clear that the personal appropriation of
> faith depends on the faith already lived by others.[24]

That is to say, awareness of our relationship to God is very unlikely
to arise if we live in an environment where genuine relationship
with others, in this case our teachers, is present. The nurture of

[22] Yoshikawa, op. cit., p. 321.
[23] Sobrino, op. cit., p. 268.
[24] Ibid, p. 271.

commitment comes about from the totality of a proclamation that is lived out by the person who proclaims.

There is another more subtle but extremely important aspect of evangelization that arises out of the insight that God is not a tribal god. Sobrino notes that:

> It has all too often been taken for granted that evangelizers preach a God whom others do not yet know but whom they (the evangelizers) already know. Such a pattern may make sense for a philosophical concept of God, but it does not hold for the Christian God.[25]

In this passage Sobrino is writing specifically about the evangelization of the poor. He is anxious to make it clear that this is not a matter of patronizing people. Why? Because of the mutual respect that I have suggested is implied in Yoshikawa's final category. We learn from those we evangelize because God the Holy Spirit is already at work in them. Indeed there is a real sense in which they evangelize us. Here a genuine dialectic takes place, rather than the false dialectics referred to by Yoshikawa. Sobrino is emphasizing the special concern of Jesus for the poor and their importance in the economy of salvation. But I believe there is also something important to be learned here about the outcome of genuine encounter between Catholic teachers and the secularized young people they meet in their classrooms.

Nurturing Relational Consciousness

To summarize what has gone before, without a genuine relationship between teacher and pupils the proclamation of Christian truth is not merely empty, it is counterproductive. It engenders contempt for the message. The first step must be to nurture such a relationship by respecting and recognizing the relational consciousness that is in ourselves and protecting it and encouraging it in the children in our care. I have suggested elsewhere[26] that there are four aspects to this task and I shall conclude by summarizing these.

1. *Helping children to keep an open mind*: It is clear from what I have
    said above that a purely rational approach to the nurture of

[25] Sobrino, op. cit., p. 294.
[26] Hay with Nye, op. cit., chapter 9.

spirituality is not enough. Social conformity is often too strong. My colleagues and I at the Centre for the Study of Human Relations in Nottingham University have found that a good way to help someone to free themselves from constrictions on their awareness is through experiential exercises. One helpful discovery is the unique nature of every individual's sense of the world (emphasizing once more the difference between this and the isolating aspects of certain forms of individualism). A typical exercise to demonstrate this is borrowed from the philosopher of science Karl Popper.[27] The members of the class are invited to 'observe' for five minutes and write down what they observe. As Popper notes, such a request usually provokes puzzlement. 'Observe what?' they want to ask, because of course there is an infinity of possible things to observe. For example, is it to be the objects in the room, or the people, or the person who made the request; or what lies outside the window? Or might it be an observation of oneself, either what one is wearing, the posture of one's body, or one's physical feelings? Or might it refer to the random thoughts that are entering the mind over the five minutes – perhaps resentment at the person who made such a foolish request, or obsessive concerns about a personal anxiety? Participants in this exercise are regularly surprised to discover how unique their personal world is, never corresponding exactly with anyone else's world and often diverging massively from others in the room. The outcome is the realization that there is no one right way to interpret reality and that conformity to a particular view is something imposed by culture rather than the truth of people's personal experience. This of course is also true of people's response to the Gospel, as anyone who has regularly undertaken the *lectio divina* is able to confirm; the way the Gospel speaks to us personally is always unique.

2. *Exploring ways of seeing*: Dogmatic certainty about a dominant mode of interpreting reality is the intellectual equivalent of physically blindfolding oneself. Pupils in the Religious Education class who 'know' ahead of time that the content of the class is implausible are in this condition. This is where exercises in deconstruction can be helpful in freeing the mind from secular prejudices. One of the easiest and most concrete ways

[27] See Popper, K., *The Logic of Scientific Discovery* (London, Hutchinson Press, 1959).

of explaining this to pupils is through the use of ambiguous drawing. Following the philosopher Don Ihde (1979)[28] I have often used the well-known Necker cube for this purpose.

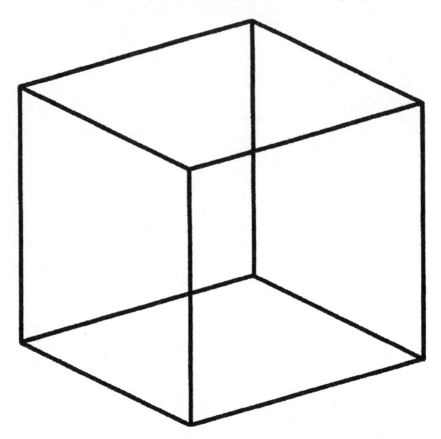

People always recognize this diagram at once as a cube. This is a socially constructed response, based on the fact that a cubical shape is probably the most familiar human artifice we encounter. It is the approximate shape of most rooms, almost certainly including the room in which we were born. But there are many other possibilities. The array of lines might be seen as a badly cut diamond, or a curiously shaped pyramid with the top cut off, or it might even be seen as flat, though usually people say that this last is difficult. Cultural construction lies

[28] Ihde, D., *Experimental Phenomenology: An Introduction* (New York, Paragon Books, 1979).

behind this difficulty. Ihde shows this by telling a different story about the diagram. Suppose that in fact it represents the totem badge worn from birth by all family members of a clan of Amazonian Indians. The badge is a highly stylized representation of an insect, with its six legs sticking out sideways to the edge of the hexagonal shape. Pupils usually say that with this story in mind they can see the diagram as flat, though it quite quickly reverts to a cube. But suppose a Westerner were to show the clan members what a cube is (living in the rain forest, they have never seen one before) and then point out that the badge can be seen as a cube. The likelihood is that the Indians would similarly say that they could see the cube briefly, but it would quickly revert to the insect. The analogy with what happens in the case of sceptical pupils in an RE class is clear. If those pupils have been socialized into a dogmatic scepticism, it is difficult for them to 'see' other interpretations of reality. But the use of such deconstructive exercises can loosen up their awareness and allow space for other ways of seeing – including the religious one (there are also of course important implications for those who hold in a rigidly dogmatic way to religious beliefs and are unwilling to countenance that there *are* other ways of 'seeing').

3. *Encouraging personal awareness*: At the heart of my relationship with God lies prayer, in which I place myself in his presence in the here-and-now. As I mentioned earlier the 'point mode' is largely replaced in adult life by the 'line mode'. This latter mode is inappropriate for the personal relationship that lies at the heart of prayer. Prayer undertaken in the latter mode is prayer that has become desiccated, and can often seem to pupils to be little more than the mouthing of religious platitudes. To be frank, that is often how it comes across in public ceremonial. Therefore it is important to underline the nature of attentiveness, particularly with pupils at secondary level, since teenagers are often quite far removed from the 'point mode' of their early childhood. They can be reminded of the power of this mode by the use of practical exercises that are not in themselves religious, yet point to the frame of mind that is appropriate to prayer. One exercise that I have often used is borrowed from Patrick Pietroni[29] and simply requires the eating of an apple, slowly and awarely. What emerges strongly

[29] Pietroni, P., *Holistic Living* (London, J.M. Dent, 1986).

is the consciousness of relationship, in this case with a physical object. Even adults who undertake this exercise are usually very surprised by the intensity of their awareness of the physical properties of the apple and they frequently say that they have made discoveries about it of which they had never been aware before. It is this kind of focused awareness in prayer that enables us to be alert as we wait upon God.

4. *Encouraging awareness of the social and political dimensions of spirituality:* I mentioned earlier the link between relational consciousness and ethics. One of the assumptions often made by secularized young people, even those who persist in their religious practice, is that the spiritual life is a private matter having nothing to do with the practicalities of life. In fact the unspoken interdict on bringing spirituality into the realities of everyday life is immensely damaging to our society. Determined political action to relieve poverty has little chance of appealing to people who have lost touch with their relational consciousness. In my view this is a major reason for the difficulties we are currently facing in creating a socially cohesive moral community where people feel responsible for each other. It is therefore of the greatest importance that the political and social implications of spiritual insight/relational consciousness are explored in the Religious Education class. This is particularly appropriate in Catholic schools because of the strong emphasis on the social dimension of religion as compared with some of our sister churches. 'We come to God in one another's company' as I was told by a Cistercian monk many years ago. That is a political statement. It is also a statement about the centrality of relational consciousness to our spiritual journey. Without it there can be no true nurture of faith and no genuine religious commitment.

Chapter 12

Inter-Faith Perspectives:
More Questions Than Answers

Michael J.G. Cooke

Reflecting on inter-faith issues in a book on Catholic education is not simply a question of asking 'How should we teach World Religions in a Catholic School?' Whilst that may be a pressing question it is not the only matter to be considered in this regard. This chapter explores the relationship between the Catholic Church and other world religions and the impact of that relationship upon Religious Education. I have subtitled the chapter 'more questions than answers' because I believe that aptly describes both the nature of this chapter and the nature of reality! My intention is to raise issues for consideration and to provide some background material for those who wish to think these things through. It would be beyond the scope of this chapter to provide answers to the many questions that arise when inter-faith perspectives are addressed. The new Catholic approach to other faiths, adopted by the Church at the Second Vatican Council, puts forward a vision of how other faiths relate to the Church and some progress is being made in working through the implications of that vision.[1] So, answers to the questions are not readily available. However, my overall concern would be that whenever such matters are addressed in Religious Education in a Catholic context, then whatever is offered to participants should reflect the Vatican II vision – the true relationship that the Church considers itself to have with these religions.

In case anyone should consider 'inter-faith perspectives' to be simply a dry and academic concern, let me spell out a few of the

---

[1] There are Vatican Congregations concerned with inter-religious dialogue and these are reflected at the level of the Bishops' Conference of England and Wales.

real questions which ground this subject in everyday experience. For those concerned with Catholic schools (as teachers, governors, clergy or parents), there are questions about whether or not we should admit pupils of other faiths. If we do, can we provide for their religious development, or do we simply expect them to endure our Catholic input and find their 'faith support' elsewhere? How important is it for us to educate our pupils for life in a multi-faith society and how do we go about this, especially for pupils who do not live in a particularly multi-faith neighbourhood? Then there are questions about whether multi-faith education should be part of the Religious Education Curriculum (with related questions about content and methodology) or part of the general provision made by the school. When it comes to adults, how can we ensure that they know what the Church says about these matters, so that they can overcome any prejudice they may have personally or encounter in others? How can we equip them to genuinely reflect upon inter-faith matters that arise in the news (such as the Salman Rushdie controversy some years ago and ongoing conflicts in the Holy Land)? Then there may be very practical issues about how the Church becomes involved in chaplaincy work, say in a hospital or university, where things are set up for a multi-faith or inter-faith team. And at the academic level, there are questions about what scope can be given to theologians to undertake rigorous study and engage in inter-faith dialogue.

So, there are a whole host of questions and I believe that adopting a realistic approach to other world religions will best equip Catholics for life in the modern world and help them to continually meet the challenge of multi-faith neighbours.

The Reality of Religious Pluralism

As we begin to explore the situation that confronts us in Britain today, we should note that the term 'religious pluralism' is used in two senses. It is *descriptive* of contemporary reality (the diversity which exists and our contact with it) and *prescriptive* in terms of offering a way to achieve the ideal situation (harmonious relationships).[2] In both senses it offers a challenge to those involved in religious education, so I want to give some consideration to each

---

[2] Cf. Morris, P., 'Judaism and pluralism: The price of "religious freedom"' in I. Hamnett (ed.), *Religious Pluralism and Unbelief – Studies Critical and Comparative* (London and New York, Routledge, 1990).

of them, even though the first (the descriptive) is really self-evident:

> Britain has traditionally been a multi-cultural society made up of
> diverse national cultures – English, Scottish, Welsh and Irish. Our
> history of Empire and Commonwealth has accentuated this charac-
> teristic by bringing people of many races and backgrounds to these
> islands. We accepted into our society other communities who
> sought refuge from persecution. All have been changed in coming
> here and we have been changed in welcoming them. Through a
> long and constant process, therefore, Britain has become irre-
> versibly a multi-racial, multi-cultural society.[3]

Anyone seeking to consider the relationship between Christianity
and other religions in Britain must take on board this statement
and insert a further epithet into its final sentence: multi-faith.
Many of the books that deal with this topic contain one or more
chapters describing the condition of our modern world in terms of
the presence of a variety of world faiths (and other secular world-
views).[4] Not surprisingly, it is in these chapters that we find the
various authors expressing their agreement. Whatever diverse
theories they may eventually produce to explain how the religions
relate to one another, they are of one mind in presenting a picture
of the reality of the pluralistic society that exists at global, national
and local levels. Britain has always had a plurality of cultures but it
seems that we are now more conscious of this and of the religious
differences that form part of that plurality:

> The nineteenth century, more than any other, saw the consolidation
> of 'intra-religious' pluralism with the growth of Christian denomi-
> nations ... Since then ... other world religions have been
> introduced and have begun to flourish. This new 'inter-religious'
> pluralism ... now includes not only Christianity and Judaism but
> also Islam, Hinduism, Sikhism, Buddhism, Jainism and
> Zoroastrianism. Like Christianity, all of these religions have their
> own subdivisions, many of which are represented today in Britain. In
> common with many nations in the modern world Britain has a reli-
> gious profile which is complex and fascinating.[5]

[3] Statement from the Catholic Bishops of England and Wales, *Concerning the Revision of British Nationality Law*, July 1979.

[4] Some examples are: D'Costa, *Theology and Religious Pluralism*; Knitter, *No Other Name?*; Race, *Christians and Religious Pluralism*. Full details of each are given in the Bibliography.

[5] Knott, K., 'Other Major Religious Traditions', in T. Thomas (ed.), *The British – Their Religious Beliefs and Practices 1800–1986* (London and New York, Routledge, 1988), p. 133f.

As the Bishops' statement says, this is a position that has been arrived at 'through a long and constant process' and is now irreversible. The factors contributing to that process and the reasons for our heightened awareness of these other faiths are enumerated and listed in different ways but I think they might be summarized as follows: broader horizons, population mobility, greater knowledge, a new missionary approach and increased tolerance. Whilst recognizing that these are interconnected, I want to say a few words about each of them in turn.

I start with *broader horizons* because I believe that this represents the most characteristic change in our time. Technological advances mean that we can witness events from around the world as they actually happen, in effect 'shrinking' the globe to manageable proportions. One of the effects of this is to see at first hand (yet from the comfort of our living room) the variety of religious custom and practice that prevails in other parts of the world, perhaps influencing the whole structure of some societies in the same way that Christianity has influenced our own. The twentieth century has been marked by an increasing consciousness of the interdependence of nations and recognition that we belong to one world. *Population mobility* has had a similar effect but at a more local level. The variety of cultures present within our British society has increased and has been accompanied by a parallel expansion in the number of religions or faiths. This is evident from the number and variety of places of worship that mark the landscape of any town or city. A greater mobility also allows us (if we choose) to visit the countries where these other religions originate or predominate. All in all, then, there is available to us a *greater knowledge* of other ways of life, other sets of spiritual values, other religious rituals. This is harnessed at an academic level through a variety of courses in religious studies that allow comparison or specialization. The shelves of bookshops and libraries have an ever-increasing range of volumes on other faiths alongside their section on Christianity, making such knowledge available on a more popular level. These changes in our society have accompanied (or perhaps given rise to) a *new missionary approach*. In the past the emphasis was on going to foreign countries to convert everyone to Christianity. Now there is (at least for some) a more relaxed approach, which seeks to understand the customs of a particular country or people (including their religious customs) before looking at how the message of Christ might be appropriately brought to them without also imposing an alien culture. This new approach, at home and abroad, has generated an *increased tolerance* of other religions. As long as people obey the law of the land, society no longer looks for them to conform to its ways (social or spiritual) if they are to be members of that community. Although certain areas of cities and towns may be predominantly (if not exclusively) occupied by people of one particular religious or racial background, there is no longer the same ghetto mentality that once prevailed. With few exceptions, people of different religious persuasions live in the same neighbourhood and share common facilities. Indeed they are often supported in making provision for their own particular needs. This is not to say that there are no problems with religions living side by side, but we must be careful to distinguish those that are of a racial rather than a religious nature. Let us remember that there can be clashes of culture within a religion as well as between religions; intra-religious as well as inter-religious.

So the complexity of cultural and confessional customs is the reality of our society today. The very presence of other cultures and traditions can challenge a person's faith, on the level of custom and practice, simply through their being exposed to something different. But that same presence can also issue a more serious challenge, going right to the heart of that person's convictions and making them ask whether or not their chosen religion has the validity they have previously assumed.

A New Catholic Approach to the Challenge

Faced with the 'problems' presented by the reality of religious pluralism, scholars and practitioners tend to put forward 'answers' which consist of adopting one or other of three positions, classified as Exclusivist, Pluralist or Inclusivist.[6]

The *Exclusivist* position, as its name implies, holds that one's own religion is the only valid one and that all other views are untrue. Conversion to that one way of life, and condemnation of those who refuse to change, are the hallmarks of such a stance. This can lead to religious fanaticism, where the adherents of a particular faith expound their own view to the detriment of all others and seek to

---

[6] Race uses these terms in *Christians and Religious Pluralism* (1983), where he says: 'There is now emerging from Christian writers a spectrum of theories attempting to deal with religious pluralism as a theological issue' (p. ixf.). They are also used by D'Costa in *Theology and Religious Pluralism* (1986) and the same ideas are expressed in different terms by Knitter (*No Other Name?*, 1985) and Panikkar (*The Intra-Religious Dialogue*, 1978). For a résumé of their use in these contexts, cf. Barnes, M., *Religions in Conversation – Christian Identity and Religious Pluralism* (London, SPCK, 1989), p. 11f.

eradicate anything contrary to it. By contrast, the *Pluralist* position proposes that all religions are equally valid and that, therefore, an individual is free to choose exactly what he or she will or will not believe, whilst we live happily side by side. This view carries with it the danger of creating, or at least condoning, religious indifferentism. If it does not matter what people choose to believe, then it could be argued logically that it does not matter if they choose not to believe. *Inclusivists* would assert that their religion has the fullest insight into humanity's relationship to God but acknowledge that it may be further enriched by the diversity of faiths, some of which perhaps already contain elements of that 'fullest insight'. Such an acceptance of others, they claim, provides the basis for true religious tolerance and liberty. One is able to deepen one's own understanding from the insights of others and able to share one's own views with people who are already some way along the same road. In slightly modified form, the latter would describe the approach now put forward by the Catholic Church.

The promulgation of the *Declaration on the Relationship of the Church to Non-Christian Religions* on 28 October 1965 was a truly historic event. Although it was the shortest of the sixteen texts produced by the Second Vatican Council, it was perhaps the most controversial. Some welcomed it as a long-overdue statement; others considered that its timing was ill-advised. Some thought it had gone too far; others that it had not said enough. Whatever their opinions, no one could argue with the fact that in *Nostra Aetate* (to give the Declaration its conventional Latin title) the Church was making a positive statement about other religions for the first time in its long history and after twenty-one Ecumenical Councils:

> The Catholic Church rejects nothing of what is true and holy in these religions. She has a high regard for the manner of life and conduct, the precepts and doctrines which, although differing in many ways from her own teaching, nevertheless often reflect a ray of that truth which enlightens all...

> The Church, therefore, urges her sons to enter with prudence and charity into discussion and collaboration with members of other religions. Let Christians, while witnessing to their own faith and way of life, acknowledge, preserve and encourage the spiritual and moral truths found among non-Christians, also their social life and culture.[7]

[7] N.A., n. 2. All quotations from the Council documents in this chapter are taken from A. Flannery, (ed.), *Vatican Council II – The Conciliar and Post Conciliar Documents* (Study Edition) (New York/Michigan, Costello Publishing Company/Wm. B. Eerdmans Publishing Co., 1992 (orig. 1975)).

There is no consensus of opinion regarding other world faiths within the wider Christian tradition, so it is not possible to talk about a Christian approach except in a very broad sense. *Nostra Aetate* is very much a Catholic document, addressed in the first instance to the Catholic community. As such, it *is* Catholic theology and advocates a new approach that the Catholic Church can pursue. The document specifically refers to Judaism, Islam, Hinduism and Buddhism, whilst including a rather general reference to 'other religions which are not found throughout the world'.[8] It does not develop this new approach in much detail but that is hardly surprising given the background to the document. The original intention was to produce a statement simply about Catholic-Jewish relationships as part of one of the other Conciliar documents but this was broadened out, and separated out, in the process of deliberation and reference is also made to this new understanding of world religions in other Vatican II documents – particularly the document on the Church.[9]

I believe that the content and import of this historic document have a significant contribution to make to the Church's task of religious education in the world today. The opening words of the Declaration ('*Nostra aetate*' – 'In our times') suggest a desire on the part of the Church to address an issue which was (and, for us, still is) of current concern. Relevant Religious Education must obviously in content reflect, and in methodology reflect on, the reality of the world in which the participants live.

School-based Religious Education

In this day and age, we have a duty and responsibility to include religions other than our own in our teaching. I maintain that the emphasis should not be on details or facts about them (though that will inevitably be involved) but primarily on exploring the relationship between them and ourselves. Public debate and interest often focus on religious topics regarding other faiths which could be dealt with purely at the level of facts but can also be seen in terms of the relationship which exists between our communities. So, for example, should Catholics be supporting or promoting 'rival' Muslim schools? In helping people to contemplate such matters in greater detail, we are equipping them to adopt a

[8] N.A., n. 2.
[9] *Lumen Gentium*, n. 16.

broader and more considered approach to religious issues which they may encounter in life. To be credible, Religious Education must address the real situation in our society today and the real concerns of people. It must demonstrate the value of pursuing the religious dimension of life which is inherent in each of us and which may provide a 'common denominator' in helping us to tackle some of the issues which face society.[10]

Any Religious Education syllabus from around the time of the Vatican Council, and even on into the 1970s, is very likely to display an exclusivist view of the Catholic religion. Often this may be more by omission than by any positive intent on the part of the author or compiler of the syllabus. Other faiths were not seen as a particular issue to include. This perhaps serves to emphasize just how *new* the teaching in *Nostra Aetate* and *Lumen Gentium* really was. It was perhaps fear of pupils being attracted to alternative ideologies that prevented religious educators from including more explicit material about them in their syllabuses, but I suspect it was more likely the fact that, until Vatican II, this was not considered a serious issue to address. Some did include information on the Jewish religion, but only where it impinged on the reading of the Bible or helped the understanding of the life of Christ. In other words, it was an historical study of Judaism, rather than telling us anything about the Jewish faith in the modern day.

Following the Vatican Council, and given that at that time there was a general development of child-centred learning, it would seem inevitable that there should be a change of approach. In a 1981 report on 'The Educative Task of the Catholic Community', the authors paralleled this task with the *aggiornamento* of Vatican II as 'the process of interaction and refinement between faith and culture'.[11] The 1984 report, *Learning from Diversity*, confirmed that this was a priority for the community, recognizing that other faiths are part of the multi-racial, multi-cultural society from which we can learn. Indeed it encouraged a shared approach, and recognized that developments were already in hand at grass-roots level:

[10] Cf. H. Küng, and K.-J. Kuschel, (eds), *A Global Ethic: The Declaration of the Parliament of the World's Religions* (London, SCM Press Ltd., 1993), which seeks to present the minimum that the religions have in common as the basis for a world ethic, 'a fundamental consensus' (p. 7).

[11] *Signposts and Homecomings: The Educative Task of the Catholic Community*, A Report to the Bishops of England and Wales (Slough, St Paul Publications, 1981), p. 37.

The study of religions other than Christianity has found a place in many RE syllabuses...[12]

At the same time, not everyone was in favour of a new approach and a further factor to consider here is the debate leading up to the *Education Reform Act 1988*. In arriving at that Act, there were a series of discussions on the place of Religious Education within the curriculum and the nature of worship within the school context. Many argued for a more diverse multi-faith approach to reflect the situation of the wider community in our country. However, those who wanted to maintain that we live in a Christian country won the day and the outcome of all this was the phrase enshrined in the 1988 Act that collective worship should be 'wholly or mainly of a broadly Christian character'.[13] As for Religious Education, the Act states that any new agreed syllabus:

> ... shall reflect the fact that the religious traditions in Great Britain are in the main Christian whilst taking account of the teaching and practices of the other principal religions present in Great Britain.[14]

Those who were unhappy with this outcome have ensured that the debate continues to this day. Whilst these sections of the Act do not apply to Catholic schools, they indicate a pattern of thought and development within our society which we cannot afford to ignore. In a nutshell, even the 'secular' claim is to a Christian pre-eminence.

The debate over that phrase in the Act was reflected within Catholic circles with the publication of a new syllabus for secondary schools, *Weaving the Web*.[15] This caused controversy, with some bishops, religious education advisers and teachers taking exception to its portrayal of other religions and its supposed denigration (or demotion) of Christianity. The ensuing debate over its relative merits and drawbacks took place in public, particularly in the pages of the Catholic press. Some years later, the main criticisms levelled against the programme were summarized as follows:

---

[12] *Learning from Diversity: A Challenge for Catholic Education*, Report of the Working Party on Catholic Education in a Multiracial, Multicultural Society (London, Catholic Media Office, 1984) p. 32.

[13] *Education Reform Act 1988*, Section 7 (1).

[14] Ibid., Section 8 (3).

[15] Lohan, R. and McClure, M. SND, *Weaving the Web: A modular programme of Religious Education* (teacher's book and six pupil texts), (London, Collins, 1988).

(1) It has the wrong priorities, is incomplete and superficial, and omits several key truths of Catholic doctrine.

(2) Too much emphasis is placed on the young people exploring their own experiences, and too many of the learning intentions are experimental.

(3) There is excessive study of non-Christian religions, which could lead to syncretism, while underplaying Christianity and the Catholic tradition.

(4) Too much attention is paid to things like liberation theology and feminism.

(5) It justifies its content by describing itself as Religious Education and distinguishing this from catechesis.

This useful summary is provided by Damian Lundy and Jim Gallagher, two people who (as the co-ordinators of the National Project that published the work) were very much in the firing line of the critics.[16] I am not trying to make light of these criticisms when I say that all five of them really belong in the much wider debate about Catholic education that is an ongoing feature of Church life today. They only apply specifically to *Weaving the Web* in so far as that programme represents a drawing together of a number of the elements from that wider debate. My sadness is that the controversy's narrower focus could just as easily stifle as stimulate the debate.

With reference to the specific syllabus, it ought to be stressed that the intention was to provide sufficient material for the teacher to *choose* what to use. This choice was to be based on a number of criteria, including the 'relevant life experience of the learner', the 'contemporary situation in modern religious groupings' and the 'setting of the school'.[17] These are important criteria and it may have been a failure to properly understand or implement the methodology envisaged in *Weaving the Web* that often led the critics to experience disappointment.[18] I hope that the new schemes of

[16] Lundy, D. and Gallagher, J., '*Weaving the Web: problem or opportunity?*', *The Tablet*, Vol. 246 No. 7907, 22 February 1992, pp. 230–233. In that same edition (pp. 234–236) there is an article – 'Where do we go from here?' – by John Redford, one of the leading critics.

[17] Cf. *Weaving the Web*, Teacher's Book, p. 15.

[18] Lundy and Gallagher comment: 'There is no perfect text which will overcome all the deficiencies in some schools and individual teachers.' (*Tablet*, 22 February 1992, p. 231.)

work and resources currently being developed for Religious Education (at both primary and secondary levels) will take account of the criticisms levelled at this earlier work and incorporate insights from the ongoing debate about the place of world religions in the Catholic framework.

Religious Education in a Wider Context

I think Religious Education is best taught from within a faith community, with the ultimate desire for those we teach to share the life of that community more fully, whilst at the same time recognizing people of other faiths. So it must not be taught as though the faith community existed in isolation or was the only such community in the world. The objective is not to present all the faith traditions as though they were goods in a shop, with people choosing the one they like best. The intention is to show how another particular faith tradition fits into the pattern of the religious life of the world, how it makes sense of life, and how its adherents are expected to live. Even if our Religious Education confined itself to a study of Catholicism, then we would still have to include other religions because, in the aftermath of *Lumen Gentium* and *Nostra Aetate*, other religions have an accredited place on the Catholic agenda.

There are tendencies within Religious Education which follow each of the main theological positions proposed for relating one religion to another. All have something to offer but we must ensure that we follow the one that most accurately reflects the actual position of the Church in this matter. We must seek to teach about other religions in a way that reflects our theological position. As such, we must give a priority and pre-eminence to Catholicism and seek to show the place and value of the other religions in relation to it. In order to do that, we must obviously bring other religions into our study but, again, that must be done in a way which reflects their handling at a theological level. I would say that the inclusivist stance is now part of the Catholic Church's self-perception and that to omit other religions from our consideration is to give a false or incomplete picture of our Church; it is to give a less than whole account of our faith. We have a relationship with these other religions both in a theoretical way (expressed in theological documents) and in a practical way (expressed in our living and meeting together). It is this *real* relationship which I think has to be reflected in Religious Education. I am not suggesting that all

Religious Education should be devoted to this issue, any more than the Church's life is devoted to it at local, national or international levels, but it is one dimension of that life and should therefore feature. It is both theoretical and tangible and, therefore, real.

We see the religions side by side in our communities and need help in interpreting how they relate to one another. The task of Religious Education is to help us achieve that interpretation and in a Catholic setting that means adopting an inclusivist approach. Some people might wonder about the difference between Pluralism and Inclusivism if both say salvation is *possible* through other faiths. Well, I see the main differences as being concerned with the centrality of Christ, the pre-eminence of Christianity as the route to salvation and the way of living, and an emphasis on the individual (more than the religion they adhere to).

The whole field of Inter-Faith Dialogue needs to be opened up (as urged by NA), for the sake of those inside and outside the Church. Real comparative theology must be entered into in a genuine spirit of searching for and deepening the relationship that exists between the religions under consideration. It is not so much a question of facts about the religions but more the fact that they are related in some way. Such theology is valueless if all the time is spent proving the other wrong. We should not become neutral observers of religion, nor leave aside our own views when we enter into dialogue. We are believers who seek to explore God's self-revelation mediated to us through the Catholic faith. If we are two people in dialogue, the purpose of our exchange is for us to understand each other's position more clearly. Other than that we have moved from dialogue to persuasion or conversion; we have turned dialogue into evangelization. I believe that dialogue lies in the field of Religious Education, since it is concerned with learning about and learning from other religions. It is not evangelization or catechesis, though it can in certain circumstances lead to both. Those conducting dialogue must seek to represent their own religion's standpoint as best they can.

Catechesis encourages individuals to grow in their own faith by reflecting upon the personal and varied experiences of their life. This naturally encompasses those experiences that are a product of living in a multi-faith society where the challenge to Catholic traditions is an ever-present reality. This new context is itself one of the reasons which demanded a radical change of style in seeking to hand on the faith. Some may consider this to be an unfortunate development but the necessity for change need not be interpreted in a purely negative way. It can also be seen as an opportunity for growth. The Catholic Church, whilst retaining the idea that what it has to offer is still the best, no longer seeks to impose that on others through a series of strict definitions but encourages them to explore it for themselves through the circumstances of their own lives. Whatever the benefits of this new approach, we need to be clear that the Church is not (as some would suspect) watering down or abandoning its doctrinal stance. It is not moving away from its tradition but seeking to express it in an appropriate way for today.

In our Liturgy, certain phrases within the Eucharistic prayers capture the spirit and essence of *Nostra Aetate* and *Lumen Gentium*, without looking for answers and explanations.[19] They are content to present us with the mystery. Yet even to acknowledge the mystery is a great step forward from the days when the question was not even addressed, when other religions were simply condemned as erroneous. I hope this new sense of mystery can be incorporated into all dimensions of Religious Education (for children and adults, formally and informally) as we move onwards in the third *Christian* millennium. I believe we must be involved in, '... opening up to wider circles of Church membership the religious enrichment of the new pluralism'.[20]

Perhaps the ideal starting point for that would be the Catholic Church putting forward more publicly than ever before its belief in 'salvation optimism' (a shorthand term to describe the import of the Vatican II teaching on other faiths). It is not a matter of simply saying of these others, 'They are good people.' That is not a natural starting point, it does not accord with previous generations and, as well as suggesting indifferentism, it is weak and patronising. We do not simply present them all as the same or equally valid but *reflect the reality of our relationship* as it is spelt out in the documents of Vatican II, whereby some are considered to be closer to us than others.

Conclusion

I believe that the inclusivist paradigm is the one that Catholics today must seek to live by. It is the only one that is credible if we

---

[19] Eucharistic Prayer III: 'Welcome into your Kingdom our departed brothers and sisters, and all who have left this world in your friendship.' Eucharistic Prayer IV: 'Remember ... all who seek you with a sincere heart ... and all the dead whose faith is known to you alone.'

[20] Hick, J., *God Has Many Names* (London and Basingstoke, The Macmillan Press Ltd, 1989) p. 41.

wish to say that God reveals himself through other religions whilst at the same time holding to the importance of the Incarnation. Jesus is *the* truth because he is God made man. He does not come to tell us the truth; he *is* it. Although he is the central avenue of Revelation and ultimately the fullness of revelation, he is not the only avenue of revelation, since God makes himself known through all means. In particular, creation itself is revelatory. Non-Christians can pick up these other broadcasts, even if they are not as finely tuned as we are or could be. By having a teaching approach which incorporates as opposed to shielding us from other faiths, we may more effectively tune their receptivity (and our own) in the process.

In April 1997, the Bishops' Conference of England and Wales produced a discussion paper on *Catholic Schools and Other Faiths*, with accompanying guidelines, which specifically concludes that the Church community needs to address the theological and philosophical issues arising from the reality of the presence of other faiths in our society.[21] The Bishops' Conference Committee on Other Faiths has, over a number of years, produced a very practical series of leaflets on the major faiths present in Britain. The Vatican Commissions continue to do their work and the Pope continues to meet with other religious leaders. His personal reflections and official pronouncements touch on these matters.[22] All in all, then, there is an invitation (if not an imperative) for Catholics to enter into serious study of inter-faith perspectives.

The Church is in a dynamic relationship to other faiths. My account touches the story of that relationship at the particular point where we experience it now. The story will only be complete in the *eschaton*. For now, Catholic education should help people to live with the tension of unity and diversity until the final fulfilment. It should encourage them to pursue rather than abandon the spiritual dimension of their lives. It should promote a sense of salvation optimism and so enable people to face the challenge of the changes provoked by our pluralist society.

Bibliography

Barnes, M., *Religions in Conversation: Christian Identity and Religious Pluralism* (London, SPCK, 1989).

---

[21] Bishops' Conference of England and Wales, *Catholic Schools and Other Faiths: A Consultation Paper*, (Chelmsford, Matthew James Publishing Ltd., 1997).
[22] John Paul II, *Crossing the Threshold of Hope* (London, Jonathan Cape, 1994) and *Tertio Millenio Adveniente* (Apostolic Letter on preparation for the Jubilee Year of 2000), Vatican, November 1994.

D'Costa, G., *Theology and Religious Pluralism: The Challenge of Other Religions* (Oxford, Basil Blackwell, 1986).

Hick, J., *God and the Universe of Faiths* (London and Basingstoke, The Macmillan Press Ltd, 1973).

Hick, J., *God Has Many Names: Britain's New Religious Pluralism* (London and Basingstoke, The Macmillan Press Ltd, 1980).

Hick, J., *An Interpretation of Religion: Human Responses to the Transcendent* (Basingstoke and London, The Macmillan Press Ltd, 1989).

Hick, J., *The Rainbow of Faiths: Critical Dialogues on Religious Pluralism* (London, SCM Press Ltd, 1995).

Knitter, P.F., *No Other Name? A Critical Survey of Christian Attitudes Towards the World Religions* (London, SCM Press Ltd, 1985).

Küng, H., *Global Responsibility: In Search of a New World Ethic* (London, SCM Press Ltd, 1991).

Küng, H. and Kuschel, K.-J. (eds), *A Global Ethic: The Declaration of the Parliament of the World's Religions* (London, SCM Press Ltd, 1993).

Oesterreicher, J.M., 'Declaration on the Relationship of the Church to Non-Christian Religions: Introduction and Commentary', in H. Vorgrimler (ed.), *Commentary on the Documents of Vatican II* (New York/London, Herder & Herder/Burns & Oates Ltd, 1969), Volume III, pp. 1–136.

Race, A., *Christians and Religious Pluralism: Patterns in the Christian theology of religions* (London, SCM Press Ltd, 1983).

Smart, N., *The World's Religions: Old Traditions and Modern Transformations* (Cambridge, Cambridge University Press, 1989).

Sullivan, F.A., *Salvation Outside the Church? Tracing the History of the Catholic Response* (London, Geoffrey Chapman, 1992).

Chapter 13

The Idea of a University: The Church Dimension in Higher Education

Liam Gearon

Introduction

In a volume on Catholic schools, this chapter presents some headings for reflection on the importance of the theological dimension to university life and some thoughts on the place of university education within the continuing professional development of educators. The chapter looks back to the mid-nineteenth century, borrowing its main heading from John Henry Newman's classic *The Idea of a University*, as a starting point from which to examine some of the distinct challenges and opportunities within Catholic colleges within the university system today. The chapter's subheading is taken from the title of a report of the Conference proceedings of the Council of Church and Associated Colleges (CCAC, now the CCC) held in Canterbury in September 2000. A further meeting was held at St Mary's at the same time the following year (Fisher and Coombes, 2001). That this was a meeting of representatives of all the Church colleges in England and Wales – Anglican, Catholic and Methodist – is itself a sign of the changes in university education in colleges with Christian foundations in the one hundred and fifty years since Newman published *The Idea of a University*.

The Idea of a University

The story of John Henry Newman (1801–1890) and his struggle to define an ideal of university education remains today an instructive narrative for the Church in contemporary higher education. This is so even as an entire century now separates Newman's nineteenth-century concerns with our own at the beginning of the twenty-first century. Newman was born in London in 1801 and privately educated at Ealing. Here he experienced a lasting conversion under evangelical influence, he matriculated to Trinity College Oxford in 1816, taking his BA degree in 1820. Ordained a member of the Church of England clergy in 1824 he became a tutor at Oriel College, Oxford, two years later and made Vicar of the University Church of St Mary's in 1828 where the power of his sermons gained him acclaim For the next fifteen years he remained at Oxford and delivered his famous Tracts for the Times which conceptualized, as he saw it, a middle way between unscriptural developments within the Church of Rome and the post-reformation failings of Protestantism, including its involvement with the politics of state and establishment. Newman's *via media* sought out the ancient catholic tradition which he saw as being at the heart of the Church of England. But the middle way resulted in a final rift with Anglicanism which culminated with Newman's reception into the Roman Catholic Church in 1845. Newman founded the Oratory of St Philip Neri in Maryvale in 1848 and moved the community to Birmingham where he was to spend much of the rest of his life until his death in 1890, eleven years after being made a cardinal in 1879.

A great literary figure as well as one of considerable theological influence, Newman's best known and most highly regarded work combined his literary skills and theological vision with an inspiring vision of university education. Newman's *The Idea of a University* was written originally as a series of lectures delivered in Dublin in 1852 as Rector of the new Catholic University instituted by Rome to counter the absence of development of 'mixed university' in the new Queen's Colleges of Ireland at Belfast, Cork and Limerick. A distinctive feature of these would be that they would educate both Catholic and Protestant but that 'no religious instruction would be given except at the expense of each denomination' (Svaglic, p. xii); and the Dublin-based university, of which Newman was the first Rector, opened in 1854 and became the forerunner of today's national university in Ireland. There was much opposition to this development at the time in a world unused to the separation of religious and secular education (Svaglic, p. xiii) but Newman's justification must be seen also in the context of a severely limited access of Catholics to higher education in any part of the United Kingdom or Great Britain (Eaton et al., 2000), which then of course included *all* of Ireland.

John Henry Newman's *The Idea of a University*, however, promoted a liberal intellectual education, a university education defined as much by its critical openness as by its Christian world-view, its catholicity integrated with a literal universality in the pursuit of knowledge:

> The view taken of a university in these Discourses is the following: that it is a place of teaching of universal knowledge. This implies that its object is, on the one hand, intellectual, not moral; and, on the other, that it is the diffusion and extension of knowledge rather than the advancement.
>
> Such is a university in its essence, and independently of its relation to the Church. But, practically speaking, it cannot fulfil its object duly, such as I have described it, without the Church's assistance; or, to use the theological term, the Church is necessary for its integrity. Not that its main characters are changed by this incorporation: it still has the office of intellectual education; but the Church steadies it in its performance of that office. (Newman, 1984, p. xxxvii)

Newman describes the task, 'taken in its bare idea, and before we use it as an instrument of the Church', of this refinement as the perfection of the intellect by the name of enlargement of mind or illumination and 'has this object and mission', to contemplate 'neither moral impression nor mechanical production', nor to profess 'to exercise the mind neither in art nor in duty'. Its primary function is 'intellectual culture': and it has done its work when it has done as much as this. It educates the intellect to reason well in all matters, to reach out toward truth and to grasp it (Newman, pp. 94–95). This, to Newman, was 'the object of a university, viewed in itself, and apart from the Catholic Church, or from the state, or from any other power which may use it ... the intellect must have an excellence of its own' as opposed to mere utility, 'a process of training, by which the intellect, instead of being formed or sacrificed to some particular or accidental purpose, some specific trade or profession, or study or science, is disciplined for its own sake, for the perception of its own proper subject, and for its own highest culture' (Newman, 1984, p. 115). This is what Newman calls Liberal Education.

There are six remaining Catholic colleges within England: Liverpool Hope (a joint Anglican-Catholic Foundation); Newman (Birmingham); Roehampton (more specifically Digby Stuart College as a Catholic foundation within Roehampton's four London colleges), St Mary's (Twickenham), Trinity and All Saints

(Leeds). All of these in varying degrees have moved considerably beyond their original missions as places of teacher education while retaining their training of educator functions. All offer courses which Newman would consider 'liberal', in other words demonstrating an openness to knowledge unprejudiced by dogma or theology. Such an institutional combination of liberal education and training would have been conceivable to Newman but without precedent in his time. So Newman reserved some of his harshest words in his Idea of a University for 'those who insist that education should be confined to some particular and narrow end' and 'should issue in some definite work, which can be weighed and measured' which 'they call making Education and Instruction' and where 'useful' and 'utility' become their watchword (pp. 115–116). Clearly today there is less aversion to institutions of higher learning providing training, a distinction which disappeared even from older universities after 1992 when the distinction between polytechnic and universities disappeared by government statute.

In this regard, post-1992 Catholic and other Christian colleges became ever more anxious to determine their identity in this new and ever more competitive world of higher education. Without wishing to alienate those of all faiths or none to their institutions, the place of distinctiveness was only cautiously given over to the theological dimension of the colleges' missions. Some Catholic colleges have strengthened the Catholic dimension by identifying catholicity as an important and distinctive aspect of the higher education market (Newman, St Mary's, Trinity and All Saints) or adopted for an ecumenical alliance (Liverpool Hope) as a way of promoting an ethical Christian identity while retaining links with secular universities for the purposes of degree validation. Roehampton has sought to retain the ecumenical and humanistic alliance of its four colleges (Anglican, Catholic, Methodist and Humanist) while entering into a formal federal alliance with the University of Surrey. In all instances the question of the need to retain a Christian distinctiveness is apparent alongside the recognition of the need to retain the same standards of quality assurance to which secular universities are bound. And if the definition of mental cultivation (a quality assurance benchmark of the nineteenth century) was highest on Newman's list of university ideals, of importance too was Newman's defence of theology within the context of the university as a haven of knowledge transmission. The reader of Newman becomes aware at this point of the author's acerbic intellect:

It is the fashion just now, as you very well know, to erect so-called
universities, without making any provision in them at all for theological chairs. Such a procedure, though defended by writers of the
generation just passed with much plausible argument and not a
little wit, seems to me an intellectual absurdity; and my reason for
saying so runs, with whatever abruptness, into the form of syllogism:
A University, I should lay down, by its very name professes to teach
universal knowledge: theology is surely a branch of knowledge: how
then is it possible for it to profess all branches of knowledge, and yet
to exclude from the subjects of its teaching one which, to say the
least, is as important and as large as any of them? I do not see that
either premiss of this argument is open to exception. (Newman,
1984, pp. 14–15)

The challenge for the inclusion of a theological dimension, while
retaining standards on a par with larger secular universities in
terms of teaching and research, is one of the same facing higher
education in Church colleges today.

The Church Dimension in Higher Education

A meeting of the Council of Church and Associated Colleges in
Canterbury Christ Church University College in September 2000
addressed this question directly by trying to define the Church
dimension in higher education. Bishop Vincent Nichols' address
to the Conference was a reflection on his then recent experience
of visiting Rome at a time of the seemingly great renewal among
the young of the Church at the immense gathering of around two
million young people from around the world at Rome at the turn
of the new millennium. It is this context that makes sense of the
Church's place in schools as a continuum between and through all
phases of education, from primary through secondary and further
to higher education. And in regard to the universities themselves,
Bishop Nichols chose to cite Pope John Paul II's declaration on
'The Presence of the Church in the University and in University
Culture' (Vatican 1994):

The Church's presence in the university is not, in fact, a task that
should remain, as it were, external to the mission of proclaiming the
faith. The synthesis between culture and faith is a necessity not only
for culture, but also for faith. A faith that does not become a culture
is a faith that is not fully received, not entirely thought through and
faithfully lived. The faith that the Church proclaims is always a faith
seeking understanding that must penetrate the human intellect and

heart, that must be thought out in order to be lived. The churches'
presence cannot therefore be limited to a cultural or scientific
contribution: it must be a real opportunity for meeting Christ
(Cited Nichols, 2000, p. 30)

And so, as the Bishop comments in his own words:

> The challenge and invitation which ... stand before our church
> colleges is that of being confident in the truth of the faith we share,
> ready, in every aspect of college life, to engage in study and dialogue
> about the truth and its meaning for today, steadfast and open in our
> public commitment to that faith, and welcoming, with uncompli-
> cated pleasure, all who come to join in the workshop from other
> faiths or none (Nichols, 2001, pp. 28–29)

Again, in a time of conflict between denominations, when
Catholics were effectively denied higher education, this is something that Newman in his nineteenth century context might have
found difficult to conceptualize; and the notion of an openness to
those of all faith and none would have made Bishop Nichol's now
mainline, post-Vatican II thinking the more so.

But this might all be counterpoised with the often assumed
secular presuppositions of the university sector which are challenged by Professor James Arthur:

> Christian influence and involvement in higher education is more
> extensive than we often think and manifests itself in three principal
> forms. First, through the presence of individual Christians, both
> staff and students, in all higher education institutions in England
> and Wales. Second, through the presence of Christian chaplaincies
> in most colleges and universities representing a Christian sub-unit
> within a secular institution. Third, through the presence of Church
> sponsored institutions of higher education which include theologi-
> cal colleges, religious halls, seminaries and Church colleges of
> higher education. Whether through individual Christian witness,
> active chaplaincies or the provision of religious colleges the
> Christian Churches clearly participate in higher education. (Arthur,
> 2000, p. 30)

The universities, even the secular ones, are far from places barren
of faith. The Church colleges are places where this faith context is
not only more apparent but integral to their foundational mission
and grandnarrative of their *raison d'etre*. And it was for this reason
that the CCAC (now CCC Council of Church Colleges) funded
a substantial project in the 1990s which looked at the place of

theology in the university curriculum (Newman's liberal education), with notable case studies from spirituality in education
(Thatcher, 1999), sociology, theology and the curriculum (Francis,
1999) and English literature, theology and the curriculum
(Gearon, 1999).

If 'the total activity of the church is educative' (Bishops' conference of England and Wales 19), in the other aspects of the college's
purpose at a time of vast change in society and higher education,
the book edited by Mary Eaton, Jane Longman and Arthur Naylor
(2000) to mark the one hundred and fiftieth anniversary of the
foundation of St Mary's College presented the diversity of provision
by the church colleges: from the Catholic Certificate in Religious
Studies (Hayes and Gearon, 1998) through to provision of professional training for school leadership (Sullivan, 2000). And Naylor
sets out too the challenges here for the future:

> The role of the Catholic college in relation to schools will be in
> responding to their needs in the training of teachers and in offering
> leadership and support in professional development. The key issues
> will include: sustaining and seeking to improve recruitment to meet
> the teacher supply needs of Catholic schools; developing partner-
> ship in training with Catholic schools; offering relevant continuing
> professional development opportunities and defining a more signif-
> icant contribution to research in Catholic education. (Naylor, 2000,
> p. 19)

If this will require 'new forms of partnership between Catholic
colleges, schools and dioceses' in support of the mission of the
church in education which in quite different ways is as urgent and
difficult now as it was in the 1850s when John Henry Newman
wrote *The Idea of a University*, then as Naylor points out:

> Undoubtedly the most challenging area of development will be
> establishing research bases in education in the Catholic colleges. It
> may be that this can only be brought about through collaboration
> with interested and supportive researchers in Catholic education
> whose bases are in secular universities with strong research track
> records. With the emphasis now placed on national and interna-
> tional collaboration, this may be more possible to achieve than
> might have been the case in the past ten years. (Naylor, 2000, p. 22)

There is in fact an urgent need for the teaching profession to recognize its responsibilities here. For only if those with experience in
pedagogy consider higher education as a valid alternative option to
professional development within schools will this context of train-

ing and the reciprocal relationship between schools and the Church colleges remain viable and vibrant. But the higher education field is a competitive one in which the Church colleges need to operate with quality of teaching and research. There is little evidence that, beyond training for leadership, there is a vibrant research culture amongst Catholic school teachers. Professor Gerald Grace's work at the London Institute of Education is one area where this is apparent; but teachers in schools need to realize that they have the potential to contribute to this important area of research, which is not only one of the most important defining features of a university but, as Naylor suggests, one of the most problematic for the former training colleges to achieve.

Education, Research and Social Justice: A Case Study

Set in Southwest London, the University of Surrey Roehampton has four constituent colleges dating back to the nineteenth century: Whitelands (1841), Southlands (1872), Digby Stuart (1874) and Froebel (1892). These colleges represent a distinctive collaboration between Anglican, Methodist, Roman Catholic and Humanist traditions. The original mission of the colleges was in teacher education. A century and more of development has seen considerable diversification to include a range of undergraduate, taught postgraduate and research degrees in education, humanities, languages, as well as social and life sciences. The distinctive collegiate organisation entered into a unique federation with the University of Surrey in January 2000 to form the University of Surrey Roehampton.

Within a university context of continued commitment to equity and social justice, the Centre for Research in Human Rights (CRHR) is an interdisciplinary venture aimed at promoting research, development and education within the field. With a physical base at Digby Stuart College and directed from within the Faculty of Education, the Centre for Research in Human Rights provides a synthesis of interdisciplinary perspectives from education, literary and cultural studies, the humanities and social sciences. The idea for a Centre for Research in Human Rights was conceived as way of defining a common research interest in a number of disciplines but also as a way of presenting a research agenda in which the Church colleges and Froebel at Roehampton could share a common interest. The new Centre has three main areas of operation: research, development and education.

The Centre builds upon a developing base of staff publications in the form of books, articles and professional works from staff in the Faculty of Education, the School of Sociology and Social Policy, the School of Languages and the School of Humanities and Cultural Studies. The inaugural conference, developed in collaboration with secular organizations like Amnesty International as well as groups concerned with social justice from a religious foundation like CAFOD and Pax Christi, planned for the summer of 2002 aims to be a model of co-operation not only between secular and faith perspectives but between universities and non-government organizations. With non-stipendiary visiting fellowships, funding will be sought for research studentships and a postdoctoral research fellowship. A series of advanced research seminars will be established and the potential for a uniquely interdisciplinary *International Journal of Human Rights* is being explored. There are immense opportunities here for teachers who wish to further professional reflection on social justice in schools through the rigours of research.

The Centre draws upon existing expertise at University of Surrey Roehampton and from a national and international advisory board of wide-ranging academic, educational and legal expertise. The Centre also provides education and training for the teaching of human rights. Given the history of the constituent colleges of University of Surrey Roehampton, a major focus here will be in the development of materials for teaching human rights in schools, in initial teacher training and continuing professional development. Eventually, it aims to provide consultancy for practitioners and policy-makers in areas of relevance to human rights, eventually including local educational authorities, health organizations, police and security forces, local and national governments. The Centre for Research in Human Rights represents, then, a national and international focus for research related to issues of social justice at the University of Surrey Roehampton, and its constituent colleges. The Centre for International Human Rights is also a serious attempt to harness further the University's wider academic profile and to develop, from its historical roots and contemporary place in the network of Church colleges, a significant professional and educational potential in local, national and international higher education.

Conclusion

The Christian Churches remain an important part of this global community. In nominal terms at the least over one billion of the world's population profess Roman Catholicism, and hundreds of millions of Christians are represented by Protestant denominations and the Orthodox traditions. The worldview of Christianity persists if altered by modern conditions. Indeed, the Second Vatican Council (1962–1965) was set up for this very purpose. Here, in historical terms, documents such as *Gaudium et Spes* proclaimed that the hopes and fear, the joys and anxieties of the world are equally the hopes and fears, joys and anxieties of the Church, that the political issues confronting the world today are the issues facing the Church too.

These are some of the areas where the Church colleges, their staff, their students, their trainee teachers, their postgraduate researchers, can and should engage the curriculum. There are distinctive opportunities for links with non-government (especially Church-based) organizations working in areas of human rights and social justice *and* global governmental bodies like UNESCO – which actually *advantage* the Church colleges; and which can feed into school provision directly. Creative thinking and dialogue can be developed into a constructive working relationship with local, national and global structures and organizations. The Christian Churches already operate at all three levels – the local, the national and the global – the Church's university colleges can only benefit from doing the same.

This is where the modern world has progressed beyond Newman's model of a university; pursuant of a liberal education focused on knowledge, setting aside the drudgery of utility. The historical roots of the Church colleges were in teacher education, what is now called training. As such, in Newman's terms, they would never have qualified as universities. But the Church colleges have in large part diversified acquired university status and compete (for funding, for students, for staff), if on a smaller scale, with larger secular universities, or, as a sign of academic and research credibility, entered into a federal university status with partnerships like the four colleges which constitute my own institution. (I refer to the federal university status between University of Surrey Roehampton and the University of Surrey at Guildford.)

And if Newman's claims about knowledge would seem naive today, so too might his claims to pursue knowledge for its own sake; not that the pursuit of knowledge can be claimed to be wrong but that the refinement needed here is that of Newman's hard and fast separation of this, not from 'utility', but from morality. For the intervening century between ours and Newman's saw the effects of an amoral use of knowledge: the mechanisation of death in world wars, mass death and genocide, environmental destruction on a scale all unimaginable to Newman in his time when science was seen as the inevitable harbinger of human progress. And here in particular the Church colleges have a particular part to play. Like *all* university sector places of learning, they combine courses of training (especially in teaching, but also other 'caring' professions) with the academic pursuit of knowledge in its own right. Post-1992, at least in a formal sense, the old divisions between education and training in Church colleges, polytechnics and universities became less easy to identify in institutional terms, with even old established, pre-1992 universities contributing courses of training as well as pure academic teaching and research. But it is, I would argue, the moral dimension, which Newman so strenuously sought to separate from the pursuit of knowledge which can be the particular emphasis within the Church college, not only in terms of ethos but through curriculum, and, following Arthur Naylor's suggestions about the difficulties of research in the Church colleges, through research which has a particular moral and engaged focus.

This brief paper has attempted to make a conscious – if brief – link between the past idealism of Newman and the present day realities of Catholic higher education. Though the university colleges have across all denominations developed into multi-disciplinary providers of degrees and postgraduate qualifications, the teachers and school system which the university colleges still serve have an essential role here. In the development of new knowledge, which is at its most basic the nature of research, teachers and manager should be encouraged fully to participate. Church university colleges cannot afford simply to be places of training – as simple functionaries of government or even Church policy. In order to survive at all they must engage seriously, competitively, but also in collaboration with secular universities. And this means engaging seriously with secular as well as theologically focused research in education and across all disciplines (Francis, 1999; Gearon, 1999; Thatcher, 1999). This, I suppose, is, finally, a plea for the school-based practitioner, both teacher and manager, to join in the process of knowledge and its discovery. Naive, idealistic, perhaps, but the practicalities of masters level work and higher degrees by research will strengthen for the future a sector with a noble historical tradition across all Christian denominations – Anglican, Catholic and Methodist.

Bibliography

Arthur, J., 'Changing Patterns of Church College Identity and Mission', in J. Arthur and E. Coombes (eds), *The Church Dimension in Higher Education*, 2000, pp. 30–41.

Arthur, J. and Coombes, E., *The Church Dimension in Higher Education* (CCC, 2000).

Eaton, M., Longman, J. and Naylor, A. (eds), *Commitment to Diversity: Catholic and Education in a Changing World* (London and New York, Cassell, 2000).

Fisher, R. and Coombes, E., *Collaboration for Distinctiveness* (London, CCC, 2001).

Francis, L. (ed.), *Sociology, Theology and the Curriculum* (London and New York, Cassell, 1999).

Gearon, L. (ed.), *English Literature, Theology and the Curriculum* (London and New York, Cassell, 1999).

Hayes, M.A. and Gearon, L. (eds), *Contemporary Catholic Theology* (New York, Continuum, 1999).

John Paul II 'The Presence of the Church in the University and in University Culture' (Vatican City, Vatican, 1994).

Naylor, A., 'Teacher Education in Catholic Colleges in England: Historical Context, Current Perspectives and Future Directions', in Eaton et al. (eds) *Commitment to Diversity: Catholic and Education in a Changing World*, 2000, pp. 9–23.

Newman, J.H., *The Idea of a University* (Indiana, University of Notre Dame, 1984 [1852]).

Nichols, V., 'The Role of the Church in the Mission of the Church in Education', in Arthur and Coombes (eds)

Sullivan, J., 'Wrestling with Managerialism', in Eaton et al (eds) *Commitment to Diversity: Catholic and Education in a Changing World*, 2000, pp. 240–259.

Svaglic, M., 'Introduction' in Newman, J.H., *Apologia pro vita sua: being a history of his religious opinions*, Oxford, Clarendon Press, 1990.

Thatcher, A. (ed.), *Spirituality and the Curriculum* (London and New York, Cassell, 1999).

Contributors

James C. Conroy has taught at schools and colleges in England and Scotland and is Director of Religious Education and Pastoral Care at St Andrew's College, Glasgow. His publications include *Catholic Education: Inside Out Outside In* (Dublin, Lindisfarne, 1999).

Michael Cooke was ordained priest for Salford Diocese in November 1983, having trained at UpHolland and Ushaw colleges. He has served as Curate, Religious Education Adviser, University Chaplain and, since the summer of 1999, Director of the Salford Diocese Religious Education Centre. In addition to his work in the diocese, he has been Secretary to the Bishops' Conference Department for Catholic Education and Formation since April 1996. Michael has a BA (Hons) in Theology from Durham University and an MPhil in Religious Studies from Lancaster University.

Aidan Donaldson is a teacher of Religious Education at St Mary's Christian Brothers' Grammar School, Belfast. He has published widely on philosophical and educational issues and acted as author to the Catholic Bishops of Northern Ireland in the production of their recent document on Catholic education entitled *Proclaiming the Mission: the Distinctive Philosophy and Values of Catholic Education* (Veritas, 2001). Dr Donaldson is currently editor of the journal on Catholic education *Ethos and Education*.

Gerald Grace is Visiting Professorial Fellow and Director of the Centre for Research and Development in Catholic Education. Of his numerous publications, recent books include *Catholic Schools* (London, Routledge and Falmer, 2002) and *Catholic Schools and the Common Good* (London, CRDCE).

Liam Gearon is Reader in Education and Director of Centre for Research in Human Rights at University of Surrey Roehampton. He has published numerous books, including *English Literature, Theology and the Curriculum* (London and New York, Continuum, 1999) and *Education in the United Kingdom* (London, David Fulton, 2002), and is co-editor of *Contemporary Catholic Theology: A Reader* (Leominster, Gracewing, 1998).

David Hay is a zoologist by profession. He worked for some years at the Religious Experience Research Unit set up by Alister Hardy, who was formerly Professor of Zoology at Oxford University. After Hardy's death in 1985 he became director of the Unit. Subsequently he was appointed Reader in Spiritual Education at Nottingham University, a post from which he retired in 2000.

Michael A. Hayes was formerly the Catholic Chaplain at University of Surrey Roehampton and is now Head of the School of Theology, Philosophy, and History at St Mary's College (University of Surrey), Strawberry Hill, Twickenham. His research is in psychology, counselling and theology, and he is co-editor of various books including *Contemporary Catholic Theology: A Reader* (Leominster, Gracewing, 1998); *Religion and Sexuality* (Sheffield, Sheffield Academic Press, 1998); *Resurrection* (Sheffield, Sheffield Academic Press, 1999); *Faith in the Millennium* (Sheffield, Sheffield Academic Press, 2001); *Truth and Memory: The Church and Human Rights in El Salvador and Guatemala* (Leominster, Gracewing, 2001).

Moyra Healy is Director of the Zacchaeus Centre, part of Birmingham's Catholic Support Centre. She started working as a teacher in inner city Catholic schools in Birmingham in 1972, where she held positions in charge of the Science Department, as Pastoral Head of Years 7, 10 and 11 and finally as Head of Religious Education in St John Wall School in Handsworth. From 1994–95 she worked at the Bridge Centre, part of the Pupil Referral Unit (PRU) in Birmingham from where she moved to her current position. At present she is on a Steering Committee group for improving behaviour management at the DfES and is also involved in producing a training video for NQTs with the NASUWT.

Peter Humfrey was born in Surrey and educated in local Catholic schools. After taking a degree in Classics at Trinity College, Dublin and training as a teacher, he took further degrees in Philosophy and Theology at the Gregorian University, Rome and was ordained priest for the Diocese of Arundel and Brighton. He was successively a teacher, chaplain and diocesan Religious Education Adviser, in addition to holding a number of appointments as parish priest. After being Chairman of the Diocesan Liturgical Commission and Episcopal Vicar for Education, he was appointed National Adviser (to the Bishops' Conference of England and Wales) for Religious Education and Catechesis.

Michael Holman is a Jesuit priest and has been Headmaster of Wimbledon College, a Jesuit comprehensive school, since September 1995. He has worked in Jesuit schools in Britain and the United States. He studied at Heythrop College (University of London), Oxford University and in Boston and New York.

Muriel Robinson is Vice-Principal (Academic Quality) at Newman College of Higher Education in Birmingham. Previous to this position she was Deputy Head of School in the School of Education at the University of Brighton, a post which included overall responsibility for part-time and in-service courses. During her time at Brighton she was responsible for developing the CCRS in partnership with the local diocese as a university-provided programme and she led the course for the first few years of its life. Her main research interests lie in the area of media literacy and learning and teaching in higher education. Before going to Brighton, she was a primary school teacher in London for ten years.

Christopher Storr started his career as a teacher and had experience of both primary and secondary schools in Dewsbury, Oxford and North Wales before entering education administration with Essex County Council in 1967. Senior posts followed in Kent County Council and the Inner London Education Authority before his appointment as Director of Education for the Archdiocese of Southwark in 1982, a post he held until 2001. He was particularly interested in governor support and training, and pioneered a number of initiatives in this field. He is now a member of the Employment Tribunals of England and Wales and an accredited adviser for headteacher performance review.

John Sullivan is Professor of Christian Education at Liverpool Hope College. He is the author of *Catholic Schools in Contention* (Dublin, Veritas, 2000), of *Catholic Education: Distinctive and Inclusive* (Dordrecht, Kluwer Academic Publishers, 2001) and of numerous articles in the field of theology and education. He was formerly Reader in Catholic Education and Director of the MA programme in Catholic School Leadership at St Mary's College, Twickenham. He has worked in secondary schools and sixth form colleges as a classroom teacher, as a middle and senior manager and as Head, as well as serving four years as a Principal Officer in a local education authority. He has been widely involved in consultancy and lecturing on Catholic education for schools and dioceses, as well as nationally and internationally.

Index